Playing in Traffic

America from the River Niagara to the Rio Grande, by Bicycle

Expanded Edition

by
Stan Purdum

CSS Publishing Company, Inc., Lima, Ohio

Playing in Traffic
Expanded Edition

CSS Publishing Company, Inc.
PO Box 4503
Lima, Ohio 45802-4503

Library of Congress Cataloging-in-Publication Data

Purdum, Stan, 1945-
   Playing in traffic : America from the river Niagara to the Rio Grande, by bicycle / by Stan Purdum. — Expanded ed.
      p. cm.
   Includes bibliographical references and index.
   ISBN 0-7880-2129-X (perfect bound : alk. paper)
   1. Bicycle touring—United States. 2. Purdum, Stan, 1945—Travel—United States. 3. Cyclists—United States—Biography. 4. United States—Description and travel. I. Title.

GV1045.P86 2004
796.6'092—dc22

20040607

Cover photo by David Barnas.

 "Stan Purdum on bicycle" from the pen of John Burns.

ISBN 0-7880-2129-X   PRINTED IN U.S.A

For
Jeanine,
Eric, Scott and Rebecca,
with appreciation and love.

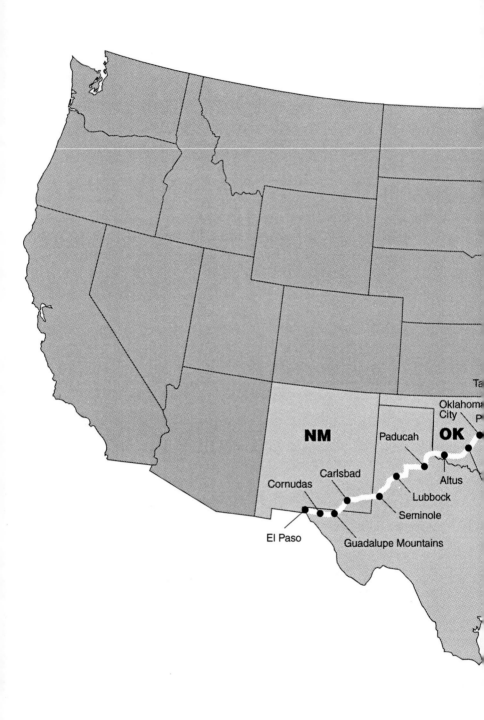

Niagara
Falls
Eden
Warren
Tionesta
Hubbard

NY
PA

Killbuck
Columbus
OH
Washington
Court
House
Maysville
Bardstown
KY
Central City

IL

MO

Eureka
Springs
Wickliffe
Sikeston
Cunningham
New Madrid
Hardy
Mountain
Home
Fayetteville
AR

uah

emah
ache

U.S. Route
62

Other books by Stan Purdum

Roll Around Heaven All Day:
A Piecemeal Journey Across America by Bicycle

New Mercies I See

Preface

If you wanted to drive from Niagara Falls, New York, to El Paso, Texas, and needed to make time, you wouldn't select U.S. Route 62. Interstate highways connect the cities in fewer miles and much less time.

But if you did take 62, you'd be rewarded with a fascinating and diverse portrait of America.

U.S. Route 62 takes 2271 miles to get from Niagara Falls to El Paso. On my bicycle, I got up close and personal with every one of them. I found the route to have many identities. Sometimes it meanders through quiet countryside. Other times it roars along as a busy expressway. Occasionally it shows an urban face. It climbs mountains, rolls over wooded hills, flirts with Interstates, stretches out in flatland boredom and crawls across blazing desert.

Route 62 travels through 10 states, spending the most time in Oklahoma and Texas (404 miles in each state) and the least in Illinois (2 miles). It connects 57 county seats, 14 of them in Kentucky alone, but only one each in New York and New Mexico. Along the way, the highway passes the highest point in Texas (Guadalupe Peak) and the lowest point in Illinois (Mississippi River). It skims by three outdoor dramas (Kentucky, Arkansas and Oklahoma), two music festivals (Kentucky and Oklahoma), four Civil War battlefields (Kentucky, Missouri, and two in Oklahoma), two rodeos (Missouri and Oklahoma). It passes through two Paducahs (Kentucky and Texas), two New Albanys in the same state (Ohio), the state with the first oil well (Pennsylvania) and the state with the most oil wells (Texas). Route 62 also crosses the path of numerous early trails, pioneer routes, historic journeys and primitive roads, the oldest dating from at least 1598.

Although 62 bears the same number over its entire length, in some places it's designated as a north-south route; at others, an east-west one. In various locales, it picks up additional monikers: Blue Star Memorial Highway, Everly Brothers Boulevard, Texas Mountain Trail, Blue Moon of Kentucky Highway, Vietnam Veterans Memorial Highway, Trail of Tears, the Ozark Trail.

If Route 62 was the medium for my journey, people who live and work near the highway were the substance of it. I listened to what they had to say, and I've let them tell you in their own words, recording their comments as faithfully as memory and post-conversation note-jotting allows.

This then is the story of a highway, of people and of a journey. Welcome along for the ride.

About the Expanded Edition: After the publication of the original edition of *Playing in Traffic*, I heard from several people who were using the book as a travel guide for their own journeys on Route 62. Some were following 62 in autos and others were using bicycles. The latter especially were interested in the alternative paths I used at those points where Route 62 joins Interstate highways on which bicycles are not allowed. "A Guide to Route 62," included in this edition, not only provides that information but also describes a few scenic alternatives that travelers using any mode of transportation might enjoy.

Chapter 1

"Doesn't riding in all that traffic scare you?" the woman asked.

I looked up from my breakfast at the middle-aged woman clutching her tray. Since I was clad in tights and a jersey, she'd had no trouble identifying me as the rider of the loaded-down bicycle outside.

"No," I said. "I respect it and I'm careful, but no, it doesn't usually scare me."

"Well, it does me!" she said. "I work in Columbus, and the traffic is just crazy there. I drive in early every day so I can beat the rush hour, and then sleep in my car until it's time for work."

I had ridden one of the major thoroughfares in Columbus the previous day and knew I could impress her. "Actually, I rode right down Broad Street yesterday during the noon hour," I said, arranging my face into a suitably humble expression.

She rolled her eyes. "Man, you've got nerve."

"Well, I try to think like a driver and be clear with them about what I'm doing. If I'm planning to make a left turn, I get in the left-turn lane. I don't cut over suddenly from the curb."

"Yeah, but you can't always tell what other drivers will do. I've totaled three cars in accidents caused by other drivers. That's why I drive in to work so early — fewer drivers to deal with."

"You're right. There is some risk," I agreed, "but generally I've found that most drivers aren't interested in causing me any problems."

This also was true, but my confident words would echo with irony later in the day when two guys in a pickup truck threw a cherry bomb at me. But that's getting ahead of myself.

Eight days earlier, a Saturday morning in May, I had begun a bicycle journey at Niagara Falls. My plan was to cycle the entire length of U.S. Route 62, from its northern terminus at Niagara Falls, New York, to where it ends in El Paso, Texas.

The falls, labeled by Oscar Wilde as "the second biggest disappointment in a newly married American woman's life," rumbled in the background as Dave, Mark and I assembled with our loaded bicycles for the launch of the trip. We stood at Prospect Point, the lip of land that juts out toward the falls on the American side. Coast-to-coast riders traditionally dip the rear wheel of their bike in the ocean from which they are starting, but attempting that here in the Niagara River as it raced toward the precipice would have been suicidal, not to mention illegal. So we settled for touching the barrier that keeps visitors from becoming part of the flotsam that plunges over the falls.

Thirty-three years before, during that same week in May, I stood watching these falls with my new bride at my side. (If she entertained either disappointment during that visit she kept it to herself.) She was still my bride but was not with me on this call at the falls. Being neither infected with the wanderlust that drove me nor enamored by lengthy jaunts by bicycle, she'd elected to remain at home while I pursued this journey.

I'd met Dave Barnas a couple of years earlier during a coast-to-coast bicycle trek across America. Then a young man a few years out of high school, Dave had been on a similar excursion. We'd met by chance along the road in Kansas and then ridden together for five days until our routes diverged. Although I was almost twice Dave's age, our interest in bike-tripping provided enough common ground for a friendship. I'd come to respect Dave's maturity and to enjoy his company. He lived near Niagara Falls, so when I conceived this new trip as beginning there, I invited him to join me for as long as his schedule allowed, which at this point was three days.

Mark was a friend of Dave's. He'd had no experience in long-distance biking, but had asked to come along, planning to ride until Dave had to leave. Because Dave and I were both seasoned riders, we wondered if Mark would have any difficulty keeping up, but he was about the same age as Dave, and I figured his youthfulness would power him along, at least for a while.

Route 62 begins at the falls. We wheeled our bikes out of Prospect Park and began pumping down the route with the enthusiasm that usually marks the first hour of a trip on which one is suddenly freed from the demands of his normal existence.

In the city of Niagara Falls, 62 first traverses some city streets, passing small businesses and houses, and then wends through an industrial and warehouse district. Eventually it settles as a four-lane highway lined with fading motels, assorted eateries and sundry other businesses in varying stages of prosperity (or the lack thereof). We rolled along easily through these areas, talking when side-by-side riding was feasible, but mostly traveling in single file, covering miles.

Before mounting up at the falls, Mark had strapped a tiny radio to his arm and implanted the attached earphone in his ear. Thereafter, every time we stopped for a red light, he had to fuss with the device. First, the earpiece fell out and dangled on its cord dangerously near his spinning wheels. He grabbed it back up, wobbling a bit as he did so. Then the radio started sliding down his arm. Mark tugged at the Velcro straps, trying to tighten it. After fooling with both parts at just about every traffic light stop during the first 15 minutes, he finally snatched the radio off his arm and shoved the whole affair into his pocket, looking disgusted.

One of the motels we passed may have been where Jeanine and I stayed on our honeymoon. That was too far back to remember for sure, but the area seemed familiar. Of course on that visit, I'd had higher priorities than memorizing the layout of the city.

The particular stretch of highway Dave, Mark and I now pedaled had a wide, paved shoulder labeled as a "bike lane," and it continued for several miles. I was surprised but glad to find it there, although I valued its existence as a paved shoulder more than the mere fact that it was marked for bicycles. My previous long-distance bike trip, the one across America, had been mostly on low-traffic back roads, so paved shoulders hadn't been particularly important. But I expected 62 to be busier. The prevailing wisdom among many cyclists is that bicycles don't mix well with heavy traffic, but I disagree. I've found that I can safely share the roads with a busy traffic stream when there is either a paved shoulder or the traffic lanes themselves are sufficiently wide to permit vehicles to pass without squeezing me off the road.

Besides, to limit bicycles to only lightly traveled roads means that there are too many places cyclists have to avoid. When I considered a new trip, I realized that just to take another back-roads journey would be a near repeat of the previous experience. It was time to stop avoiding the main thoroughfares. Cars and trucks own the roads, and ranting about that is a waste of time. So my approach has been to learn to ride in traffic. It can be done, and done with reasonable safety.

Experience helps, however, and the intersection we were then approaching separated the novice from the pros. We advanced toward it in single file with Dave in the lead, all riding the shoulder. The roadway broadened to accommodate a right-turn lane that forked off from the main track. When the right-turn lane branched, Dave, well experienced, continued straight on, nosing just to the left of the white line that demarked the straight-ahead lane from the turn lane. Mark, less cycle savvy, stayed on the berm, right of the turn lane. This meant that when he wanted to go straight ahead, he now had to cut across in front of turning traffic.

Even worse, some drivers could incorrectly assume Mark was turning right. Confusing drivers is not a good idea, but Mark, in his inexperience, didn't know he was doing so. Knowing the risk of unsolicited advice, I figured he'd catch on by watching us, and he soon did.

We left Niagara Falls behind, progressing the rest of the morning through heavily populated districts dotted with business establishments and retail stores. After skirting the edge of North Tonawanda, 62 enters Buffalo on neighborhood streets teaming with cars and people. Cars parked along both sides of the road forced us to focus our attention on them, for we never knew when a motorist would fling a car door open or pull away from the curb without looking behind him.

There were frequent traffic lights, and when we hit them on red, we stopped just as the motorized traffic did. I make this point deliberately. On a bike, it's easy and often even safe to ignore some traffic laws. Frequently, the police won't bother you for doing so, but I don't recommend it, especially in traffic. Drivers find it irksome to see cyclists flaunting the laws they have to follow, and who wants an irked driver overtaking them? Besides, when we cyclists obey traffic rules, we behave more predictably in traffic, and that makes us safer.

After rolling through the industrial and warehouse districts on the south side of Buffalo, we finally emerged into a rural environment, punctuated periodically by small towns. In the heart of Lackawana, the first of these towns, I pulled over for a photo of a massive structure that I assumed was a courthouse. Dave, however, who had visited the building years before on a grade-school field trip, insisted that the impressive stone building was a church, and further investigation proved him right. The Italian Renaissance-style edifice, built in 1921, was Our Lady of Victory Basilica and National Shrine.

As we left Lackawana, the weather, which had been warm and sunny, adopted a darker look, and we found ourselves suddenly dealing with strong wind and threatening skies. We pulled on our windbreakers and continued in the light rain that now fell.

Later, cruising through the town of Eden, we glimpsed what appeared to be a Buick-sized bug speared to the top of a building, but a longer stare revealed it to be a huge kazoo. Fascinated, we came to a standstill, trying to make sense of what we were seeing.

A sign on the building announced that we were in the presence of the Original American Kazoo Company, the only firm in the world still making metal kazoos (most are now made of plastic). The place had already closed for the day, but their website, which I visited later, informed me that the structure was a working museum devoted to the history of this humble musical instrument and that it continued to manufacture "a complete line of kazoos." It seems my education has been sorely lacking, for until that point, I was completely ignorant that there was enough variation in kazoos to constitute a "complete line." Display cases inside reportedly contain not only metal kazoos, but several wooden types, as well as — and I am being completely truthful here — kazoos shaped like liquor bottles, used to celebrate the end of prohibition. The website also points out that the kazoo "is the most democratic of instruments because any-one can play," which leaves entirely unaddressed the question of whether anyone should.

We continued, riding past fields of sprouting vegetables. The soil that nourished them was so rich that the area had earned the nickname "Garden of Eden."

There had been very little rise and fall in the terrain from Niagara Falls to Lackawana, but we now entered a region with occasional hills. Almost immediately, Mark, who'd been riding reasonably well so far, started faltering. While Dave and I pumped up the hills eas-ily, Mark slowed to a crawl and the expression on his face tele-graphed distress, though he said nothing. In fact, it was his lapse into silence that alerted us to the depth of his weariness. He was riding a mountain bike rather than a road model, and he had men-tioned earlier that the position of the handlebars — designed for off-road use — forced him to ride bent over, and that was no doubt adding to his discomfort now. We slowed to accommodate Mark, but he was clearly exhausted. Thus, we bivouacked in mid-after-noon in a restaurant in Scranton, hoping that some hot food and a rest might rejuvenate him, and he did seem to bounce back ... well, maybe not bounce, but at least trickle.

We'd already covered about 40 miles and had planned to reach Gowanda, one of the larger towns on this part of 62. That was another 20 miles, and now that he was rested, Mark thought he might be able to make it. We started out, but by the time we reached North Collins, seven miles short of Gowanda, Mark was struggling again, and wearing the sort of expression that one might wear on his way to the gallows. We spied a church, got permission from the pastor at the house next door to camp behind it, and holed up there for the night.

Noting that we had logged 53 miles, Mark casually mentioned that his previous distance record on a bike had been eight miles. Given this information, I now realized that he'd taken an admirable leap by joining our trip. With sincerity, I congratulated him on a new personal best.

A lot of long-distance riders, especially young adults, camp out when bike touring, frequently because they can't afford motels. Riders in my age group, who usually have better incomes, often prefer "credit-card camping," riding all day but hitting a motel each night. I can afford motels, but I don't mind sleeping in a tent, and I really like the flexibility camping gives me to stop wherever I happen to be when I run out of steam. I save motels for bad weather nights.

I'd been camping ever since I was a Boy Scout of 12. Starting that early, I have learned what to take to accomplish it comfortably. In my 20s and 30s, I undertook several wilderness trips, some by canoe and others on foot wearing a backpack. I enjoyed it all, though I never cared much for the cooking part. So with bike touring, I usually sleep out, but eat in restaurants. And since I don't have to expend energy on cooking and cleaning up afterward, I can ride more hours, which is what I want to do.

Dave too had a lot of camping experience, but Mark did not. He had last camped at age 10 with his family. In preparing for this trip, Mark had relied on Dave's advice as to what to bring. They had planned to share a tent, but it never occurred to Dave that Mark wouldn't think of some of the most basic equipment, so Dave never mentioned the obvious things. Mark had brought such crucial items as his portable radio and earphones, a CD player, a gadget that transmitted the sound from the CD to a more powerful speaker (which he had also brought along) and a portable phone. But he had missed a few other things.

Earlier in the day, riding behind Mark, I'd glanced idly at the bundle on the rack of his bike. "That's a pretty small sleeping bag," I said.

"That's not a sleeping bag. It's Dave's tent."

"Oh. Well, where's your sleeping bag?"

Silence.

Then Mark said quietly, "I didn't bring a sleeping bag."

Dave exclaimed, "You didn't bring a sleeping bag?! What are you going to do?"

Silence.

As it happened, our route took us to within a few blocks of Dave's parents' home. They were away, but Dave had a key, so we stopped by to borrow some blankets. Unfortunately, Dave was unable to locate any. He did find a fleece couch throw, which we took, leaving his parents a note.

"That one cover may not be enough," I said to Mark. "But if you sleep in your long pants and sweater you'll probably be okay."

"Oh. Was I supposed to bring some?" Mark asked.

In the ensuing silence, Dave and I exchanged looks of concern.

When we were camped, Mark no doubt missed those items as the rain, which had started earlier, continued. It was not heavy, and Mark did at least have a windbreaker. He and Dave opted for cooking their supper on Dave's camp stove. While Dave got the meal going, Mark hooked up his electronic gadgetry and played music. I headed for a restaurant in North Collin's tiny business district and supped heartily.

Later in the evening, with little else to do, all three of us visited a bar, where we watched the locals play pool. Dave and Mark each had a beer while I sipped a Coke, and we all appreciated sitting quietly without our legs spinning around. It didn't take long to recognize that we were tired, and by 9:30, all three of us were ensconced in our tents for the night. Mark, swathed in trousers and a flannel shirt I'd loaned him, wrapped himself in the fleece throw.

I've been interested in roads for as long as I can remember. Every time I encounter one I've not seen before, it beckons enticingly, promising adventure somewhere along its length. One reason I love riding my bicycle is because it gives me an enjoyable way to explore the byways and the roads less traveled. That interest eventually led to my ride across America, a trip I detailed in a previous book, *Roll Around Heaven All Day*.

For most of its mileage, that trip avoided the major traffic routes, although in some places, particularly in the West, the only paved passage was a numbered federal highway. While riding across the panhandle of Idaho from Kooskia to Lolo Pass, for example, there was no alternative but the two-lane U.S. 12. And later, as I worked my way down the western border of Montana, U.S. 93 was the only viable through route for a road bicycle.

For my new trip, I was already thinking along the lines of following a numbered federal highway from start to finish when I happened across the information that Route 62 runs all the way from Niagara Falls to El Paso. Coincidentally, Route 62 passes through Canton, Ohio, just a few miles from my home. I drive on it frequently, but I'd never thought about where it went beyond the scope of my daily travels. It was time to find out.

I briefly considered exploring 62 as a motor trip, but quickly abandoned that idea. For one thing, I love bicycle touring. For another, bicycle touring itself occasions a lot more interaction with both the terrain and the people along the route. I would make the trip by bike.

Chapter 2

By morning the rain had stopped, although the day dawned cool and overcast. As we packed up our camping gear, Mark announced that he'd decided to pull out, indicating that he was still weary and hadn't been warm enough to sleep well. Using his cell phone, he called a family member who agreed to pick him up.

We hoped at least to eat breakfast together, but being Sunday, there was nothing in the little community open. Mark told us to go ahead, and he settled down outside a store to await his pick up. It was hard to tell whether Mark was feeling disappointment or relief. Some of both, I expect. Dave and I bid him goodbye and rode south. Though neither of us voiced it, we were relieved not to be bound by the limits of Mark's cycling ability, though we wished it were otherwise.

For the most part, the highway continued to offer us paved shoulders, and when it didn't, there were wide enough lanes that traffic had no trouble rumbling by us. Probably because this was a Sunday, there wasn't much traffic anyway.

Beyond Gowanda, where we breakfasted, 62 trudges upward continuously for five miles, giving us the first significant climb of the trip. On backroad hills, the roadways often follow the contours of the land, sometimes shifting abruptly from moderate to very steep inclines. Unlike those, this one had been evened out so that the degree of rise was reasonably constant and not too severe. Cycling the climb was still sweaty work, especially now that the weather had cleared and warmed up, but I found myself appreciating the grade standards that applied to the U.S. numbered highways.

"Standards," in the plural, is the right word, for there is no single percent of grade than can be uniformly applied, and that's not just because the hills themselves differ. Highway engineers have a table of maximum allowable grade percentages based on several variables: Is the road urban or rural? What is its functional classification — freeway, arterial, collector or local? Is the terrain level, rolling or hilly? For what speed is the road designed?

For example, the maximum grade on a rural freeway designed for 60 to 69 miles per hour over rolling terrain is 4 percent. An urban local street in hilly terrain designed for 20 to 29 miles per hour can have grades as steep as 15 percent. Route 62, where we were at that moment, was in a rural area and had a posted speed of 55. I judged the terrain to be hilly, which meant the grade was allowed to be as much as 7 percent. Thankfully, it was nowhere near that.

Stupidly, we'd forgotten to fill our water bottles at breakfast, so by the time we arrived at Dayton, perched at the pinnacle, we were, to put it mildly, thirsty. Only after we refilled our bottles at a convenience store did the clerk advise us not to drink the stuff. She said the local people preferred bottled water due to the strong sulfur taste in the liquid from the tap. But it was safe to drink, she assured us, and we needed it, so we used it anyway. I added a scoop of a powdered sports drink, which sufficiently camouflaged the sulfur taste, and we continued.

With the sky now blue and the temperature moderate, the day proved to be a perfect one for cycling. The rural region was quiet, lacking weekday traffic. We rode on through a land of rolling hills, enjoying conversation, the sunshine, and the small climbs and gentle descents.

Coming upon a tidy farmhouse, we saw about a dozen young Amish children standing in the front yard studying our approach. The girls were all attired in dresses of medium blue, and the boys wore shirts of the same color, tucked into black trousers. I waved, and after a second's hesitation, during which the kids considered the strange spectacle we presented in our spandex shorts and muscle shirts, the tallest of the boys waved back.

The hesitation didn't surprise me. Viewing their way of life as separate from the mainstream, the Amish don't encourage lots of contact with the outside world. But having been around the Ohio

Amish, I'd discovered that a friendly salutation generally brought a polite, if somewhat stiff, response.

What did surprise me was coming upon this Amish home at all. I knew that Route 62 traverses a region in Ohio that boasts a large Amish settlement, but until that moment, I hadn't realized that this part of New York was also a home to these plain people.

"That yard full of kids would have made a great picture," Dave said.

"Yeah, it would have," I said. "But I think it would have seemed intrusive to stop and shoot the picture. The Amish aren't crazy about having their picture taken."

As we continued in the crisp morning, we met occasional Amish buggies pulled by trotting horses. We waved each time, and invariably, an occupant of the buggy waved back. A deeply religious people, the Amish do not build church buildings, but rather gather at a community member's home to worship. Since the children we'd seen appeared too close in age to all belong to one family, I speculated that that house was the designated gathering place for this particular Sunday.

In addition to the usual route signs, this stretch of highway also sprouted smaller signs at regular intervals of perhaps a 10th of a mile. Unlike the Route 62 emblems, these signs topped short posts — about three feet tall — and were apparently installed for some other purpose than to be read from moving vehicles. A series of three numbers appeared on each one: at the top, a four-digit number that remained the same on every sign; in the middle, the number 62, which we assumed referred to the route; and on the bottom, another four-digit number that dropped by two with each sign. We concluded that the signs served as some kind of marker for service vehicles or to enable police to pinpoint accident locations.

Feeling pleased with my powers of observation and deduction, I declared, "With these signs, we'll have no possibility of losing our way."

Yeah, well, pride goeth before destruction.

Frewsburg is the last town in New York on 62. The route travels the small burg's main street, which curves eastward and briefly joins 60, a local road that runs to nearby Jamestown. Then, according to our map, 62 bends south and makes a beeline for Pennsylvania while 60 continues eastward.

We rolled out of Frewsburg watching for the turn. After a couple of miles, I noticed that these small signs now had "60" as their second number. Since 62 was the federal route, I assumed that its number would be the one to appear on the sign when two routes shared the roadway. Peering ahead, I saw none of the tall 62 signs and began to suspect we'd missed the turn. The condition of the pavement, which was more broken and patched than any we'd been on all day, added to my suspicion.

"Have you seen a 62 sign recently?" I called to Dave.

"No. Have we missed the turn?" He was kind enough not to comment on my previous cocksure declaration.

"Possibly," I said.

We stopped to study the map and looked both ways on the highway for signs. Seeing none, we finally decided to pedal back toward Frewsburg before getting too far astray.

We did that with due alacrity, continuing all the way to the town without finding the turnoff, so we finally inquired at a gas station. "That's the road right there," the attendant said, pointing where we'd just been. He described the turn as merely another quarter mile beyond where we had turned around. Sheepishly, we comported ourselves through the hamlet for a third time and, as we passed the edge of town, we spied a Route 62 sign that we had somehow missed on our first pass.

Dave said, "In a car, we'd have covered these two miles so quickly we'd have gotten to the turn without thinking we were off route." Well, that was a better excuse than none at all.

When we arrived at the junction, we propelled ourselves around the corner and noticed that the small signs, which continued on this road, again had "62" as their second number. Now they tell us.

Roughly five miles later, we entered Pennsylvania. We had set our sights on Warren, another 12 miles down the road. A few miles before the city, we stopped at a roadside ice cream stand. As we placed our orders, the smiling girls behind the windows handed us complimentary bottles of spring water, saying we looked hot. But they didn't fool me. It wasn't *my* welfare they were being solicitous of. I received my complimentary drink because the girls saw I was accompanying Dave, the babe magnet. He's tall, with striking good looks, and I've noticed that young ladies frequently start conversations with us — ostensibly about cycling — when Dave's along. When I'm cycling alone, the only way my presence registers with young females is if I run into them with my bike.

I asked a fellow customer about camping possibilities near Warren. He didn't know of any, but a large, middle-aged woman who overheard us suggested Buckaloons, a national forest camping area, which she described as being "just on the far edge of Warren, right on Highway 62."

Normally, when noncyclists give directions, I assume they are underestimating the distances involved. The difference between three miles and seven miles, for example, is virtually insignificant from the seat of a car. But on a bike it can involve an expenditure of more energy than the rider has left late in the day. This woman, however, said she rode a bicycle often and even had dreams of someday riding across the country, so I granted her distance estimate a bit more credibility than usual — though given her size, I suspected she had some fitness work to do before departure on such an expedition.

My odometer registered 70 miles for the day as we entered Warren. We were still riding strongly but felt ready to stop, so we looked forward with some relish to arriving at the camping area. In Warren, Route 62 turns west on a broad street lined with large old homes, many handsomely restored. We proceeded along it and followed 62 to what appeared to be the edge of town without spotting the promised campsite. Not wanting to miss it, we dismounted and clattered into a convenience store, where the clerk told us the location we sought was still three miles further on.

"Only three miles?" I asked.

"Yes, not more than that," and he gave us directions, indicating that Buckaloons was situated right after 62 made a decisive left turn. I glanced at my map and saw the turn, but it looked a good bit more than three miles away.

"You're certain about the distance?" I said.

"Absolutely," he replied in a confident tone. "No more than three miles at the most."

It was eight.

Route 62 leaves Warren heading west, sharing a four-lane highway with U.S. Route 6. Being Sunday evening, the traffic was light, and we pedaled these last miles of the day quickly, if a bit wearily. Aside from being grossly mistaken on his mileage estimate, the clerk was right about Buckaloons being right after the turn. We rolled in, registered for a campsite, and then cooked supper on Dave's camp stove. With no restaurant nearby, we had no other choice.

Buckaloons Recreation Area, located within Allegheny National Forest, rests on the site of a former Indian Village and is named for the Seneca tribe that once lived there. Now it is a quiet camping area with sites well insulated from one another by trees and undergrowth. A brief after-dinner walk sapped us of all remaining energy, so that by the time the daylight faded, so did we, slipping gladly into our tents.

Some people we'd talked to along the way seemed truly incredulous that anyone would want to bike as far as I was planning to, but bikes actually have a special connection with America's highway system. In fact, the history of both is intertwined.

While hard-surfaced highways have been a fact of life for our lifetime, that wasn't the case for our grandparents.

The first national road survey took place in 1904. It revealed that there were then 2.15 million miles of rural highways in our nation, but only 14 percent of those were anything more than dirt lanes. And most of the so-called improved miles had only gravel, plank or shell coverings. A meager 38,622 miles boasted a surface of water-bound macadam. In the entire country, only 141 miles had any better form of paving.

But all of that was an improvement over what had been. In the closing decades of the 19th century, roads were far worse, many of them little more than mud troughs for months every year. Although several state governors pushed for improvements, little happened. The federal government hadn't done much road building since before 1840, and some of that had been for military purposes. Once the military need had ended, most of that mileage had not been maintained.

Federal inaction on road building was based on interpretation of the Constitution. During the first three decades of the 19th century, a series of presidential vetoes blocked efforts to federally fund highway construction. President Madison, for example, argued that the federal government had no right to infringe on the sovereignty of a state by exercising jurisdiction on a highway within the state's borders. Thus, these presidents held, the federal government had no Constitutional authority to build and maintain roads.

Besides that, during much of the 1800s, transportation efforts were put first into building canals and later into laying track for railroads. Roads, so the thinking ran, existed for local travel and for getting goods to and from railways stations. Many people had never seen good roads and thus had no idea of their value.

The introduction of the bicycle into the United States in 1877 changed things. The first bikes were called "penny farthings" or "ordinaries," and had enormous front wheels and tiny rear ones. By 1880, hundreds of people along the eastern seaboard pedaled these ordinaries, and the cycling craze swept westward rapidly.

Also in that year, the first national bicycle organization emerged, the League of American Wheelmen. By 1893, it listed over 100,000 dues-paying members, but even that figure was only a fraction of the riders in America. By then, cycling had spread to nearly every town and village.

Local chapters of the League began sponsoring two-wheeled tours, and this sport exposed riders to the deplorable conditions of the country's roads. On their high-wheeled steeds, cyclists were very susceptible to injury when uneven surfaces resulted in falls. But the ease of travel by bike on the few good highways that existed helped many people see the need for road improvement.

Early on, some towns banned bikes from streets as menaces to public safety, and in other places they were taxed, so the League's initial emphasis was on the legal rights of cyclists. Soon, however, the focus shifted to campaigning for road improvements. In 1888, the League made that effort official when it established a National Committee for the Improvement of Highways. Over the next 17 years, the Wheelmen poured thousands of man-hours and several hundred thousand dollars into the cause of better roads. Among other things, the organization printed millions of pamphlets on the road problem, published a monthly magazine called *Good Roads*, wrote articles on road-improvement for major journals and held good-road meetings and conventions.

At one point, the group even sponsored an International Road Congress in Port Huron, Michigan, where it displayed the latest road machinery and constructed a sample section of macadam-paved roadway.

These activities finally paid off when, in 1893, the U.S. Congress established within the Department of Agriculture the Office of Road Inquiry, a move that eventually led to the previously mentioned national road survey and subsequent road improvements.

Naturally the introduction of the automobile in the 1890s gave added impetus to the drive for good roads, but it was cyclists that had drummed the effort that far.

In 1905, the Office of Road Inquiry was enlarged and renamed the Bureau of Public Roads. Two highway acts, one in 1916 and the other in 1921 made it through Congress, and federal money was soon funneled to the states for highway construction and improvement. The age of modern roads had begun.

And all because of bicyclists. As a beneficiary of their efforts, I for one am impressed and appreciative.

In the lead during the pouring rain, Dave suddenly swerved to a stop. I pulled in behind him. "What's up?" I asked.

He looked miserable. "My feet are swimming," he said. With that, he sat down on the metal guardrail at the edge of the highway and began removing his shoes. I stood shivering as the steady hard rain continued to drench us.

The precipitation had started sometime during the night. Its patter on my tent woke me only long enough to hope it would end by morning. It didn't, and it continued to fall — chillingly — as we struck our tents and packed up in the 50-degree daylight.

On our separate rides across America, Dave and I had handled rainy days differently. Since he had been on no fixed schedule, he simply hung around camp when rain fell. I had a limited time allotment, so I rode rain or shine. But on this trip, Dave had to be back at work the next morning, and so there was no consideration of hanging about. We mounted up and rode out, hoping to find a restaurant or store where we could get breakfast and possibly wait out the downpour.

The evening before I'd asked the campground manager, a retiree volunteer, if we'd find any place to eat. He explained that he wasn't from the area, but was fairly sure there were some places within a very few miles.

From the Buckaloons area southward, 62 runs on the hem of Allegheny National Forest, slipping between the wooded hillside and the Allegheny River. On a clear day, it would surely be a scenic ride, but on this particular morning, we rode hunkered down against the rain as it soaked through our several layers of clothing and filled our shoes.

Within the first mile, we saw a sign for a restaurant, but it pointed down a side road with no indication of how far off track it lay. Because the campground manager had assured us there were other places to eat not much farther on, I suggested we continue.

Big mistake.

When we'd dressed against the rain that morning, Dave had produced a pair of supposedly waterproof socks, which he slipped on over his regular ones. Now at the roadside he pulled them off and upended first one then the other. A tankard of water gushed out of each. "Are they filling from the top?" I asked, thinking the moisture had run down his legs and into the socks.

"Hard to tell," he said. "I'm soaked everywhere. What about your feet?"

"I'm sloshing too, but at least the water isn't getting trapped in my socks. It's running right through."

Dave pulled his shoes back on, minus the high-tech socks, looking distinctly disheartened.

Route 62 though the National Forest was narrow, lacked paved shoulders and showed signs of hard use. For the first time since leaving Niagara Falls, we were on roadway with none of the three prerequisites for safe motor vehicle-bicycle road sharing — wide lanes, paved shoulders or low usage. A good bit of the traffic on this stretch consisted of coal trucks, which flew by seemingly heedless that we were on the road — and the spray spewing from their big tires added a lovely layer of grime to our already drenched clothing. A few semis also passed, but they were more mannerly, willing to wait for assured clear distance before sheeting us with the contents of a puddle.

With each pluvial minute, my regret at not checking out that first restaurant grew. We cycled on forlornly for 14 miles without finding any such establishments, and when we finally did, near Tidioute, we were thoroughly chilled.

Hot coffee and tea in the little restaurant we at last found revived us somewhat, and after placing a breakfast order with the 30-ish waitress with intricate tattoos slithering up both legs, we took turns using the restroom to change into dry clothes ... well, drier clothes anyway. By that point, the deluge had seeped deeply into our panniers, though the plastic bags with which we routinely lined the packs had offered moderate protection to the contents. Despite the less wet clothing, however, we shivered most of the time we ate.

By the time we emerged, the storm had finally taken a breather, although gray still dominated the sky, and I suspected that the rain was not done with us. Still, it held off long enough for us to pedal the next 13 miles, which brought us to the village of Tionesta, an Indian name meaning "home of the wolves." Tionesta was a nice enough place, but the facility we most appreciated about it that day was its laundromat, where we dried our wet stuff. While we were indoors, rain suddenly hurtled down again with vigor and then, just as suddenly, stopped. We debated whether to continue or halt the day's ride where we were. Earlier we had set Franklin as our destination, and we both hated to quit that early in the day. I, ever the optimist, urged continuation and Dave, trusting friend of the optimist, agreed. Maybe someday he'll learn.

Sixteen miles lay between us and Oil City, the next community on 62. Franklin was another eight miles beyond that. We rode bravely out of the shelter Tionesta provided, and began the run to Oil City. The highway, also recently repaved, continued to follow the river, crossing it twice on bridges. The forest environment continued and

62 rose and fell through it, more or less following the topography of the land.

Then we began another climb. This one, however, did not drop back down as quickly as previous ones had done and we continued upward, making our way over a mountain. Until this point, the only substantial hill we'd met was in New York, the five-mile climb coming out of Gowanda. This new one was perhaps three miles shorter, but significantly steeper. The ascent was hot, thirsty labor. The chill we'd felt earlier completely dissipated, and we stopped to remove outer clothing before reaching the top.

That all changed when we finally achieved the summit. As if on cue, rain started and the temperature dropped suddenly as if the floor had been pulled out from under it. The downhill side of the mountain was about as steep as the climb had been, so even though we put our jackets back on and controlled our speed somewhat on the descent, the frigidity from the wind whipping us was bone-chilling.

Oil City lay at the bottom of the mountain. By the time we got there, Dave was shivering.

"Let's stop here," I said. "Enough is enough."

"I agree. I'm not up to eight more miles of this."

We had ridden just over 50 miles since the Buckaloons.

I had no interest in camping in the unrelenting wet, so I presented myself at the town's only motel and rented a room for the night. Dave phoned his friend who was to pick him up and changed the rendezvous from Franklin to Oil City. We found a restaurant for supper and waited for Dave's ride home.

"Pretty miserable day, wasn't it?" Dave said.

"You can say that again."

"Would you do it again?"

"Would you?"

We both grinned and knew the answer.

In a heartbeat.

After Dave left, I pulled out my maps to figure how far I'd be likely to get the next day. For my coast-to-coast journey, I'd purchased a set of maps from Adventure Cycling Association, an organization that has mapped several scenic, low-traffic routes up and down and across America. Designed especially for cycle tourists, those excellent maps indicate route elevations, and the location of food services, bike shops, campgrounds and so forth.

But no such bike routing has been done for 62, and probably never will be. Bike route planners seldom consider major highways. I'd briefly considered whether I needed anything at all beyond standard state road maps. After all, as a federal highway, 62 would be well signed along its entire length. But a cursory survey of 62 in my road atlas revealed that it lopes onto stretches of Interstate and other restricted-access roads now and then, and I'd need local maps to find paths around them. So for this trip, I'd solicited help from the American Automobile Association, but at first, I'd had difficulty getting what I wanted across.

"Er ... I think you want Ernie's Bike Shop," the AAA receptionist had said. "We don't have maps for bicycle trails."

"Yes, I know. I'm not looking for a bike trail."

"But we map highway trips." The poor woman spoke politely but no doubt she was beginning to wonder what to do with the obviously addled chap standing before her.

I tried again. "I'm planning to follow Route 62, only on a bicycle."

"Oh," she said, brightening. "We can map that." And she directed me to a "travel consultant" across the room. My packet of maps, with my route marked clearly in green ink, was ready a few days later.

Chapter 3

At Oil City, the Allegheny River still flows southwest. Oil Creek, coming down from Titusville, flows into the Allegheny at that bend, cutting the land on the main river's north shore in two. With a population of 12,000, Oil City spreads over all three banks created by the juncture of the two rivers. The town is united by means of two bridges over the Allegheny and one across Oil Creek.

As the community's name suggests, it owes its beginning to oil. The nation's first oil well was drilled in Titusville, 15 miles to the north, in 1859. Oil City sprang up quickly thereafter as 17 million barrels of oil were produced along the Oil Creek ravine in the first decade after the discovery, a yield that earned the Oil Creek region the label, "the valley that changed the world." One of the first wells, drilled in 1861, is still producing.

It was not oil that was on my mind as I awoke the next morning, however, but rain. I peered out the door of my motel room to see it still falling. I flipped on the television and watched the weather report. It promised scattered areas of rain all day long throughout the region. Fixing my hope to the notion that "scattered" meant the rain would not be falling nonstop, I walked next door to McDonald's for breakfast. Rain still fell as I returned to the motel, so I took my time packing my panniers and loading the bike. Finally, resigning myself to getting wet again, I checked out and pulled onto the highway. To my relief, the precipitation stopped almost at once.

The sky remained overcast, however. I rode across the bridge that carries 62 and turned eastward on the level four-lane that 62 becomes as it follows the Allegheny Valley between Oil City and Franklin. A strong, cold headwind smacked me as I pushed on along the edge of the busy road. My hands were freezing, so I switched from my fingerless riding gloves to the full ones I had in my saddlebags. Riding into the wind was tiring, but it wasn't rain, and I was abundantly grateful.

For much of the way between the two towns, 62 offered a paved shoulder, but since some of the highway had been hacked out of hillside, shale, fallen from the chopped banks, littered the berm in places, forcing me to swerve into the traffic lane periodically to avoid the rocky debris.

By the time I got to Franklin, I realized that I simply did not have enough clothing with me to stay warm in the persistent wind. Riding during the last week of May, I hadn't expected the low temperatures and had left my cold-weather gear at home. Spotting a discount department store, I stopped in, but discovered only summer items on display. A bit farther on, however, I came upon a Goodwill used-clothing store. Inside, I found a heavy wool sweater for $4. I layered it on beneath my windbreaker and immediately felt warmer.

Franklin is built at the confluence of the Allegheny River and French Creek. The main river flows southwest into Franklin and then swings southeast, meaning that I would now leave the waterway I'd been paralleling ever since Warren.

Franklin's recorded history dates back to a fort named Machault built by the French in 1753 at the juncture of the two rivers. Seven years later, the British also built one, Fort Venango. According to one story, Indians often played ball near the British fort. If, on occasion, the ball flew over the fort's wall, the soldiers would let the Indians inside to retrieve it. In 1763, during Pontiac's War, more Indians than usual were "playing." The ball went over the wall, and when the British opened the gate, the Indians rushed in and seized the fort — sort of an inverse Trojan horse tactic.

Franklin itself was just a backwater town until the discovery of oil nearby in 1859. In record time, refineries were thrown up, and by 1868, Franklin had blossomed into a city.

Route 62 exits Franklin by climbing an enormous hill. Although the lanes would normally have been wide enough to accommodate bicycles and motor vehicles, they were not on this particular day. Highway crews were working on the downhill side widening the shoulder and adding a concrete curb. The widening work had not yet been done on the uphill side, so I was forced to the very edge of the pavement by the narrow, temporary lanes that had been established to sustain traffic. Fortunately, although there were a lot of vehicles moving up and down the hill, the uphill stream had frequent gaps due to the heavy trucks that lumbered upward, slowing the train of vehicles behind them. During these gaps, I pounded over as much ground as possible, and then pulled over when overtaken by the huge trucks. Thus, in sprints, I made my way through the construction zone and up the hill.

The labor of pumping uphill at least warmed me, and halfway up I stopped to remove the sweater. But once I achieved the top, the wind lambasted me as coldly as before, and I put it back on.

A plodding ride over rolling ground brought me to the little community of Polk, named in 1886 for President James K. Polk. As I drew near it, an impressive looking campus of brick buildings captured my attention. A college perhaps?

Beginning to tire from the constant buffeting from the wind, I pulled into Polk's little eatery, "Laurie's Restaurant." Maybe it was because of the cold, but the hot meal I had inside seemed as tasty a lunch as I'd ever had. The large bowl of homemade soup featured massive chunks of turkey in concert with thick egg noodles in hot broth. A grilled cheese sandwich completed the main course.

The youngish woman who waited on me seemed to have a proprietary interest in the place, and I assumed her to be the Laurie named on the sign. I asked her about the college-like buildings across the street. The state mental hospital, Laurie said.

Maybe she ought to look into supplying the food for the institution, I thought. It was certainly doing *my* mental health some good.

"Where are you headed?" called a middle-aged woman at the next table.

"I'm following 62," I said, and told her my destination for the day.

"You can save a couple of miles and big hill if you take 965, just up the road. It rejoins 62 later."

"Thanks, but I'm purposely following 62."

"Yeah, but there's a long hill that way. Everybody around here uses 965."

"Well, thanks." I saw no point in continuing to debate it.

"Of course, 965 has a hill too ...," she said, as if to herself, "but it's a short one." This last part she addressed to me.

"Okay. Thanks."

"I know a man who walks up it every day."

"I see."

"You really should consider it."

Obviously she wasn't going to let go of this, so I told her I would consider it, a reply she seemed to accept. I did consider it — as a non-option for my journey.

Laurie approached my table. "Would you like any dessert?"

"Do you have pie?"

"Certainly," she said, and listed three kinds.

"Homemade?"

"Made them myself."

I ordered the cherry crumb, and received a large slice. Each bite reminded me why pies have long been the most popular dessert in diners across America.

As I walked out, the woman at the next table gave me a friendly smile and said, "Good luck!"

"Thanks."

"And don't forget 965. It's just up the road. You can't miss it."

The hill she had tried to warn me off proved to be quite moderate. The grade crept more than leapt, and I crested the top before I had worked up much of a sweat.

Earlier, while adjusting the equipment tied on the rack over my back tire, I had knocked the battery-powered rear light, cracking off a piece of the red plastic reflector. So when I spotted a hardware store in the next town, Sandy Lake, I went it to buy some glue. A woman stood behind the counter reading a magazine.

She led me to the display where I selected a glue, and then we returned to the cash register. While she rang up my sale, I glanced down idly at her magazine, still lying open on the counter. My eyes opened wide with surprised recognition. Even looking at it upside down, I recognized it. "You're reading *Homiletics*," I said.

"Yes?"

"I'm the editor of that publication."

She looked skeptical.

"No, really." I flipped back a few pages to the masthead. "See, right there. 'Executive Editor: Stan Purdum.'"

"That's you?"

"Yes. Here." I pulled out my wallet and handed her my business card. "That's me."

"Well, this is a surprise."

"For me, too, to find it here, that is. Are you a minister?" *Homiletics* is a preaching journal, published bimonthly with sermon ideas for clergy. And although it circulates widely among the clergy, it was a surprise to find a copy as hardware store reading.

"No, I just saw an ad for it and ordered it to show to my pastor." She took a deep breath and then blurted, "To tell you the truth, I think it's worldly!"

"Well, we do try to help pastors address people in the mainstream of life."

She considered this briefly and then brightened. "I do like some of the children's sermons, though."

I laughed inwardly. She referred to the short talks we included for pastors to use with children during the worship service. Almost invariably, they make the same point as the main material, only in simplified form.

The day continued dry but cold and windy. I pushed on, passing through Mercer, the seat of Mercer County, and Hermitage. In Mercer, I passed "The Avenue of 444 Flags," a park drive lined with 444 American flags, one for each day that 53 American hostages were held captive in Iran during the reign of Ayatollah Khomeini in 1979-1981. There is also a monument to the eight U.S. servicemen who died trying to rescue the hostages.

About 5 p.m., I neared Sharon. With a population of 17,500, it was the largest of the Pennsylvania cities on 62. At the east edge of town, "Business 62" splits off the main route, and I took it, looking for a restaurant for supper. After eating, I continued through town, riding next to the curb as traffic passed on my left.

Ahead was a side street running off to the right. As I rolled near it, a passing minivan made a sudden right turn in front of me onto that street, forcing me to brake hard to avert an accident. After some fleeting nasty thoughts about that driver, I wondered if he had even been aware of the problem he almost caused.

Probably not. Percentage-wise, inattentive and preoccupied drivers are a greater threat to cyclists than those who deliberately cause problems. There is no "Riding in traffic" rule to prevent the dangerous situations careless drivers create except perhaps to remember that some drivers don't think like cyclists and really don't consider such issues as how much distance a rider needs to stop. America's first documented auto accident involved a bicycle. It occurred in New York City on May 30, 1896, where a bicyclist was struck by a car. The driver was at fault.

Of course, there are occasional drivers who for some perverted reason deliberately maneuver dangerously around cyclists. Almost every rider has a tale of some malevolent motorist who, by malicious action, struck fear into the heart of the cyclist.

I can recount a few myself. Once, on a solo ride, a pickup truck started to pull past me and as it did, I swerved toward the shoulder to give the vehicle more room. Apparently that action took me out of range of an impending surprise attack. The pickup was now ahead of me and starting to pull away. A young man sat in the truck bed, waving a stick and wearing a venomous look. Indicating his stick, he shouted, "Boy, are you lucky!" On a few other occasions I've also been the target of teenage boys or young men trying to jolt me by suddenly screaming as the vehicle they rode in streamed past.

But unsettling as those occasional acts of deliberate meanness are, the primary traffic risk to cyclists on the road is still from drivers with no ill intent but who aren't thinking about what it's like on the bike. Some drivers seem unaware or unconcerned about how closely they impinge on a cyclist riding legally near the right-hand edge of the road, and simply do not allow enough clearance. The too-close proximity of the vehicle can force riders into the gravel, where they lose control and upset, sometimes with injury. There have even been cases where the protruding mirror of a too-close truck or RV whacks a rider and knocks him off his bike.

One of my own scariest moments on my bike occurred right in my hometown. I was riding a short stretch of a heavily traveled street, one with no shoulder. The passing cars had all been pulling slightly left to avoid me, but then a motorhome overtook me. With traffic in the other lane, his wider vehicle could not swerve left, but we were only a short distance from a side road, and had he exercised a bit of patience, I'd have pulled over to give him clear passage. Instead, he decided to pass me immediately. Creeping up beside me, he left me no place to go. I clung to the edge of the road trying my best not to wobble or bob at all while his massive vehicle slid by not more than two inches from my shoulder. Once past me, he sped up, leaving me shaken and angry.

Considering the number of cars on the road, the drivers who cause these harrowing incidents are a definite minority. Most motorists are cautious, and many are even courteous. And while it takes only one careless driver to cause an accident, I don't head out to ride feeling apprehensive. Actually, with all the riding I've done over the years, I'm surprised by how few car-bike incidents I've experienced. I do try to avoid narrow, busy roadways with no shoulders whenever possible, but I don't let fear of traffic keep me off the roads.

A survey of 700 cyclists I'd seen a couple of months before my trip verified my perception that most drivers are careful around cyclists. When asked how they felt about the statement, "I get more respect from motorists these days," 39.7 percent of the riders agreed. A smaller percent — 32.1 — disagreed.

A full 65 percent agreed that they were "allowed by motorists to behave as a vehicle," and just over 46 percent felt they were "allowed ample room on the side of the road."

Still, it was a bit disconcerting when, three weeks before my departure, a motorist in Chicago was charged with murder for deliberately running down a cyclist with his sports utility vehicle during a fit of road rage. The incident began when the driver cut off the cyclist. The rider responded by pointing at the side of the vehicle with his fist. The driver then allowed the rider to pass, after which he rammed his vehicle into the bike and rider several times. When he succeeded in unseating the cyclist, he drove over him and sped away. He later surrendered to police.

Clearly the driver behaved criminally, and I hope he spends years and years in prison. But given the emotional climate on the road, the cyclist made a mistake when he shook his fist. It is simply unwise to respond to provocative acts by drivers. Like it or not — and I don't like it — it's better to swallow my anger, keep riding and do nothing at all. That doesn't come naturally, but there is too much potential for violence in such confrontations. And even if I do emerge unscathed, the driver may take out his anger on the next cyclist he encounters.

Besides, I always get a little tingle of pleasure in realizing that my non-response is a big disappointment to the jerk who had hoped to provoke or startle me.

Business 62 reunites with the main route on the west side of Sharon, and minutes later, 62 enters Ohio. I tooled across the state line and rode the few miles to Hubbard, a city within the metropolitan area of Youngstown. I'd logged 60 miles, most of the way into a headwind, and was ready to stop.

I had once lived in the Youngstown area, so I knew in advance that finding a place to camp would be difficult. Instead, I checked in at the motel attached to "Truck World." This is a huge, full-service stop for the big rigs that run the I-80 Interstate, which crosses 62 on an overpass at the north edge of Hubbard.

Although not restricted to truckers, they are clearly the target market for Truck World, no surprise given the name. In addition to the services outside — tire and mechanical repair, and numerous pumps for diesel fuel — the establishment also offers a mini-mall with a passel of shops, most of which are open 24 hours a day.

Wandering inside, I found two restaurants, three game rooms, a pub, a driver's license bureau, a news stand, a specialty candy-and-nuts store, a road-permit center, a gift shop, a decorative sign store, a bank of telephones, an ATM, a shoeshine stand and a tool store with really BIG wrenches and an extensive display of savage-looking knives. One of the busiest shops was a convenience-store type, but with merchandise slanted toward on-the-road needs, including audio-books, truck electronics, over-the-counter medicines, maps, forms for filing various trucker reports and assorted personal items. One rack included an assortment of "stay-awake" pills, each packing a high-caffeine whammy. I'm never sure whether to be glad for these — on the idea that they help truck drivers to stay alert — or to worry that they keep tired drivers on the road when they should be laying over.

There was also a hair salon, which surprised me at first, but then I noticed the number of drivers who had women (their wives, I assume) traveling with them. I also saw a couple of women who, judging from their conversation, snatches of which I overheard, may have been drivers themselves.

Only one area was marked as restricted to truckers: a lounge with a laundromat and shower rooms leading off it. Disregarding the "Truckers Only" sign, I wandered in, and when nobody stopped me, I took a gander around. Near the shower area, a male attendant was collecting some sort of chit from drivers before issuing them towels and unlocking a shower unit. The chits were issued as a bonus when drivers filled their rigs with diesel fuel.

On the mammoth parking lot out back, more than 200 18-wheelers, most of them with motors idling, stood waiting for their drivers. There was almost constant movement as big trucks entered and left the lot.

Of course I'd seen trucks on 62, but not as many as I expected for a major route. And many of those I did see were of the smaller variety, the sort used for local deliveries. Even the occasional tractor-trailers on 62 often had cabs minus the sleeper units that characterized the long-haul semis. I knew most trucks used the Interstates for long-distance runs, but since Interstates don't go everywhere, I had still expected more truck movement on the numbered highways. In any case, Truck World reminded me of the vital role the big rigs play in the movement of goods in America.

When I had checked in to the motel, the desk clerk, a cheerful man in his late 60s, looked at my bike and inquired about my trip. Later, as I passed his desk after my wander around the mini-mall, I noticed he had a national highway map out and was tracing 62 with his finger. "That's going to be quite a trip," he said.

I allowed that he was right. "How do you train for a thing like that?" he asked.

I explained that it was mostly just by riding two or three times a week.

"Yeah, but what do you do in the winter?"

"I Spin," I said, and went on to tell him about it. "Spinning" is the trademarked name for a series of intense exercise classes conducted entirely on stationary bicycles.

I first learned about it a few years previously from a magazine article, when the activity was just being introduced in a few locations around the country. What captured my attention was that Spinning ran as a group activity. Over the years, I've had enough exercise setups in my home to outfit a small gym, including a couple of different stationary bikes, but I've never managed to keep myself going for long on a solitary workout program. It's a mystery to me how I can love bicycling outdoors but hate the same activity in my basement. In any case, I wondered if Spinning's group dynamic would make a difference.

So when Spinning was instituted at my local YMCA, I showed up for a demo class. Though subsequent sessions convinced me that the instructor took it easy on us that first time, the session was strenuous enough that I worked up a good sweat. The only trouble I had was getting out to my car afterward; people kept stepping on my hands.

Okay, that's an exaggeration, but you get my meaning. I signed up, and was pleased to discover that working out in a group and with an instructor did enable me to stick with the program, in part because I didn't want to be the only guy who wimped out in front of my fellow exercisees, especially since nearly half of them were female. The group endeavor also injected some enjoyment into the pursuit — probably along the lines of the old cliché that misery loves company.

Each class is 40 minutes long, and the basic idea is that once it starts, you never stop pedaling until the class ends. The bikes, specifically constructed for this activity, have 38-pound freewheels that make coasting impossible. Built to match the geometry and feel of road bikes, the stationary cycles have quick, nifty adjustments to accommodate riders of almost any size.

The real workout comes not just from spinning the crank, but from what you do in addition. At the direction of the instructor, you turn up the resistance and, for measured amounts of time and at varying speeds, you pedal against it. At other times, you rise out of the saddle for "jumps," "runs," "breakaways" and "standing climbs."

The real killer is the "sprint." That's where, against moderate resistance, you pedal as fast as you absolutely can for 15 to 30 seconds. You go all out and you end up all in. Sprints are done both in seated and standing variations. The more merciful instructors save sprints for the last exercise before cool-down. Those who've studied the techniques of the Spanish Inquisition stick sprints in the middle of the session.

Other than the sprint, none of the individual moves is that hard. But when strung together, repeated in combination and at varying speeds, under load and for increasingly longer amounts of time, they amount to a significant cardiovascular workout, not to mention how they build the muscles of your legs and make you want to cry "Uncle." The measure of your progress over the weeks is that you are able to do these exercises with less and less recovery time in between. ("Recovery" is spinning the cranks with little or no resistance, during which the acid burn in your legs subsides. Also, your chest stops heaving and you subdue the need to throw up.)

After several months of attendance at the twice-a-week sessions, I found that my road riding had indeed improved. I powered up hills better and recovered from strenuous activity quicker. During a checkup prior to my giving blood, the nurse commented on the slow, steady beat of my pulse. "You must exercise some," she said.

"Some," I replied modestly.

Well, heck, I wouldn't want to brag.

Back in the clean but plain motel room, I lay on the bed and wondered how many truckers had slept in that room before me. If they'd had to stay overnight, they must have been long-haul drivers, many with families at home. Maybe that was the reason for the gift shop in the mini-mall. After being on the road for a while, no matter how legitimate the reason, you begin to feel guilty about not being home with the people waiting for you, and perhaps you buy gifts to assuage your guilt. Even for those like me, infected with restless feet, the joy of being on the move can be shadowed by intensely lonely moments, and I was having one right then. My itinerary called for me to "camp" in my own home the next night, and I was looking forward to seeing my wife and kids. Home and hearth would feel good.

The only trouble is ... I keep wanting to see where the road goes next.

Chapter 4

Dawn brought another gray and cold day, but, as I was pleased to note, no rain. I ate breakfast in the Truck World restaurant, where I noticed telephones on the wall above every table and at frequent intervals along the counter, where I sat. I eavesdropped as a driver seated next to me used one of these phones to speak with his dispatcher about a load he was to pick up. The driver seemed to know the location where he was being sent, and accepted the assignment matter of factly.

After generous portions of sausage and eggs, I wheeled out onto 62, which winds through Hubbard and on into Youngstown, the biggest city on 62 since Buffalo. In Hubbard, I saw the first "bike-killer" storm-sewer grate I'd noticed on the trip. These grates consist of a series of steel bars aligned parallel with the street. The open spaces between the bars are ready-made traps for bike wheels. When an unsuspecting rider rolls over one of these grates, a wheel can drop up to the axle without warning, usually causing the rider to take a header over the handlebars.

This very thing happened to my brother-in-law. We were riding together one day when his front wheel suddenly dropped between the slats of a grate, upending his bike and tossing him to the ground. He sustained a nasty groin injury and his bike frame was stove in so badly it had to be discarded.

Thankfully, as highway improvements occur, this type of grate is being replaced with grid-type sewer covers that leave no opening large enough to ensnare narrow tires. But in some cities, the old, dangerous grates are still in use. Ohio, for example, is a home-rule state, meaning that in cities of 5,000 or more, it's up to the city government to maintain the highway within the city limits. Even though the state standards call for bike-friendly grates, the cities aren't bound by that regulation unless the state is contributing money to the city's road work.

I pedaled the road between Hubbard and Youngstown, dodging gravel and other detritus that littered the road's edge. At the edge of Youngstown, 62 travels though a district of rundown industrial buildings and low-income housing. The route drops onto a city street that, during my visit, was in the process of being ripped up prior to repaving. The scalped road was so bad that I considered moving to the sidewalk, until I saw it heavily overlaid with loose stones thrown up by traffic. I gritted my teeth and rolled over the ravaged surface as slowly as I could.

Because 62 joins the I-680 inner-belt in town, I had to take an alternative route through the community. My route, which at one time was the path of 62, ran downhill past Youngstown State University — my alma mater — and into the city center, half of which, it seemed, was boarded up. Although the end of the main street nearest the city center had been converted into a plaza, the rest of the street had taken on a skid row appearance. I left the downtown by means of a bridge across the Mahoning River that put me back on 62, now called Market Street, for the long climb out of the valley through the city's south side. Although the community had some fine old buildings, it exuded an air of faded prosperity, which was not helped by the worn appearance of the south-side businesses lining Market Street.

Up through the 1970s, Youngstown's economy had been built on steel mills. Then the influx of cheaper foreign steel plus the failure of many American mills to replace antiquated equipment led to financial crisis, and Youngstown became part of the infamous "rust belt." According to the Auto Club guidebook, the community now has "a strong and diversified industrial base." That may be, but there are some neighborhoods in Youngstown that haven't gotten the word yet.

Continuing on 62 out of Youngstown took me into the suburbs where things looked a lot more prosperous. On the way, 62 crossed Mill Creek on a bridge. Looking to the north, I could see the magnificent old Lanterman's Mill, built in 1845 and now fully restored and open to the public.

Although I hadn't yet traveled a lot of miles, I was beginning to tire. As they had the day before, cold headwinds batted me and made me feel as if I were pedaling through molasses. By the time I got to Canfield, a village that looked as if it had been imported from New England, I was tired and cold. One of the well-kept buildings on the town's oval-shaped green was a coffee shop, and I hustled in. It was one of those places that serve deluxe pastries and cappuccino in several different flavors. I ordered a hot tea, for which they charged me twice what I'd pay in a diner.

While I sat sipping my beverage, two women and a girl of about 10 came in. One woman proceeded to the counter to place their order. The other woman ushered the girl toward a table. The whole time, the girl was loudly instructing the woman with her what to order for her. The child spoke in a rude, demanding tone, so I assumed the woman was her mother.

The girl wanted a large, cream-filled pastry. "No," her mother said, "you never finish those. You can share mine."

"Then I'll ask Aunt Peg," the girl said. "She'll get it for me." The girl jumped up, marched to the other woman and in a sweet voice, repeated to her what she wanted. Aunt Peg said, "Okay, dear."

Mom looked exasperated.

I recalled when my own offspring were at the age where getting food ordered was an ordeal. Typically, we'd try to head off trouble on the trip to the restaurant. "We're going to Wendy's," my wife would say to our brood. "Decide now what you are going to eat."

"What do they have?" the kids asked.

"The same things they've had the last 80 times we eaten there," my wife said. "The usual hamburgers, chicken, and french fries."

The kids appeared deep in thought so we assumed they were contemplating the menu.

The children said no more about food until we were in line waiting our turn. "Have you decided what you're having?" my wife asked. They nodded yes.

"Why don't you tell us what you want," I said. "We'll place the order for you."

"No. We want to do it ourselves."

I should have smelled trouble. "Well, make sure you're ready.

We don't want to be all night getting our food. Any questions before we get to the cash register?" They said no.

No questions that is until we were ready to place our order. As my wife was speaking to the cashier, my youngest yanked on her mother's coat. "Mom, can I have —"

"Don't interrupt your mother while she's placing her order," I said. "You're supposed to have your mind made up before this."

"But I want to change my order," my daughter said in a loud voice.

"Don't speak so loudly," I said. "Besides, how can you change an order you haven't even placed yet?"

It came my daughter's turn. "I want mumble, mumble, mumble," she said to the cashier.

The cashier looked to us for help. "Speak up," I said to the girl whose volume had been too high moments before.

"I want mumble, mumble, mumble," she repeated. This time I translated. I hadn't actually heard what she said either, but she had the same thing every time we ate at that restaurant, so it wasn't difficult. Apparently I got it right, since my daughter didn't contradict me.

Next my number two son. "I want a large Coke."

"Not a large, Scott," my wife said. "You never finish it."

"But I'm really hungry tonight," he protested.

By now the folks behind us were getting a bit restless, so we gave in. "Okay, a large. But I expect you to finish it," my wife said.

He finished placing his order. He wanted a large everything.

Number one son was easier. He's been at it longer.

After we were seated and got the food on our tray sorted out, there were the usual three more trips to the counter for ketchup packets, salt, more ketchup packets and other items the children had neglected to mention they wanted the first time we were there.

When we were getting ready to go, I looked at number two's place. "You haven't finished your hamburger, your french fries or your Coke," I observed.

"I wasn't that hungry," he said. "Besides, you always order me too much."

I finished my tea and mounted up. I began plodding southwest toward Salem through open country. A few miles above that community, I crossed an intersection identified as New Albany. If there had once been a town there, all that remained of it was an ice cream stand. The spot was unremarkable, except that I had noticed on my map that 62 traveled through another New Albany, also in Ohio. I'd hit that one a couple of days later.

Salem, a shortened version of Jerusalem, was founded by Quakers who moved to the area from Salem, New Jersey, in 1803, bringing the name with them. In the late 18th and early 19th centuries, Ohio and other parts of what was the Northwest Territory drew Quakers because of two provisions in the Northwest Ordinance of 1787. One declared that no one was to be "molested" for religious beliefs, and the other pronounced the territory forever free of slavery. This second stipulation especially attracted Quakers from the South, who saw migration to the Northwest Territory as an opportunity to escape an oppressive slave environment. By 1800, 800 Quaker families, including the entire membership of one North Carolina congregation, had migrated to the Ohio territory.

Just a few weeks before my visit, 62 had been rerouted to bypass Salem on a four-lane that had just opened but was still under construction. I had the road almost all to myself.

After a couple of miles, 62 left the new four-lane and deposited me on the busy two-lane road that is a straight shot from Salem to Alliance. It also proved to be one of the most frustrating sections of 62. The shoulder was unpaved except where household mailboxes stood beside the road. In front of each mailbox, an apron of pavement had been installed, apparently for the convenience of the rural mail carrier. But in between these aprons, the berm remained gravel. Sighting ahead, I could see a series of aprons as blips wandering away from the road edge and back again, like the edge of a serrated knife. From my perspective, this on-again-off-again shoulder paving was a problem. The gravel portions in between where too rough for my skinny bike tires, and were a couple of inches lower than the aprons at that. And I found it dangerous to be dipping back and forth from the blacktopped shoulder to the highway proper. Whenever I pulled onto an apron, drivers evidently assumed that I was going to stay on the shoulder and passed me without hesitation, forcing me to stop abruptly when the apron ran out. In the end, I decided to ignore the aprons and ride on the highway. The lane was just wide enough to share it with cars, but there was little room for error.

Continuing on 62 into the unrelenting headwind, I eventually came to Damascus. Little more than a crossroads community, it did have a general store where I acquired the makings of a sandwich for lunch.

Damascus is a biblical city name, and like Salem, the community was settled by Quaker pioneers. The town was never very large, but from 1866 until 1977, it was the headquarters of the Ohio Quakers. Though the central office has since moved to Canton, Ohio, there's still a sizeable Quaker meeting house, now called Damascus Friends Church. A 19th-century split among Quakers resulted in one branch following the "silent-meeting" path and retaining the Quaker name. The other group adopted regular services with hymns, prayers and preaching, and took the name Evangelical Friends Church.

During the days of stagecoach travel, Damascus had a hotel located on what is now Route 62, and to the consternation of the Quakers, liquor was sold there. To rid the town of this blight, the local Friends church purchased the inn, and then resold it to someone more sympathetic with their viewpoint, who banned the booze and renamed the establishment "The Temperance House."

Continuing my journey I passed what I'd come to consider a standard part of the scenery in Ohio — oil well tanks. Ohio ranks fourth nationally in the number of wells drilled, behind only Texas, Oklahoma and Pennsylvania. These small tanks dot the landscape, especially in eastern Ohio, sitting near wellheads. According to the most recent figures I'd seen, Ohio currently had over 64,500 active wells producing oil and/or gas.

Of these, the majority were "strippers," wells that produce less than 10 barrels of oil or 60,000 cubit feet of gas per day. Many of Ohio's wells generate only one barrel of oil (or the equivalent in gas) daily. While their outputs may not be phenomenal, most strippers have long lives and produce reliably. All but 12 of Ohio's 88 counties have gas and oil wells.

Cyclists tend to be more intimately acquainted with oil well tanks than the general public. That's because the tanks are to cyclists what fireplugs are to dogs. At least that's so in Ohio, where trees and other cover are often too far back from the road to be of immediate service. For many cyclists, the oil tanks are the refuge of last resort in moments of urgency far from the nearest convenience store. The tank I saw now bore the name of a company I'd never heard of, but that was no surprise. Most of those companies that drill wells in Ohio are not "Big Oil." Generally, they're entrepreneurs, small operators with a modest numbers of wells, often five or less, and some have only one. The largest single producer owns only about 50 wells. In fact, this is typical of the United States as a whole. In our nation, independents drill about 85 percent of domestic wells, and locate more than half of all new gas and oil reserves.

So my advice to fellow cyclists: The next time you wheel into a well site, give a moment's thought not to the big name oil producers, but to the little guy who has so kindly provided these bicyclists' comfort stations at convenient intervals along the byways we pedal.

Alliance, the next town on my itinerary, also owes its start to Quakers. With three communities in a row all founded by this religious group, I wondered in what ways the Quaker influence still showed in the region. The label is prevalent: Several shops in Salem have the word "Quaker" worked into their business names, but those are more commercial uses of the name than statements of theology or lifestyle. Even the Salem high school football team is called "The Quakers."

To find out about the true impact, I talked to Kenneth Albright, senior pastor of the Damascus Friends Church. He freely admitted that things uniquely Quaker are hard to identify in the communities today. "It's more of a memory," he said.

"Do members of your church think of themselves as Quakers?" I asked.

"Only in a historical sense. Our focus is more on helping people find Jesus Christ as their personal Savior."

It's an endeavor in which the Damascus church was apparently having some success. Their building, already surprisingly large for such a tiny community, was slated for expansion to accommodate the growing congregation, and Reverend Albright was looking for an additional full-time minister to help with pastoring responsibilities.

"Damascus is a tight-knit community," the pastor said. "I think our faith plays a role in that."

I asked Reverend Albright about The Temperance House story, and he laughed.

"Did Quakers succeed in making Damascus a dry community?" I asked.

"No, though we wish it was. You can buy alcohol at the store. While we're still not in favor of drinking, we stay focused on our main mission, bringing people to Christ."

Before I moved on, Reverend Albright mentioned that he and his son had recently ridden RAGBRAI, the annual bicycle ride across Iowa sponsored by the Des Moines Register. "We really enjoyed it," he said. "I also ride a motorcycle but the cycling is something special. I love it."

On the street outside the church, I watched a team of men with surveying instruments take sightings and measurements in preparation for some road work. I knew, of course, that surveying played an important role in the laying out of modern roads, but for a long time, I had assumed that most of America's first roads had developed haphazardly, overlaying the course of animal and Indian trails and often following the path of least resistance. Some initial arteries did start that way, allowing the first forays into the American wilderness. And in some cases, early roads were simply a widening and clearing of these trails. But in the long run, these trail roads were not the main solution in settling the land, and in fact, most that started that way were often later relocated, at least in part, to surveyed routes. Most roads, it turns out, were laid out not by animals or Indians but by surveyors.

For example, the Natchez Trace, an early road that basically followed an Indian trail between Nashville, Tennessee, and Natchez, Mississippi, did provide settlers access to the southern frontier, but it was gradually abandoned in favor of surveyed routes. The problem was that like many trails, the one that had become the Natchez road avoided lowlands and thus missed most natural water sources. In addition, the ridgelines the trail followed did not offer the rich soil farmers needed. In other words, the road traversed places nobody wanted to live.

Even the use of the Trace as a post road increased the likelihood of its eventual disuse. Better farmland lay to the east of the Trace, and with each new settlement in that area, the outcry built for the postal riders to travel through places where there were actually people to send and receive mail. Thus surveyed routes to where people wanted to live eventually replaced many of these trail-to-roads routes.

As the young nation acquired additional territory, surveys were crucial to settlement. The land ordinance of 1785, passed by Congress to regulate the sale of land in the Northwest Territory, provided for surveying the large region into townships six-mile square, along lines running east-west and north-south. The townships were further subdivided into 36 lots or "sections." Later, as roads were built in these areas, they were generally routed along the survey lines.

Road surveys also played a role in the early years of Ohio's settlement. The 1802 act of Congress that set the stage for Ohio's admission into statehood provided that three percent of the proceeds of the sale of Ohio public lands would be used for building roads within the state. Fine and good, but as historian William T. Utter points out, the money "was largely expended for locating or 'laying out' roads rather than for their construction." While Utter mentioned that as one reason road-building efforts crawled in the early years, it also shows that when it came to road construction, route location and surveys were among the first things people thought about.

There were roads that simply grew up alongside railroad lines, but the rail route had been surveyed, so the roads simply took advantage of that existing layout work.

Route 62 chugs straight through Alliance as State Street, a five-mile retail strip, which is four lanes wide from the eastern edge of town to its western boundary. Since Alliance is not far from my hometown, I've driven through it frequently. And every time, State Street has been busy with constant traffic. That was true this day too, as I cycled through.

Alliance's territory seems out of proportion to its population of 23,000. At one time, I thought I'd found out why. The community is an amalgamation of four towns. (I assume they named it Alliance because Amalgamation doesn't fit as well on the signs at the city limits.) I guessed the four villages had been spaced out along this highway. But I learned that the four were actually quite near each other, clustered around what is today the downtown area. Evidently, the extended area is simply city sprawl. The oldest of the original villages, Mount Union, was founded in 1824 but all four weren't united until 1891.

At the western edge of Alliance, Route 62 drops onto a four-lane highway on which bicycles are not permitted. This situation continues with 62 most of the way through Canton and well beyond, so I followed 62's pre-freeway path. This was a 24-mile departure from current 62, but made necessary because of the prohibition — although what harm a cyclist would do riding on the lane-wide shoulder of the four-lane highway is beyond me. The old route, however, was more interesting.

It started at the west edge of Alliance as State Route 173 and then became Columbus Road all the way to Canton. The highway ran through rolling farm country, with some nonfarm homes scattered along the way. It had one drawback: no paved shoulders. Why wide shoulders on some roads, narrow shoulders on others and none at all on still others?

One of the reasons was shortsightedness. When the state highway departments first acquired the right-of-ways, they often had plenty of width, but couldn't envision why they'd ever need it all. In some cases, they turned the unused portions back over to the adjacent landowners. Later, when the highway officials wanted to widen the road or add more shoulder, the landowners, who were often farming right up to the road edges, were unwilling to sell the land back cheaply.

Of course, shoulders, paved or otherwise, are not added primarily for the benefit of cyclists. One of the specification manuals highway engineers use states that shoulders are to provide an area for stopped vehicles, for roadside emergencies and to maintain traffic through construction work zones. Not one word about cyclists.

Still, the move today, whenever space and funding allow, is to add wider shoulders, with the portion adjacent to the lanes "treated" in some fashion. Pavement is the best form of treatment, but depending on the classification of the road, lesser treatments can be acceptable (but not to cyclists!).

Although the road I was then pedaling had no shoulders at all, the traffic was moderate, so the only problem I had was when pedaling up the short hills. Motorists behind me couldn't see over the crests, and so naturally, they did not want to pull into the other lane for fear of oncoming traffic. But if I rode near the edge of the highway, some drivers would try to squeeze by me, too close for comfort, and I'd be forced off the road. So on the upgrades, I practiced a riding technique known as "taking the lane."

Instead of hugging the white line, I rode about three feet left of it. This placed me far enough into the traffic stream that overtaking vehicles could not crowd by me without swerving well into the left lane. Thus they had no choice but to wait to pass until it was safe for them and me. When I neared the top and could see the other lane was clear, I moved over to the white line and waved the following cars around me.

My alternate route eventually delivered me to downtown Canton.

Like Youngstown, Canton once relied heavily on the steel industry for its employment, but has diversified since the crisis in steel manufacturing. With a population of 84,000, Canton is the county seat of Stark County. Laid out in 1806, it incorporated as a village in 1815, as a town in 1834 and as a city in 1854. (Are you paying attention? There will be a test!) The original surveyor named the community in honor of a deceased friend. The friend, who had transported the first cargo to arrive at Baltimore, Maryland, from Canton, China, had christened his Baltimore estate "Canton."

Canton claims fame as the home of President William McKinley, and there's a large national memorial to him in an attractive city park, with an excellent museum of history, science and industry adjacent to it. Reportedly, thousands of people visit it every year, but when I tell people I'm from the Canton area, nobody ever says, "Oh yes, the home of William McKinley." To about half, the name means nothing; the other half light up and exclaim, "The Pro Football Hall of Fame!"

Indeed, in terms of renown, that attraction dropkicks the

McKinley Memorial off the field. There's even a weeklong festival associated with the Hall of Fame every summer. Although the community does not have a major league football team, it was the founding site of the American Professional Football Association, the direct forerunner of the National Football League. In 1920, several football enthusiasts met in an auto showroom and anted up $100 each to get the league started. Even before the formation of the league, the Canton Bulldogs were an early pro football power, including in their lineup the now legendary Jim Thorpe.

Market Avenue took me through the city center, where I found a four-block section torn up in preparation for a new brick-paved plaza. That was typical of what's been gradually going on as the community struggles to renew its downtown. Like many urban areas, Canton's downtown has been eroded by suburban shopping centers, malls and outlying professional buildings. Still, with its wide streets, massive old buildings, plazas and small parks, Canton's downtown projects a substantial, if slightly threadbare, allure.

Canton's main downtown street is Tuscarawas. For years, Tuscarawas was the path through Canton of the old Lincoln Highway, later rechristened U.S. Route 30, though that route now bypasses the downtown as a four-lane freeway. The Lincoln Highway was the brainchild of Carl Graham Fisher, an Indianapolis businessman who helped promote the Indianapolis Speedway. In 1911, Fisher (who, by the way, had once been a bicycle salesman and racer), proposed a hard-surface, "Coast-to-Coast Rock Highway," as the first continuous transcontinental route. It was to run from New York City's Times Square to San Francisco's Lincoln Park. Henry Joy, president of the Packard Motor Company, supported Fisher in this idea, and proposed the highway name in memory of President Abraham Lincoln.

Joy, an adventurer at heart, had previously tried to drive across the country and found that the roads ran out in Nebraska. In Omaha, he got directions from a resident. He was to drive west from town until he reached a fence. Open the gate, drive through, close the gate and continue, repeating this process several times. Joy did this, until finally the fences ran out and there was nothing but twin ruts across the plains.

Fisher and Joy together formed the Lincoln Highway Association in 1913. Using their own money, they publicized the idea, which soon attracted strong support from the auto industry and the general public. Their initial target was to have the road ready for Association members to drive to San Francisco for the 1915 Panama-Pacific Exposition.

Though they received $10 million in pledges, this wasn't nearly enough to build the road, so the Association dropped to Plan B. First, they marked the entire route, using existing roads, gravel paths and tracks in the prairie to designate a connected route from ocean to ocean. Next, they petitioned cities, towns and counties to rename local parts with the Lincoln name. (In Massillon, the next town west of Canton, the main street still bears the name Lincoln Way.) And third, to raise public consciousness of the value of a paved cross-nation road, the Association used its money to construct a number of "seedling" miles, paved with concrete, spaced out along the route.

Although much of the route, especially in the Midwest, remained a mud track for years, the route was actually used. In 1915, several hundred parties motored across it heading for the Exposition, and thousands of others followed in the next years for both touring and commercial purposes. With the federal funds made available from the Federal-Aid Road Acts of 1916 and 1921, the paving was eventually completed, and for several years, the Lincoln Highway was the main middle route across America.

But in 1926 when the national system of route numbering was imposed, the Lincoln Highway as an entity came to an end. While much of the Lincoln's course, from Pennsylvania into Utah, became Route 30, the remaining portions were assigned other numbers or became state or local routes. Route 30 was a coast-to-coast road, but with the new routing, it now began in Atlantic City, New Jersey, and ended in Astoria, Oregon. In the later part of the century, after the Interstates were built, I-80 became the middle route across America that the Lincoln Highway was initially envisioned to be.

Before the freeways, 62 departed Canton by means of Navarre Road, the course I now followed. On Canton's west side, the road paralleled a railroad track and took me past blue-collar housing, light industry and several trucking depots. Nearer Navarre, there were some newer, more upscale homes.

About a mile north of the town whose name it bears, Navarre Road ends. Maneuvering around the corner, I found myself back on 62, with the bike-restricted segment behind me at last.

The extended rerouting of 62 in the Canton area is an example of a trend affecting the entire Numbered Highway System — that of relocating portions of the routes to newer, faster and shorter paths. Since 1955, the body responsible for designating the federal routes has considered the Numbered Highway System essentially complete. From that point on they stopped establishing new routes and instead, began perfecting existing ones. Often this involved reworking inadequate sections that had been accepted to get the system established. This extensive reworking has resulted in an overall mileage reduction. In 1969, the U.S. Numbered Route System had 167,231 total miles; by 1989, it had dropped by nearly 10,000 to 157,724.

Navarre was once a port town on an earlier sort of American highway, the Ohio and Erie Canal. Some canal-era buildings remain yet today, and a log cabin dating from 1808 is reportedly the oldest remaining building in Stark County.

The town was named by the French-speaking wife of the community's founder in honor of Henry IV, King of France and Navarre. In Henry's day, Navarre was in independent kingdom located mostly within the Pyrenees Mountains. Henry, who died more than 200 years before Ohio's Navarre was founded, had absolutely nothing to do with the town, but the name did prove to its citizens that the founder's wife knew her history.

As far as I was concerned, Navarre was the best-smelling community on 62. Nickles Bakery, a supplier of grocery-store bread, perfumed the air with the scent of fresh-baked loaves from its plant just a block off 62.

Propelling my mount out of town, I had the sense that I was plunging into the first full-fledged farm country since entering Ohio. I'd passed other Ohio farms, but much of the land along 62 from Youngstown to Canton supports a mix of suburbia, rural housing, township services and small businesses, not to mention the industrial belt in the two cities themselves. Below Navarre, however, the landscape is unapologetically cropland.

Cruising southwest, I soon landed in Wilmot, the last community before entering Holmes County, which is home to the world's largest colony of Amish people. Wilmot touts itself as the "Gateway to Amish country." Although the hamlet has only 300 souls, I have seen traffic jams at its single traffic light when people by the busload flock in during the high-color foliage days of October. The view of manually harvested shocks of corn on Amish fields against the variegated autumn backdrop is the stuff calendar pictures are made of.

The first confirmation that I was in Amish country became apparent as I headed out of town: buggy tracks in the gravel beyond the highway berm. In this region, 62 has some of the broadest paved shoulders I'd seen — four- to five-feet wide — making a roomy corridor for my bike. The wood-spoked Amish buggies use the shoulders as well, but often run with their right wheels in the gravel beyond. They find the asphalt a glabrous surface for their horses and have to weld borium to their steeds' shoes to keep them from slipping. I was glad for the paving, though. Other than dodging occasional scatterings of horse droppings, my way was smooth and unobstructed.

The terrain changes below Wilmot. Within minutes, I was puffing up steep ridges and bounding over the rolling hills in between. I ambled on, surrounded by fields greened with spring growth and punctuated by Amish residences.

These are easy to spot. They are usually tidy, white wooden structures, often two-story or three-story and generally featuring generous front porches, often enclosed as living space. It is not uncommon for two homes to be joined, with the generations living separately but together in extended-family fashion. The smaller house is the *daadihaus*, for the grandparents.

Other giveaways include the absence of electric lines entering the buildings and Amish clothing hanging on backyard clotheslines. But, at least with one strand of the Holmes County Amish, the most obvious sign is curtains gathered only to one side of the windows, rather than split in the middle and gathered to both sides as in the homes of the *englisch*, one Amish name for their non-Amish neighbors. Another name is "yankee."

The Amish are of Swiss and German descent, and from the same religious root as the Mennonites, who are also well represented in this area. The two groups together comprise 80 percent of the population of eastern Holmes County. The Swiss-German ancestry is evident in the family names I saw on mailboxes. It seemed as if every other name was either Troyer or Yoder.

Following a motor route, I was especially interested in why the Amish eschew motor vehicles. As a people bound together by religion, the Amish feel called to live separately from mainstream culture but together in tight families and communities. They have observed that people who leave their group and begin driving cars seem to lose some quality of life. The families of those who leave become more scattered, have fewer meals as a family unit and become too busy to visit one another, a key activity among the Amish. To car owners, nowhere seems too far, say the Amish, and the automobile gives people a sense of power that can distort self-importance.

The Amish are not foolish about motor vehicles, however. When they need to travel beyond the area that they can reasonably go by buggy, they will hire a van or a car-owning neighbor to drive them. But they will not own or drive the auto themselves, nor will they become dependent upon it.

And so they live their quieter, industrious lives, generally within a circumscribed area. While I wouldn't want to live with such restrictions, it makes me feel good that such enclaves exist and that people are free to follow this simpler way if they choose.

I ended my exploration of 62 that day in Winesburg, a town so small that its one-room general emporium with Amish buggies parked in front has to be considered an anchor store. I celebrated my progress — 74 miles that day — with a delicious supper in the modestly named "Winesburg Restaurant."

Winesburg is near enough to my hometown that I intended to sleep at home this night. I phoned my wife, who drove out to pick me up.

While waiting for her, I thought about how Winesburg is occasionally mistaken for the setting of Sherwood Anderson's 1919 classic short story collection, *Winesburg, Ohio*, in which, despite name changes, residents of Anderson's hometown of Clyde, Ohio, recognized their dirty laundry. For years after the publication of the book, some people claimed that Anderson had smeared the good name of the real Winesburg, Ohio. In his defense, Anderson claimed to have consulted a list of Ohio community names and found no Winesburg on it. Unfortunately for this Holmes County community, the roster Anderson supposedly perused contained only the names of towns and cities served by railroads. Since the genuine Winesburg had no train service, it did not appear in that listing.

Actually, the misidentification of this community with Anderson's might have been avoided had it stayed with its original spelling. Laid out and occupied by people of Swiss and German extraction, the town was called Weinsburg after a town in Germany. The Post Office Department later changed the spelling.

Anderson's purpose in writing *Winesburg, Ohio*, according to one of his biographers, was to detail the lives of unimportant and unhappy small-town residents who, while seldom leaving their provincial community, never really fit life there either — people who live lives of lonely misery. Whether such a description would fit any of the souls in the real Winesburg I certainly couldn't say after a mere 45-minute visit. But in terms of physical environment and general atmosphere, this tidy little town of 300 was a delightful place, and appeared a good spot for someone who is at peace within to make a quiet home.

Chapter 5

After a comfortable night in my own bed, I returned to Winesburg to resume my ride, thanks to the kind shuttle services of my wife. The weather had changed dramatically and the forecast promised several warm, dry days. Though still cool enough for my long-sleeved jersey and tights, I left my sweater behind. The way I figured it, the tights already looked ludicrous on a man of my age and girth, so the less bulk on my upper body for contrast, the better.

The gleaming sunshine of this day felt especially good after the three gloomy, cold days preceding it. There was still a headwind, but at least it wasn't icy.

I was soon rolling along past well-groomed farms and tidy homesteads. Not all of them belonged to the Amish, but those of the *englisch* were equally well groomed, a classic case of keeping up with the Yoders.

I soon chugged into Berlin, a town that capitalizes on being quaint. It is both an Amish shopping town and a tourist mecca, and even on this weekday tourists flocked on the sidewalks. Virtually every house on the main street had been converted into a quilt shop or a craft store or a bed-and-breakfast or a restaurant featuring "Amish cooking." Many of the latter do have some Amish women and girls among their wait staff and, for all I know, as cooks as well, but the establishments are owned by non-Amish people.

While there is no argument that the food in these restaurants is gratifying, I've never been able to see what's different about "Amish" cooking from mainstream America's home cooking. The so-called Amish meals usually consist of meat, potatoes and gravy, vegetable and salad, with pie for dessert, just like American home cooking elsewhere. Yet people travel for miles to eat an Amish dinner. On Saturdays, eateries with names like "Der Dutchman," "The Amish

Door" and "Dutch Country Kitchen" sprout lines of people a block long waiting to get in. I think the appeal is not just good food in picturesque surroundings, but also that with most women now in the workplace, home cooking isn't happening much at home anymore. In other words, you have to eat out to get home cooking.

In Berlin, I leaned my bike against the wall of a grocery store and went inside to get a snack. When I came back out, I found two young Amish men and a yankee companion admiring my bike and paying special attention to the load — four saddlebags, a handlebar bag, sleeping bag, tent and air mattress — I had attached to it.

"Does that load slow you down?" one of the Amish men asked. Many Amish use bikes to run errands, but usually have little more than a basket on them.

"A little when climbing hills," I said. "But most of the time, once I'm on the bike, I hardly know it's there."

"That's good," the other Amish man said.

They next asked the usual questions about how far I was going, how many miles I averaged daily, and so forth, which I answered.

"You must burn a lot of energy," the first man said. When I agreed with that, he pulled a business card from his pocket and, pointing to a product named on the card, he said, "You should try this. It's an energy bar, loaded with nutrients." He went on to make some claims about the bar's energy-enhancing ability — something about fructose bonding delivering minerals directly to my cells. It all sounded dubious to me.

I glanced at the card. It gave his name and identified him and his wife as "Independent Marketing Executives."

Thanking him for the advice, I watched as the trio climbed into the front seat of a pickup truck, which the yankee drove. They waved and pulled away.

I found the whole episode unsettling. The Amish favor farming, viewing it as a godly profession and believing that it is vital to preserving their way of life. But as their colonies grow, there isn't enough land for everyone to farm, so many Amish men work in the building trades or in home shops providing such services as cabinet making, harness repair, blacksmithing and cheese processing. Apparently the young man whose card I now held had chosen instead participation in an up-to-date home-marketing venture. I wasn't sure whether to admire him for his industry or to view his choice as a sellout to the modernism his people disavow.

From Berlin, 62, now a broad, smooth highway, lopes west over rolling terrain to Millersburg, the seat of Holmes County. Wheeling by the courthouse in the center of that town, I noticed an adjacent area for buggy parking, complete with hitching rails for tying horses.

When I slowed for a red light, a man of about 35 in a coat and tie called to me from the sidewalk: "Where are you headed?" I pulled to the curb and stopped. When I described my journey, his eyes lit up with a passion I recognized — the longing to be on the road. Sure enough, he began telling me about the bike he had recently purchased and how he had been riding progressively longer jaunts in the area.

His next questions showed that he had thought about some of the obstacles to footloose travel. How did I manage enough time off work? I explained that I was doing the trip in stages, using more than one vacation block. Did I feel any threat on the road riding alone? I said I didn't and told him how difficult it was to find riding companions able to take the time for such a journey.

He set his briefcase down and pressed on with other specific questions about bike equipment and clothing. From previous experience, I suspected where the discussion was headed. And sure enough, there we soon were, two grown men, complete strangers, comparing notes about our underpants.

One of the things riders discover when they begin distance cycling is that the saddle that works just fine on short spins through the neighborhood becomes an instrument of torture on longer outings. Most novices jump to the seemingly logical conclusion that what they need is a softer seat, and they repair to their local bike shop where they lay out good money for specialty saddles padded with layers of foam or gel. And bike shop employees who should know better cheerfully accept the lucre.

These plush saddles actually feel great — for about the first five minutes one is astride them. After that, they feel no better than the hard seat they replaced, and sometimes feel worse, maybe because the foam disperses the support the saddle ought to provide. The truth is, there isn't a saddle made that feels great after planting one's tush on it for eight or more hours, but some do better than others, and there are ways to minimize the discomfort. One of these is to wear cling-type bike shorts sans underwear.

The shorts have some slight padding, but more for the absorption of dribbles and sweat than for insulation from the bike seat. These garments benefit the rider primarily because of the support their high-tech fabric gives to one's entire sit-down region. Underpants negate that comfort. After a couple of hours, the seams and finished edges of the standard pair of briefs and the rumpled acre of extra yardage on boxers burrow into the rider's flesh, giving rise to painfully inflamed saddle sores. So the formula is 1) find an unpadded seat shaped best for your anatomy, 2) wear bike shorts and 3) leave your underpants at home — or in your saddlebags for evening wear.

Understandably, a lot of people have trouble with this last instruction, viewing it as somehow unwholesome. Novices hope to find another alternative, and so they question seasoned riders: "Do you really go without underpants?" Once and for all, the answer is yes. And, now, dear reader, we're going to leave that right there.

Finally my questioner asked, "Would you mind if I ask how old you are?"

"Not at all. I'm 53."

His face lit up, and I understood why: *He still had time.* Even if his current responsibilities prevented him from taking an extended trip at present, he now had hope that he would not be too old when his life duties slackened enough to set him on the road.

I understood this completely. I had lived with the same hope myself for years. It had been the approach of my 50th birthday and concern about waiting too long that had set me to serious planning and eventually, led to my previous trip across America.

His concerns were not unfounded. While I've met several long-distance riders in their 60s and one in his 70s, bike touring at any age is physically demanding. It requires the rider to be in reasonably good health. It is possible to put off some dreams too long.

Route 62 makes a left turn in Millersburg and runs south briefly before heading west again. Zipping downhill out of town, I overtook a string of cars plodding so slowly that I had to brake firmly to reduce my speed. Scanning ahead, I saw a horse-drawn wagon at the head of the line, with an Amish man driving and a boy on the seat beside him. Though the horse clipped right along, it still moved much slower than the posted speed limit. Traffic flowed copiously in the northbound lane, denying the southbound bunch opportunity to pass the wagon. And there was no room for the wagon to pull over. There was enough shoulder for me, however, and I slipped past the crawling cars until I was directly behind the wagon. It was running far enough to the right that I was able to swing around it on its left without crossing the yellow line and break free of the bottled stream. I rolled on at full throttle and had the road to myself for a couple of minutes until the traffic, finally uncorked, overtook and flowed by me.

The man and boy in the wagon were the last Amish people I saw, and the region I now traveled was significantly different from the Amish farm land I'd seen since Wilmot. I had entered the Killbuck Valley. Although I have traveled quite widely in Ohio and even lived in a few different regions of the state, the appearance of this valley came as a surprise. It looked unlike any other part of Ohio I could think of. In fact, had I been plopped down in it without introduction, I would have guessed I was in Kentucky or West Virginia.

Instead of farms, forested hillside came to the edge of the highway on one side. A narrow strip of bottomland lay beyond the other. Frequently, this bottomland wandered into marshes and swamps. The few homes I passed were built on narrow shelves near the road or in hollows where the hillside gapped.

Eventually the valley broadened out. On the right-hand side of the highway, the town of Killbuck lazed in the sunlight, but 62 bypassed it, running instead between two large ponds surrounded by marshland.

I backtracked to explore the town. As I suspected, 62 originally wound through Killbuck. The old way enters Killbuck on its main street, hits the center of the small downtown and hangs a right. There were a few stores, a bank, an insurance office and a library on this street, but the storefront marked "Restaurant" was closed and had a "For Sale" sign posted. Next door to it stood a building labeled "Killbuck Valley Museum." It had an "Open" sign, so I went in.

Inside, my curiosity turned to amazement. Nothing in the appearance of this out-of-the-way, unassuming village led me to expect the substantial natural-history collection I found inside this ordinary-looking building. The museum included rocks and minerals, fossils and zoological specimens, all from the area. There were archaeological artifacts from Indians living nearby some 12,000 years before Europeans arrived, and some tools and other materials from the first white settlers. But what astonished me was a display case containing mastodon bones that had been unearthed near Berlin in 1993 by college archeology students. A typed description beside the bones explained that because flint flakes had been found scattered among them, archaeologists concluded that the discovery site had been a butchering area for some Native American about 11,000 years ago.

Recalling that Berlin was doing a booming business in tourism, it surprised me that that community had not made something of the bones found in its environs. At the very least, some restaurant there could be offering mock "mastodon burgers." On second thought, it's probably just as well that they don't. A wax museum couldn't be far behind.

The Killbuck museum was owned and operated by the local historical society. As I was the only visitor, I fell into conversation with the woman who had opened the building and was apparently the entire volunteer staff. She introduced herself as Glenda Arnold.

I asked her how Killbuck got its name. "It depends on what you want to believe," she said. "Some say it was because of a big deer shot near here. Others say it was for an Indian named Killbuck." She hauled out a book of local history and let me see the pages regarding the town. Naming the place after a deer kill sounded like a spurious tale to me, but sure enough, it was repeated in the book.

As to the other possibility, there was not one Indian, but three and maybe even four. No birth dates were given, but the first Killbuck's father died in 1776. Killbuck, the son, was a Delaware chief. His sons, Killbuck II and Killbuck III were also chiefs. These two later assumed the names John Henry and Charles Henry, out of respect for the patriot Patrick Henry. Regrettably, the book didn't explain that connection. These two sons of Killbuck I, along with one Francis Henry, signed a 1798 agreement between the U.S government and the Society of United Brethren allowing the latter group to "assume 12,000 acres for the propagation of the Gospel," though what that much land has to do with missionary work eludes me completely. In any case, it's possible that Francis Henry was Killbuck IV, a brother to II and III. (Hey, if you've got a catchy name, there's no sense dreaming up new ones just because more kids come along.)

One of the displays consisted of two huge millstones and some photos dating from the 1930s of a large mill. I asked if the building still stood.

"No, but it used to be right there," Mrs. Arnold said. She pointed out the window to a parking lot at the end of the street next to a bridge. "It had gotten in pretty bad shape, and until a few years ago, they weren't thinking of historical preservation." The book she'd shown me also had an item about the mill. The flour ground there bore the brand name White Lily, and later, the area basketball team carried that name. I wondered how the players felt about being the "White Lilies" when other teams were adopting names like "Vikings" and "Bulldogs."

The stream behind the mill site was Killbuck Creek. "It's pretty quiet now," Mrs. Arnold said, "but there's been times when it flooded right up into town. Back in '69 it did. We live up on the hill so we were okay, but it was into most of these buildings down here."

Finally ready to leave, I inquired about a place to get lunch, and Mrs. Arnold directed me to an ice cream stand back down Main Street. She added, "Time was, before they moved 62, we had a couple of good restaurants here, but we couldn't support 'em once they bypassed us with the highway. We used to even have bus service here. I went to school up in Canton and I used to ride the bus, but that doesn't come by anymore."

When I told Mrs. Arnold about my ride on Route 62, she said, "There's a country band by that name, you know." Actually I had already heard of it and intended to look them up, so I was pleasantly surprised when she added that her daughter and son-in-law were in the band.

The group had chosen the "Route 62" name because four of the five members live in Killbuck. They have day jobs and so limit their gigs to Ohio, but when I got to hear them later, I found them to be every bit as good as many nationally recognized groups. Mrs. Arnold's daughter, Toni, and Toni's husband Brad, write most of the music the band performs, and the songs range from bluesy to rockabilly to southern rock. Toni, the only female member, has a soulful voice that echoes the loneliness of the highway.

I left town that day by the bridge over Killbuck Creek and headed out onto the pavement that, due to the relocation of 62, had now become a back road. Later, the bridge and stream and the road came back to me when I heard Toni sing with the band:

> Driving these old back roads
> Searching the same ones in my mind
> Makes me ask the question
> Why I was so inclined
> To take every detour
> Avoiding a crossroad I couldn't face
> It's led me to that same desperate place
>
> I've got too many rivers to cross
> But I've burned every bridge along the way
> And though you'd love to save me
> There's nothing you can do to change me
> I've got too many rivers to cross

Beyond Killbuck, the valley widened, allowing some farming between the hills on the valley floor. Unlike some other small valley areas in America, this one did not look impoverished, but neither did it appear affluent. It was simply work-a-day Ohio, and I enjoyed seeing it.

Stillwell is a cluster of houses right on 62, but the hamlet is so tiny it wasn't even named on my AAA map. The sole commercial enterprise I saw was an auto junkyard, and I didn't notice any activity around that. A church sat on the hillside immediately beside the road, with its front steps coming down right to the edge of the berm.

The day had warmed generously, and I stopped there to remove my outer layer of clothing, stripping down to riding shorts and T-shirt. Needing a rest, I sat on the church steps and gazed across the narrow valley. A pasture opposite me wrapped up the hill on the other side of the valley, and a few cows grazed its grass. They were the only signs of life I saw, and that surprised me. It was now early afternoon; the sky was blue and the temperature pleasantly warm — perfect weather to be outside. Where were the residents? Perhaps all at work in larger communities? There certainly didn't appear to be many jobs in Stillwell. Even the small farm didn't look like a full-time endeavor.

Continuing on, I rolled by Brinkhaven, another village bypassed by 62. It may have once had a store or a business, but now it is just three streets of houses and a couple of small churches. Before being bypassed, Brinkhaven embraced 62 as its main street, and sent the highway on its way via a one-lane steel bridge over the nearby stream. That bridge was now closed, with barricades at each end. Out on the main highway, traffic rumbled by on 62, crossing the water on a modern concrete span while Brinkhaven, nearly forgotten, dozed at the wayside.

I sauntered on, eventually arriving in Danville, a small, pleasant-looking community. Route 62 turns south at the town's four-way stop, and as if on command, the terrain changes as dramatically as it had below Millersburg. Now, instead of valley, I spun through rolling open countryside, encircled by farmland that bounded off into the distance. The scenery continued similarly for the next several miles and the traffic was light. Though the weather remained agreeable, the wind continued to slug me, and I began to feel drained beyond what the single day's ride should have exacted. Apparently the battle into the wind over the last three days had taken a toll. I slogged on, completing a 60-mile day and finally calling a halt in early evening at Utica, a small town on the Licking River. The community has modest fame in Ohio as the home of Velvet Ice Cream, a brand widely distributed around the state.

At the family-style restaurant where I ate dinner, I inquired about campgrounds. No one could think of any nearby, so I rode slowly around the town hoping to find someplace where I could beg a site for the night. I stopped to talk to a man working in his yard, and he offered a perfect solution. He was a member of the Church of Christ across the street. He felt certain no one would object to my camping in that yard. He even walked over with me and showed me the area.

Later, when I had my tent up, the pastor came by. The church was happy to extend its hospitality, he said, and inquired if I needed anything. A woman with him even offered the key to the church so I'd have restroom access during the night. I declined the key, but was impressed by the level of welcome this church provided to a stranger.

Setting up camp can consume a lot of time if you don't have a routine about it, and it's all too easy to misplace things if you are too disorganized. So over my years of camping, I've developed a setup pattern by which I do the same tasks in the same order every time. For example, before unpacking anything else, I set up the tent. Once it's erected, I toss the tent stuffsack into the foot of the sleeping area so I'll know where it is when I break camp in the morning. Next, I place the sleeping pad in the tent, followed by the sleeping bag, placing both of their stuffsacks in the foot of the tent as well. I proceed in a similar fashion with the rest of my equipment, and in the morning, I simply reverse the pattern, taking the tent down last.

Yes, I know it sounds compulsive, but so far, it's usually prevented me from losing things, and it has kept setup and takedown time to a minimum. Where I get into trouble is when I try to impose my approach to routine tasks upon my wife. Consider, for example, how we load the dishwasher.

When I fill the machine, I keep all the bowls in orderly file along the front side of the lower rack. Plates are ranked according to size in the rear section, all facing the same direction. Glasses and cups go in the upper rack, with plastic cups between each pair of glass ones. (I developed this procedure on the theory that the glass ones might crack if allowed to clink together during the wash cycle.) I insert remaining items wherever they will fit.

Jeanine, on the other hand, dumps the dishes into the dishwasher in more or less whatever order she picks them up, so that a row might contain a bowl followed by a plate followed by a saucer followed by another bowl followed by a cup and so forth.

One day, while watching Jeanine fill the dishwasher, I graciously pointed out to her the superiority of my method, to which she responded, "Who cares?"

"You should," I sputtered. "My way lets you get more dishes into the machine. It leaves fewer to wash by hand."

"Yes," she said, "but your way also takes three times as long. I've got too much to do around here to spend that long loading the dishwasher."

"But my way is tidier. It's better organized."

Jeanine looked at me as though I were crazy. "And this," she said, "from a man who can't keep track of his keys and who leaves dirty socks in every room of the house." She exited the kitchen shaking her head.

After she left, I spent the next several minutes using my system to rearrange the dirty dishes she'd already loaded, and was able to shoehorn two more plates in. When I later told Jeanine of this accomplishment, she pointed out that the whole load could have been washed by hand in the time I'd spent marshaling our tableware by categories.

Of course, with more than three decades of marriage behind us, we've had similar discussions before. One that occurred in our first year of matrimony concerned the toothpaste tube: I always squeeze from the bottom and roll up the tube as it is emptied. Jeanine squeezes from the middle. When the contents are reasonably depleted, she starts another tube. This is obviously a disorganized approach to toothpaste usage. I demonstrated that for Jeanine's benefit on several occasions that first year by placing her discarded tube on the floor and stepping on it, triumphantly revealing that there was at least one more serving of toothpaste to be had.

After the first year, though, I abandoned such demonstrations; it's hard to convince someone who volunteers that you are "making a big deal out of nothing." But at least she now leaves the old tubes around for me to step on to load my own brush.

I will give her the point about the dirty socks, though. She works a lot harder at keeping our house clean than I do. Nonetheless, she's not nearly as bothered by a disorganized closet as I am. Jeanine reminds me of this difference in our makeups every time we have company coming. She wants the house spotless and tidy; I want to rearrange a closet our guests will probably never look into. Facing that kind of logic, it's difficult to be persuasive that my priorities are best.

Jeanine is our family treasurer. Throughout the year, she manages our budget, pays the bills and regulates how much money I'm allowed to have in my wallet. However, I prepare our annual income tax return, so at that point, she turns her records over to me. I always find this a frustrating moment, because her filing system for receipts and paid bills consist of a paper bag.

Her figures usually come out right, and, if I dig in the bag long enough, I can generally find the receipts I need, but to me, her system is dispiriting.

This year I decided to suggest a better method, patterned after the one I use to store our family records and important papers. Jeanine listened patiently while I outlined my plan, and then totally surprised me by saying, "You're right."

"I am?"

"Yes, and you're just the man to refile the receipts. I've even got an idea where you can organize them."

"That's great," I said. "Where?"

"Use the dishwasher."

Alone in my tent as darkness descended, I drifted off to the sounds of the quiet community — a voice as someone arrived at a nearby house, a car passing on the street, the chirp of crickets, the rustle of leaves in the wind — and I was soon enjoying the sweet slumber that follows a good day's effort.

Chapter 6

Running southwest on 62 toward Columbus, Ohio's capital, the next morning, I noticed the traffic increasing the nearer I got to the city. Also, the land flattened out. The day warmed rapidly in a muggy sort of a way, and I stripped off my long sleeves and tights not more than 10 minutes into the day's expedition. (I'm assuming you understand that I had my shorts on underneath; I was not flashing the passing motorists.)

I next came to Ohio's second New Albany, an outskirt town to Columbus, and maneuvered quickly through it. Below the town, a blacktopped side path unrolled beside the highway, separated from it by a strip of lawn. Though not marked as a bike path, it clearly wasn't a typical sidewalk. I assumed it was a multi-use path, and since it had no other traffic, I decided to try it. After about three-quarters of a mile, however, it turned away from the highway and into the grounds of some sort of cultural center, so I pulled back onto the highway.

I wasn't particularly disappointed. Bike paths can offer cyclists some pleasant riding, but there are major problems with them.

First, they seldom go anywhere you actually want to go.

Second, even if you are content to travel where the path leads, none of them are bike-*only* paths. They are all multi-use trails, and some are so heavily frequented by walkers, skaters and people of all ages on all manner of bikes that the potential for accidents is much higher for the cyclist than riding on a busy highway. On the road at least, everyone, motorists and cyclists alike, is governed by traffic rules and thus usually behaves more or less predictably. But pedestrians, skaters and children on bikes (and on some paths, even tricycles) recognize no standard rules of movement on the paths. John Forester, in his book *Effective Cycling*, calls bike paths "the most dangerous facility" for cyclists, quoting an accident rate of 2.6 times higher than that of an average roadway.

A bike path not far from my home travels an especially attractive route. Laid out on the towpath of the aforementioned Ohio and Erie Canal, the path journeys through history. Users of the trail thread through scenic wooded areas, view the remains of old locks, visit museums in old canal buildings and in some places, walk beside sections of the canal that are still intact. The path is a true linear park, and I have ridden its length. But on good-weather weekends, so many people use the path that cyclists wanting to travel at even a moderate speed endanger both themselves and other trail users. When I rode it, I often came upon family groups on bicycles, all traveling at the speed of their youngest members, who were on tricycles. I then had to wait for a break in the stream of oncoming people to attempt to pass the slow-moving group.

That's not a complaint. I'm glad the park is so well used. It's a pleasant respite from the congested area around it, but it's simply not a good choice for bike travel. When I go there, I go for some other experience than bike touring; for that, you need roads.

A third problem with bike paths is the contingent of legislators who want bikes off the highways. Their idea is to provide bike paths for cyclists and then restrict cyclists to them. But no matter how many bike paths are opened, they will never go all the places highways go. Regarding legislation, I much prefer that which sets highway standards to include wide traffic lanes, paved shoulders and bike-safe sewer grates. I also favor any efforts that educate motorists that bike riders are legitimate users of the highways.

In Columbus, 62 runs for about four miles on I-670, which as a cyclist I had to avoid. At a bike shop in outlying Gahanna, I inquired for a workaround and was directed to "old 62." This took me to a busy but navigable four-laner adjacent to Port Columbus International Airport and then to Broad Street, the primary east-west concourse through Ohio's capital city. Route 62 joins Broad Street part way along.

Broad Street also carries U.S. Route 40, the highway begun in 1811 to connect the headwaters of the Potomac River with Ohio and thus provide a corridor for settlers in the states of the old North-west Territory to ship their produce to eastern markets, and to help additional settlers to get to Ohio and beyond.

Actually, in 1784, 19 years before Ohio was admitted into state-hood, George Washington saw the need for such a road. With access to the eastern seaboard difficult, Washington feared that western settlers would be drawn into trade instead with the Spanish or the British, both of whom had enterprises in the New World. To avoid that, Washington urged that the nation "open a wide door, and make a smooth way for the Produce of that Country to pass to our Markets before the trade may get into another channel ...." That wide door eventually took the form of a highway from Cumberland, Maryland, to Wheeling. Dubbed the National Road, it was one of the very few highways directly authorized by the federal government.

With strong sentiments afoot in the new nation about maintaining states' rights, many Americans considered federal funding of internal improvements unconstitutional. In the case of the National Road, Congress got around this concern with an agreement that a percentage of the proceeds of public land sales in the Northwest Territory would be used for roads within the territory and for access to it. That worked, but the National Road was to be the last major federally financed road for more than a century.

In fact, except for the Interstate highways that came along later in the mid-1900s, almost none of the American road system was built by the federal government, at least not in any direct way. After the successive presidential vetoes of road-building acts in the first third of the 19th century, it became accepted principle that the federal government had no constitutional right to build and maintain roads in the separate states.

The National Road was completed to Wheeling by 1818 and immediately carried heavy traffic. With additional congressional appropriations, the road was extended to Vandalia, Illinois, by 1839. But in keeping with the states' rights thinking, the federal government relinquished each section, upon its completion, to the state in which it lay.

Congress considered extending the National Road on into Missouri, but a controversy over the proposed route stalled the work until, with the advent of the railroad, which now provided rapid transit of the region, few people saw the need to push the road any farther. Within a few years, trains carried virtually all the cross-county passenger and freight traffic, and for the balance of the century, railroads became the focus of national transportation efforts. The National Road continued to serve local traffic, but its glory days appeared at an end, and the states through which it ran had little incentive to maintain it.

Late in the 19th century, two inventions — the bicycle and the automobile — changed that, and the old National Road again became an important thoroughfare. In 1926, the National Road became part of U.S. 40 and was once more a major component in interstate travel.

By the logic of assigning east-west roads even numbers (and, conversely, north-south routes odd numbers) my path, 62, would be an east-west route. But, of course, it wasn't. Strictly speaking, it runs northeast-southwest, slicing diagonally across the nation. And I discovered that the route signage changed according to which direction the local chunk of the route happened to be aiming. In New York, the signs read "62 North" and "62 South," but in Pennsylvania, it was more often signed as "62 East" and "62 West."

If I'd had the time, the ride through Columbus could have offered plenty of diversions. Near where 62 joins Broad Street sits the Franklin Park Conservatory and Botanical Gardens, which, if nothing else, has a great lawn on which weary cyclists can grab a brief snooze. That's what I did. Afterward, I wheeled past the Museum of Art and the original Wendy's restaurant, both fronting on Broad. The latter opened in 1969 and was still in operation. (I guess there are worse things than being known as the birthplace of "Biggie Fries.")

In the busy downtown, I straddled my bike waiting for a light to change. Three young adults in an overpowered foreign car braked to halt next to me. The bloke in the back seat called out, asking where I was going. I told him. He looked startled, and then said, "Man, that's craaazy!" Just then the light changed. The spokesman for the carload gave a wave, and the vehicle roared off.

At Third Street, 62 jogs south a couple blocks, slipping behind the Ohio Statehouse, before launching west again on a street paralleling Broad. But to be truthful, in keeping a sharp eye on the busy center city traffic boiling around me, I missed the turn and continued west on Broad Street, crossing the Scioto River on a bridge a few blocks above the one carrying 62. Actually, I realized my blunder before entering the bridge, but my rudimentary knowledge of Columbus assured me I'd connect with the route again a few blocks later. And anyway, spotting the Santa Maria docked at river edge made me glad I'd not veered off.

Obviously old Christopher himself never sailed up the Scioto, but the name linkage between this city and the explorer was apparently sufficient excuse for the municipality to sanction permanent dockage rights for a full-scale re-creation of Columbus' 15th-century vessel. It was open to the public as a floating museum. I detoured to it, and spent a few minutes poking around on board, noting how small the vessel actually was.

I plodded on along Broad toward the west end of the metropolis where a cross street put me again on 62. Once that street cleared Columbus proper and suburban Grove City, it became a highway that bounded southwest into level, open country.

From then until early evening, I rolled over relatively monotonous miles. Fields and pastures unfurled on both sides of the highway. The reading I'd done indicated that stock-raising was the primary form farming took in this region. The farms and homes looked prosperous, although I didn't notice any particularly large herds along 62. Much of this region was flat enough to be a slightly greener version of western Kansas, though I doubted it would seem that way to drivers. Despite the initial impression, there were occasional undulations in the terrain, which on the bike were spaced sufficiently far apart to invite fixation on the tableland in between. In a car, I suspected, the modest humps would arise only minutes apart, thus never giving cause for one's mind to think of the Great Plains.

On my later homeward journey by car, I paid special attention in this area and confirmed my speculation: It was only while drifting through at bicycle speed that the Kansas comparison held up.

In midafternoon I took a break from the road in Mount Sterling, which, despite its name was not much more elevated than the surrounding land. It was a pleasant-looking community, and I enjoyed a brief siesta in the shade of a tree on the city hall lawn.

There is an enduring notion in America that small towns are more wholesome places to live than the major urban areas, and at least on the surface, there may be some truth to that. But cracks continue to appear in the myth. The week after my brief sojourn in this quiet, appealing place, an item appeared in an area newspaper reporting that Mount Sterling's 61-year-old mayor had been accused of domestic assault, specifically, attacking his 18-year-old granddaughter. This followed on the heels of an accusation that his honor had been using building regulations, zoning codes and the authority of his job to harass and intimidate villagers. And before that, he'd threatened his wife with a gun. The latest incident had local critics calling for his resignation as mayor. One wonders what took them so long.

I cite this report not to single Mount Sterling out. Every town has its share of aberrant individuals. But when incidents like these occur in small towns, almost everyone knows the people involved. The damage to the community's self-image can be greater than in a bigger community where the offender is unknown to most of the population.

In late afternoon, I came to a junction where a large wooden barricade blocked further progress down 62. Behind that was a large piece of earth-moving machinery parked crosswise on the road with its bucket stretched out ahead of it, creating an additional barrier. A sign posted nearby said ROUTE 62 DETOUR and an arrow pointed left to a side road.

I dislike detours. Highway people think nothing of sending traffic on a five- or 10-mile loop to get around a quarter mile of torn-up road. That's usually not a huge problem for cars and trucks, but it can be an hour of extra riding for a tired cyclist. But maybe this detour was a short one, I thought. I peered down the side road and watched cars disappearing in the distance without turning. No such luck.

But cyclists do have an advantage over autos; frequently, we can get through the section under construction. Bear in mind that this is no doubt illegal, but I've never had a problem. I've even slipped through some construction areas when workers were there. Sometimes they ignored me; other times they said hi. Here however, the workday was over and there appeared to be no one on the construction site. I decided to check it out. I walked my bike around the end of the double blockade. Behind the earthmover, I saw that a highway bridge had been completely removed. Beneath where it had been ran a stream perhaps 10-yards in width. But of interest to me were two steel I-beams that had been laid side by side across the water, no doubt to enable the workers to cross.

I first had to get down an embankment to the stream level. Pushing my loaded bike ahead of me, I started down, only to find the earth so loose that my shoes had trouble getting purchase. Almost at once I started sliding into my bike, and a vision of my broken body lying across it at the bottom of the ravine flashed into my head. Of course, there'd be no hope of being found until morning, and then only if the crew worked Saturday. Fortunately, I stumbled to the bottom of the slope just before totally losing control and averted disaster. I wheeled the bike onto one I-beam, planted my feet on the other, and clanked across the creek in seconds. After scrabbling up the other dirt bank, I wove around more road machinery and another barricade, and remounted.

Ten minutes later, I ambled into Washington Court House, population, 12,600. Hungry for supper, my first priority was to find a restaurant but the first I saw displayed a large sign that proclaimed BUFFET, DISCOUNT FOR SENIORS, 55 AND OVER. The whole idea of that suddenly struck me as funny. There I was, just 13 months away from qualifying for the "senior" discount. I'd just ridden a 78-mile day, cruised without problem down one of the busiest streets in the state and successfully avoided injury while shortcutting through the detour. And now I was nearly eligible for the over-the-hill crowd. I selected another diner for my meal.

I had hoped to camp that night near Washington Court House, but no suitable location presented itself. With my energy waning, I proceeded to a local motel where I was granted a room at a tiny discount — in deference to my Automobile Club membership card — by a young woman who apparently had not been issued a personality.

This seat of Fayette County, originally dubbed just "Washington," latched onto its three-word moniker in the late 1820s to distinguish itself from four other Ohio communities that had also baptized themselves with our first president's name. Apparently all the other towns did some similar adjusting of their names, for the current official listing of Ohio communities includes a New Washington, an Old Washington, a Port Washington and a Washingtonville, but no just plain Washington. I assume that means the name is thus available to any existing Ohio community that wishes to upgrade its designation. After examining the Ohio community list, it occurs to me that Funk, Gore, Roundhead and Dilles Bottom might be contenders.

The area around Washington Court House is known for its horse farms, and as I pedaled out of town the next morning, I passed the county fairgrounds where a number of these splendid animals were being put through their paces whizzing sulky carts around a racetrack in the brilliant sunshine. Although I'd been in long sleeves at breakfast, I'd stripped down to shorts and T-shirt almost immediately afterward as the day rapidly warmed.

Within a few miles, the landscape, although still generally flat, had a few more ripples than the region I'd covered the previous afternoon. Still, when the high point of the morning was a bend in the otherwise straight roadway, I knew I was ready for a more dramatic change of scenery.

Occasional cars and delivery trunks zipped by. A postal vehicle overtook me and then pulled over to slide letters into the mail receptacle in front of a farmhouse. Just as I caught up, the postal carrier pulled away and bobbed on down to the next mailbox. In this hopscotch fashion, the carrier continued the delivery route until gradually outdistancing me.

Seeing the mail being delivered along this rural highway reminded me of the role postal delivery played in the development of the American road system. The precedent that the federal government had no constitutional authority to build and maintain roads left road building to states, counties and smaller jurisdictions. Thus, at the close of the 19th century, there was no national highway plan. But with the advent of the automobile and pressure from the good-roads movement, Congress began looking for ways to get around that impasse. The solution it found was its constitutionally granted power to establish a postal system. The delivery of mail in rural areas required roads. Congress could legitimately fund any road designated as a post road, so the thinking ran.

This was not entirely subterfuge. In the late 19th and early 20th centuries, most farm families lived with a high degree of isolation, having neither telephone nor rural mail delivery. To get their mail, farmers had to go to the post office in town — for many, a trip of several miles and certainly not something one did every day. During bad weather and spring thaw, road conditions ranged from risky to impassable, preventing farm families not only from getting to town, but also from getting to church, to school and even out to see neighbors. Even in better weather, roads could be so bad that horse-drawn wagons had difficulty and "horseless" carriages were routinely equipped with planks, canvas and other materials for bridging ruts and working wheels out of the mud.

Advocates of good highways pointed out that improved roads would not only reduce this rural isolation, but would also make rural delivery of mail feasible. In time, Congress agreed, appropriating $10,000 for an experimental program. The first rural delivery route began in 1896 in West Virginia. In less than a year, 44 rural routes were running. Congress then appropriated more money, so that by 1903, nearly five million rural Americans were receiving free delivery of mail.

Standards imposed by the Post Office Department aided the drive for improved roads. The Department ruled that rural delivery routes would only be established along reasonably good roads. It also declared that carriers were not obligated to deliver, even on established routes, if the roads were not in decent condition. This, in turn, added volume to the public outcry for better roads, and Congress responded by beefing up appropriations for the postal service, often granting more money than the Post Office asked for.

A 1912 Post Office appropriation bill adopted by Congress specifically stated that the funds were not only to improve existing post roads, but also to determine *additional* areas that could be served by rural post carriers as roads were amended.

The act required that state or local governments receiving the aid put up two-thirds of the cost. In execution of the legislation, the Office of Public Roads, working in cooperation with the Postmaster General, learned a valuable lesson — that federal aid for roads should be dispersed only through state governments. Dealing with county and other local governments proved far too complex. This wisdom became an important piece of subsequent highway legislation and ultimately valuable for the connection of highways from one state to another.

Significantly, the 1912 act also authorized a joint Congressional committee to study the entire matter of federal aid to highways. The report of this committee, issued three years later, included two important conclusions. First, that federal aid for highways was needed, desirable and constitutional. Second, that there should *not* be centralized control of the road program from Washington.

All of this was background for the momentous Federal Aid Road Act of 1916. Though still characterizing the funding as being for "the construction and maintenance of rural post roads," it asserted that this was to be done by aiding the states in their highway building. To this end, it required all states receiving the aid to have a state highway department. It gave the Secretary of Agriculture the authority to establish standards these federally funded roads would have to meet. The bill specified that construction of these roads would be the responsibility of the states, with each state putting up 50 percent of its project costs. Maintenance of the roads, when complete, was totally up to the states, and a state's failure to do so meant that state received no further federal road aid until the road was restored.

Under pretext of expanding the postal system, the 1916 act took America's highway program a giant step forward. All pretense ended when, in an amendment to a 1919 Post Office appropriation bill, the term "rural post road" was redefined to mean "any public road a major portion of which is now used, or can be used, or forms a connecting link ... of any road or roads now or hereafter used for the transportation of the United States mail."

Objecting to this definition, a senator from New York, de-

clared, "I am convinced that any road that can be made suitable for carrying mail includes any and every road in the United States." Exactly.
The bill passed by a strong majority.

By midmorning, I needed a break, and finding no formal rest area, I plopped down in the shade cast by a utility substation at roadside. Later, I came upon a beautiful highway rest area, complete with picnic tables, mowed lawn and restrooms, but the site must have been selected on some criteria other than the needs of the weary traveler, for it had been situated not more than a mile north of Hillsboro, the only community of any size between Washington Court House and the Ohio River. Silly me, I'd have planted the rest area somewhere *in between* these towns that rise up like oases in this otherwise open land, so that the motorist with a full bladder might find relief where no gas station or restaurant was already available.

Actually, the convenience of the traveler probably was not the guiding factor in situating the rest area. Many of these wayside relief stations were built during the Great Depression of the 1930s by the Works Progress Administration. Intended as a way to address the massive unemployment of the era, the WPA put legions of people to work on projects for the public good. WPA workers built roads, schools and airports, improved waterways and parks, and produced books, plays, concerts and maps. Many of these proved to be invaluable contributions for generations to come. But others, to keep people employed, were "make-work" undertakings, sometimes branded as "boondoggling." This particular rest area may have been one of the latter, built to keep people working on land that happened to be available, even though the location was less than ideal. Of course, in the 30s, the fast-food restaurants that often serve as pit stops today were nonexistent, so maybe this rest area served a purpose in its time.

The fact is, except for the modern rest areas on the Interstates and other freeways, many highway departments are divesting themselves of roadside rests as fast as they can. Environmental Protection Agency regulations no longer permit the building of pit toilets, and the cost of pumping the sewage to a municipal treatment plant or building on-site sewer systems is prohibitive. Coupling that with the cost of repairing the vandalism common to untended rest areas makes them albatrosses on the necks of the highway departments. Unless nearby local municipalities step forward to take them over, most rest areas on the numbered highways may soon be gone.

Hillsboro is appropriately named, and within its environs, I cycled up the longest hill I'd encountered since leaving Amish country. This took me to the center of town, which could lay modest claim to the term "bustling." The town supposedly encompasses seven hills, but fortunately, 62 doesn't climb them all. This seat of Highland County has a population of only 6,200, but the profusion of restaurants and stores on its outskirts indicates that the community serves a large surrounding region. A glance at the state map reveals that there are no towns to rival Hillsboro's size within a large radius.

I ate lunch there and moved on, finding considerably more rise and fall to the land as I shuffled southward. Starting about 10 miles below Hillsboro, I entered a stretch of about 20 miles marked by dilapidated barns, shabby mobile homes and unkempt homesteads. Not every home was this way, but the area, centered around the sad little community of Fincastle, was clearly less prosperous than where I had been earlier in the day.

I pushed on toward Ohio's southern boundary, sailing en route through the eye-blink town of Ash Ridge. A few miles beyond that, I was rolling along in a mindless reverie when a car I instantly recognized overtook me and pulled to the roadside ahead. Out stepped my wife.

To avoid a long absence from home, I was riding the Route 62 journey in segments. I'd slated the New York to Kentucky leg to end that night with my arrival in Maysville, the first town in Kentucky on Route 62. We had planned that Jeanine would meet me there on the morrow.

Glad to see her early, I stopped and we embraced. She'd gotten away sooner than planned and had decided to come now. "Becky said I'd never find you," Jeanine explained, referring to our daughter, "but I knew you had to be on 62 somewhere down here."

She suggested I toss my saddlebags and camping gear into the car. She'd drive ahead to Maysville and wait while I finished the day's journey unencumbered by the weight. That sounded good to me.

After she left, I cruised on, and without the luggage, I verily flew up and down the hills that were now becoming more prevalent. Back in Holmes County, I'd told the two Amish men that I hardly noticed the weight when rolling, and that was true, because you quickly get used to how the bike feels when it's doing double duty as a beast of burden. But now, with the immediate contrast of riding one minute fully loaded and the next unloaded, I had to admit there was significant difference in the way the bike bounded up the hills.

About six miles north of where 62 encounters the Ohio River, it unites with U.S. 68 and the two run together as a four-lane highway. Unfettered by accouterments and facing a glorious downgrade on a lane-wide paved shoulder, I rocketed along. Suddenly I heard an enormous BOOM close behind me. Though startled, I continued at full speed downward without losing control, but my ears rang. From the childish behavior of the two men pulling away from me in a pickup truck, I deduced that I'd been the target of a thrown cherry bomb. I refrained from indicating my opinion of them by gesture, but in my thoughts I identified them with a part of the anatomy not usually mentioned in polite conversation.

Ripley, a town of 1,800, lazes directly beside the Ohio River where 62 completes its downhill run. In its early years, Ripley workers built steamboats and pianos. The town also played a role in the abolitionist movement: A house in Ripley belonging to the Reverend John Rankin functioned as a way station on the Underground Railroad.

After a brief look around the town, I followed the highway, which now included U.S. 52 as well, southeast for eight miles as it snaked beside the water. On the way, I saw a massive new suspension bridge under construction, which, when completed, will carry 62 across the river on two 12-foot lanes, and, conveniently for cyclists, two 12-foot shoulders. The roadbed will be nearly a half-mile long.

But for the moment, the route continued another three miles into Aberdeen, population 1,500. Aberdeen grew up as the southern terminus of Zane's Trace, the first road in Ohio, though "road" is a generous description of what was little more than a forest pathway.

(Warning! Historical facts ahead!) In 1796, a speculator named Ebenezer Zane claimed the land where Wheeling, West Virginia, now stands. He soon concluded that pioneering a land route across the Ohio territory from Wheeling to Aberdeen could prove profitable. Pioneer families had been arriving in Wheeling and making their way down the Ohio River to Maysville, on the opposite shore from Aberdeen, to establish homes in the Kentucky region. Others continued on to Cincinnati. But with only rowing and poling power on the settlers' flatboats, the river was a one-way, sandbar-ridden route — and frozen part of each year at that.

Zane convinced Congress that an overland, all-weather route would not only aid settlers, but also provide a mail link to Frankfort, Kentucky. He insisted that the new road would shave 300 miles off the existing route between Philadelphia and Frankfort, but in this claim, he fudged his sums. He reported the distance from Wheeling to Maysville as 190 miles when in fact it was over 230.

In the deal Zane offered Congress, he would build the road in exchange for land grants on the three rivers the route would cross. In May of 1796, Congress agreed, but set an impossible completion date, stipulating that the road be open with ferries operating across the three rivers by January 1, 1797. Savvy enough to know then what modern highway contractors later discovered — that a contract in hand and work in progress was enough to keep the money flowing despite missed deadlines — Zane accepted the terms. He and a crew of helpers began blazing the road almost immediately, taking advantage whenever possible of existing Indian trails and paths opened by military expeditions. With his main concern the completion of a blazed path, he didn't worry about surveying the most direct route. Instead, he took the easier, though more circuitous course, avoiding wetlands and hills. Even at that, however, the route was not completed until the summer of 1797. And it was autumn before the first ferry, a makeshift affair consisting of two canoes tied together, went into operation.

Still, the path was the beginning. Originally only passable by packhorse teams, it was widened to a wagon road in 1803 under the direction of township supervisors. And unlike the Natchez Trace described earlier, Zane's road opened land that settlers actually wanted. Zane too, made out just fine. His three land grants eventually became the cities of Zanesville, Lancaster and Chillicothe.

In essence, Zane's Trace still exists, underlying portions of federal and state routes from Wheeling to Maysville. It also has important connections to two previously mentioned items. In 1825, when Congress appropriated funds to continue the National Road beyond Wheeling, the Ohio road builders used the portion of Zane's Trace between Wheeling and Zanesville as the basic route. They brought it up to National Road standards and veered from the Trace only when surveyors found a better course.

The Trace also figured into the controversy about the federal government's right to finance internal improvements within the states. In 1830, Congress authorized funds to extend the Trace from Maysville to Lexington, Kentucky, but President Andrew Jackson, using what seems like shortsighted logic from a later viewpoint, vetoed the legislation, stating that the national government should not fund improvements of purely local character.

From the time the Trace first linked to Aberdeen until well into the 20th century, all traffic for the opposite shore traversed by ferry. Now, however, both 62 and I crossed the wide Ohio River on an aging but impressive span built in 1931. The bridge, named for Simon Kenton, an area pioneer, was reputedly a prototype for San Francisco's famous Golden Gate Bridge.

Maysville, and my good wife, waited on the other side.

Chapter 7

In the late 1700s, the Ohio River landing at Limestone was one of the main doorways into Kentucky, and through it flowed scouts, hunters and eventually settlers. By 1780, the town growing at the landing became a major port for river rafts and later, steamboat traffic. In 1792 it was renamed Maysville after John May, the Virginian on whose land the community was built.

My brother Scott and I landed there in a more prosaic fashion on a beautiful day in mid-September: We came by car, with our bikes loaded in the back. Over the years, Scott has been my most frequent companion on various adventures — canoeing, backpacking and bicycling. On my transcontinental bike journey, he'd ridden with me from Astoria, Oregon, to Yellowstone Park, Wyoming. This time, his schedule didn't permit him to join me for an extended period, but we had two days, and we intended to ride a portion of 62 together.

These days, Maysville, a town of 7,000, harbors one of the largest burley tobacco markets in the world. Several large loose-leaf warehouses support the tobacco industry and are open to the public during the winter auction season.

Maysville also promotes its history. Immediately at the foot of the Simon Kenton Bridge we found a visitor center that housed an Underground Railroad Museum, highlighting the area's role as an escape route for thousands of slaves, though whether it's a good museum, I couldn't say. It's open only a meager six hours a day, a schedule I'd not found particularly convenient. When I'd completed the first leg of my Route 62 odyssey, Jeanine had been waiting for me in the parking lot of the visitor center/museum. But since it was a little past their daily closing time of 4 p.m., we couldn't go in. Now Scott and I were in town at 8:30 in the morning, an hour and a half before its opening time. We couldn't afford the time to wait around for it to open. There's also a walking tour of the town that features 48 National Register buildings. The tour, naturally, runs on the same 10 to 4 schedule.

After securing a place to leave the car and settling for a quick look around the attractive little community, Scott and I mounted our bikes and rolled into the gorgeous morning. With temperatures in the upper 60's and a bright blue sky overhead, the day was ideal for cycling. We started out wearing tights and jerseys, but after an hour or so, we stripped down to our warm weather cycling apparel.

As middle aged, paunchy men, neither of us cut a figure in spandex bike shorts that could be described as "dashing," but as I've already explained, there are good reasons to wear them when riding long distances. In a small store where we later stopped for refreshments, a local man asked Scott about whether the girdle-like shorts were comfortable.

"They are," Scott said, "though we wear them more as a fashion statement."

"Actually," I added, pointing at Scott, "*he* wears them as a fashion statement. I wear them because I have great legs."

Scott protested, "You can't explain them that way. You have to say something believable."

Route 62, running concurrent with U.S. 68, leaves downtown Maysville by climbing a steep ridge on a four-lane highway. That hill was the main reason a separate community, Washington, developed on the crest. In the days when the route up the long hill was only a primitive path, it sometimes took an entire day for oxen and mule teams to haul heavily loaded wagons to the top. When they finally got there, the teamsters were ready to stop for the night (to say nothing of the oxen and mules!), and Washington grew up to serve that traffic. Washington has now been incorporated into Maysville.

The infant form of the road that is now 68 was a wide path trampled by buffalo on their way to the natural salt springs at Blue Lick, and thus was called Buffalo Trace. In 1783, it became known as Smith's Wagon Road, after a man named Smith took the first wagon over it. In 1829, the Maysville and Washington Turnpike

Company received a charter from the state to construct a better road over that route between the two towns. The resulting four-mile turnpike, opened in 1830, was the earliest macadamized road west of the Alleghenies.

The states adopted the idea of privately built turnpikes from Britain. From 1792 to about 1850, hundreds of turnpike companies were chartered in America to build new roads or improve existing ones. The chartering states regulated the turnpike companies, established fixed tolls and set construction standards. Since the turnpikes would serve the public good, state governments granted the companies the power to invoke eminent domain to prevent obstinate landowners from blocking road development by refusing to sell right of way. The states also granted the company owners immunity from personal liability for injuries to travelers using the roads.

In return, the companies were expected to build decent roads, and most met that standard, given the road-building technology available. Surfacing materials included stone, gravel and sometimes plank. Turnpike companies built tollbooths along their roads and counted on fee collection to recoup their costs and earn a profit.

In terms of funding roads, the particular case of the Maysville Turnpike had a significance larger than the road itself. As planned, the pike would serve as a branch off the National Road via extension from Zane's Trace and eventually connect to Nashville, Tennessee, and Florence, Alabama. Thus, the Kentucky segment fit into a larger network. Viewed that way, the Kentucky legislature in 1830 called upon Congress to buy 1,500 shares of capital stock in the Maysville Turnpike Company, to fund the extension of the fledgling turnpike to Lexington. Congress saw the wisdom of this and authorized the stock purchase. But President Andrew Jackson vetoed the bill, reaffirming the policy that the federal government would not fund internal improvements it regarded as of benefit to a single state. That veto forced turnpike companies and later the railroads to be financed as private corporations rather than as public utilities.

The remaining length of the Maysville Road, Washington to Lexington, was funded by state and local subscriptions and finished five years later, complete with 13 tollhouses and six covered bridges. The company name became the "Maysville, Washington, Paris and

Lexington Turnpike Road Company." Maybe they needed to fill space on their letterhead.

Jackson's decision came back to nip the national government eight years later when a United States Mail contractor claimed the right to travel the Maysville Road free of tolls. The federal Court of Appeals ruled that the presidential refusal to assist in the construction of the road made agents of the federal government liable for the same fees as the general public.

The turnpike companies derived most of their operating revenue from long-distance travelers. Local traffic often was often exempt from tolls or simply tramped paths they dubbed "shunpikes" around the toll booths. In the Massachusetts charters, for example, the companies were required to grant exemptions to people going to church, the gristmill, to military duty or on business within the town where the tollgate was located. Overall, few turnpike companies saw profits higher than two to three percent, and in time, most companies turned their roads over to the states and withdrew from road-building pursuits. The coming of the railroads put the remaining companies out of business.

As long as 62 and 68 ran together, the road enjoyed a wide paved shoulder. But this one had something I'd not noticed before along 62. Immediately right of the white line, a series of depressions, about three inches wide and 18 inches long and spaced about three inches apart, had been pressed into the asphalt, creating a continuous rumble strip. This had been placed there, I imagine, to give a vibration warning to sleepy or drunk drivers who might be drifting off the traffic lane, but it formed too rough a surface for the bike. This particular shoulder was wide enough that we could ride to the right of the rumblers. But a few miles later, when 62 branched off on its own and the berm narrowed to a mere 18 inches, the rumble stripping continued, spanning the entire shoulder. This left us no choice but to ride in the traffic lane. On the road ahead, I would discover that rumble strips continued all the way across Kentucky whenever paved shoulders were available, and would show up periodically in other states. I hope the rumblers save drivers' lives, but they do nothing to help cyclists.

About five miles south of the river, 62 split from 68 and began a southwesterly jaunt across Kentucky, running as a narrow two-lane, often shoulderless road, most of the way to Georgetown.

For much of the distance, 62 meandered on rolling ridges with scenic green valleys and wooded hills on each side. Homes were few and widely spaced apart, and we frequently had the road to ourselves. We rode side by side, talking as we pedaled. It was a grand day and a grand place to be cruising along on two wheels.

Scott asked me how my son's rock band was progressing, referring to my 20-year-old offspring who plays the drums. My son, who is also named Scott, recently organized a rock band, and they practice in our basement since none of the other band members live where a cacophonous onslaught is tolerated. I explained that though it's not my kind of music, they were actually sounding pretty good, for which Jeanine and I were grateful. As his long-suffering parents, we'd endured a lengthy musical journey with our son.

At age 11, Scott, my son, found the drum after a series of enthusiastic but short-lived experiments with — successively — piano, violin, saxophone, cello and guitar. During that era, Scott maintained a standing account at the local music store, where he was identified as a "preferred customer," and we congratulated ourselves on having the sense to only *rent* each of the instruments selected to that point. (We had, however, developed a collection of instruction method books: "Book 1" for each of the aforementioned instruments.)

Given this list of the tried and discarded, you might think Jeanine and I pushed Scott to take up an instrument. Not so. The kid just had a musical itch and was trying to find the most effective way to scratch it.

From our perspective, however, Scott's search for the right musical medium meant that we had lived through the beginner stages of each of these instruments, which, as you'll readily understand, are the most difficult for the listener. In fact, audiences at first concerts sometimes have problems recognizing that a melody is actually being played. Let it simply be said that we understood completely what the poet John Masefield meant when he wrote, "Bugles that whinnied, flageolets that crooned, and strings that whined and grunted."

Of the instruments that Scott had tried to that point, the saxophone stands out most in my memory — although at the time, I would have preferred that it stood outside my home, for it was by far the loudest of his first five forays into the elusive world of melody. Scott acquired the saxophone itself a few weeks before lessons could be scheduled, so we were treated to several ad lib concerts performed without benefit of musical instruction. In fact, he blatted on the horn so much that his lips swelled. This was a godsend since it allowed me to prescribe a complete rest from rehearsals until his lips returned to normal size.

Shortly after bringing his first drum home, Scott invited a young friend over who was also learning the drum. Scott did this so that his mother and I could be treated to a drum duel — er, duet. This visit motivated me to run several out-of-the-house errands that I'd been putting off.

But now it all seemed to be paying off. Although Jeanine and I continue to ponder the effect of the band's volume on neighborhood relations, drum-playing has become to my son what bike-riding is to me, a rich, satisfying life pleasure.

We passed a number of fields where tobacco was growing or had been recently harvested. Nearly every farm had at least one tobacco barn, painted black to absorb the sun's heat and speed the curing of the sheaves hanging inside.

Our road map indicated that a few tiny communities lay on our route, but a couple seemed to have disappeared. Others were identifiable only by a small cluster of houses and sometimes a single store or church. At the edge of some of these scanty settlements, the state had placed signs reading "Congested Area," making us believe that someone in the signage department had a healthy sense of humor.

We ate lunch in a little café in Mt. Olivet, where a young waitress hobbling on a broken foot gave us better service than I've sometimes received from servers with two sound hooves. Although the town has only 400 people, it is the seat of Robertson County and features a tightly packed main street, making the hamlet look bigger than it is. The original street through town must have been very narrow, for to expand the road to the required minimum width for the current traffic, the road builders had chopped the sidewalks severely close to the buildings, sometimes adding railings to keep pedestrians on the skinnied walkways.

After lunch we pursued 62 as it flowed off the ridgeline to cross the Licking River and then pedaled a lengthy hill out of the river valley, the first grade since Maysville steep enough to require use of our lowest gears. Over the top, we encountered another "Congested Area," this one bearing the ridiculing moniker Oddville. Its only commercial enterprise was a rundown but functioning garage where tires were sold. Noticing a pop machine out front, we pulled in and each bought a can. A boy of about 14 came out of the ramshackle office to inform us he had snacks for sale inside, and he led us to a display rack with a few bags of potato chips and small assortment of candy bars. A man I assumed to be his father was in the attached garage mounting a car tire on a rim.

Because it was a midweek day, I asked the boy if school had gotten out early. "Nah," he said. "I stayed home sick." He looked fine then, but who am I to tell? His reply did, however, remind me of a phone conversation I happened to overhear the previous summer while cycling with my daughter on the Outer Banks of North Carolina. We were eating our breakfast on the porch of a marina, when a man pranced by in a bathing suit with a bikinied babe on his arm and holding an open beer can in his hand. Using the pay phone near us, he dialed a number. After identifying himself to whoever answered, he said, "I won't be in today. The young-uns are sick and I need to stay home with them." My daughter had all she could do to keep from laughing out loud.

Scott asked the lad what he did for excitement in Oddville. "We keep the garage open," the boy replied.

A few more miles brought us to Cynthiana, another county seat, but considerably larger than Mt. Olivet. I wondered if this was because unlike Mt. Olivet, which is served only by the curvy 62 that is represented as a snaking black line on the state map, Cynthiana can be reached by both 62 and U.S. 27. On the map, 27 is a "red-line" road, indicating that it's a more important artery. Looking ahead on the map, I noted that 62 showed as a black line across most of Kentucky.

Cynthiana was the site of a battle late in the Civil War. The southern band known as Morgan's Raiders took the town June 11, 1864, but held it only one night before a Union force took it back. That victory demonstrated that the superior mobility and number of Union troops were starting to turn the tide of the war. After Cynthiana, the Confederate cavalry found they could no longer raid with impunity.

Cynthiana also has a minor claim to fame as the hometown of a colorful character known as Death Valley Scotty. Born Walter E. Scott in 1863, he later moved to California to prospect for gold. Eventually his fabulous tales of gold finds in Death Valley, made the more believable by his residency in a desert castle worth $3 million, duped several investors. The home actually belonged to a Chicago millionaire who allowed Scotty to live there. The tycoon said "he got it all back in laughs." In 1941, Scotty was found out, but by then he had become a legend. He died in 1954.

From Cynthiana to Georgetown, a distance of 19 miles, 62 is a narrow, shoulderless, roller coaster of a road, and it's heavily traveled. We were forced to ride in single file, hugging the white line as cars impatiently chugged behind us waiting for the oncoming lane to clear enough to pass. No doubt much of the traffic had to do with the shift change at the Georgetown Toyota Plant, a huge complex that dominates the area northwest of Georgetown. As we finally neared the plant, 62 dropped onto a wide expressway built as a bypass around the town to serve the Toyota plant. With 65 miles behind us, we repaired to a nearby motel for the night.

Georgetown, population 11,400, is named for George Washington, but some claim its real distinction is as the place where bourbon whiskey, America's only native liquor, was first made. An unsupported but possibly true story has it that the drink was concocted there in 1789 by, of all people, a Baptist minister, the Reverend Elijah Craig. Whether he created the first bourbon or not, Reverend Craig was responsible for several other firsts. He established a school that was to become Georgetown College. He opened Kentucky's first cloth-making mill and later started Kentucky's first paper plant. Later still, he set up a shipping business on the Kentucky River. After Kentucky became a state, Craig, along with 177 of his neighbors, were found guilty of making whiskey without a license and fined $140.

Fifty years later, the students and faculty of Georgetown College, the Baptist school Craig founded, constructed a building for the institution, firing the bricks from clay dug on the site. Reportedly, they installed a quart of bourbon under each of the six ionic columns that support the building's portico roof.

Today, 62 plows through the Georgetown area on a bypass also numbered U.S. 460. The wide paved shoulder made it easy for the bikes, although, as with many expressways, the travel wasn't especially interesting. But three miles west of Georgetown, 62 turns south on an older, two-lane road, where the views are more appealing. We wheeled through well-tended countryside, and eventually arrived in Midway. This tidy town of 1,300 was developed by a railroad company, and the tracks still course through the town. But rather than the frayed look worn by some railroad towns, Midway sports an alluring mien, with Victorian-style antique shops, gift boutiques and restaurants lining Railroad Street. The village earned its name because of its location midway between Lexington and Frankfort, two of the region's larger communities.

From Midway to Versailles Route 62 provided a visual treat. Black wood-slat fences and fieldstone walls of expansive horse farms lined both sides of the road. Overhead, branches from the numerous roadside trees formed a leafy arch that added a gentrified charm to the route. And on the bluegrass-carpeted fields beyond the fences, sleek-looking horses grazed. With light traffic and the day warm and bright, the pedaling was particularly pleasurable, and we left this stretch only reluctantly when 62 delivered us to Versailles.

Versailles, though named after the French city of the same spelling, is in Kentucky pronounced "Ver-SALES." The town was christened in recognition of the aid French King Louis XVI gave the American colonists during the Revolutionary War. Route 62 ambles into town, but a block short of the main street, it ducks out again.

From Versailles to Paducah in the western end of the state, 62 parallels continuous four-lane freeway, though that highway is known by various names over its length. At the Versailles end, it's the Blue

Grass Parkway. Further west, it becomes the Western Kentucky Parkway. And after Eddyville, it runs as I-24. Looking at the state map, it's clear that this modern, four-lane system, lying so nearly on 62's path, has taken over the cross-state responsibilities the older route once carried. But that meant that on 62 we'd have to contend only with local traffic.

A couple of miles west of Versailles, we noticed a string of old railroad passenger cars sitting quietly on the hill. A bit further on, where a track ran near the highway, a short train of other old cars rattled by, pulled by a small diesel locomotive. All of this was part of the Bluegrass Scenic Railroad and Museum, run to give visitors a taste of what riding the rails in a bygone era was like.

A short distance later, 62 plunged down a deep gorge to the Kentucky River. There, the route made a right turn onto the long Blackburn Memorial Bridge, an S-shaped span that is one of only two of its kind in the world. This one stands 175 feet above the river. Straight ahead on the far side, rising above the bluff, rose the buildings of Boulevard Distilling Company, home of Austin Nichols' Wild Turkey bourbon. To the left of the road bridge and some 90 feet above it reared Young's High Bridge, a 1,700-foot-long railroad trestle built in 1888.

Our ride so far in Kentucky put me in mind of the story, no doubt apocryphal, about the young minister, newly graduated from seminary, who was sent to pastor a church in rural Kentucky. The first Sunday, his sermon was "The Sin of Smoking." The congregation listened politely, but after the service, the elders took the pastor aside and explained that he couldn't preach on smoking since a third of the congregation grew tobacco. So the next Sunday, he preached on "The Sin of Drinking." Again the elders took him aside, this time to explain that a third of the congregation grew corn, which they sold to the distilleries for whiskey production. The next Sunday, the sermon was titled, "The Sin of Gambling," but afterward, the elders pointed out that the remaining third of the congregation raised racehorses, used on the betting tracks.

Sensing the elders were running out of patience with him, the pastor was very careful in his selection of a topic for the next Sunday, and when that day came, everyone was delighted with the sermon and many commended him for the level of conviction with which he spoke. His topic? "The Sin of Fishing in the Territorial Waters of a Foreign Nation."

Once across the bridge, we followed the road as it snaked to the right and crawled up the palisades. The road had been shoulderless all the way from Versailles, but at this point we found a wide paved shoulder attached to the uphill lane, which served us nicely as we pumped up the grade. The shoulder petered out at the top, but we continued without problem to Lawrenceburg, where we planned to eat lunch.

Lawrenceburg, a town of 6,000, was named in tribute to Captain James Lawrence, commander of the frigate *Chesapeake*, who was killed during the War of 1812. He last words made him famous: "Don't give up the ship."

The town's main street, on which 62 flows, is dominated by an exquisite white limestone courthouse. Its presence there made me think about a phenomenon I had noticed in some other county seat towns and would see more as my journey continued. With the courthouse located in the traditional town center, attorneys, county officials, office clerks, jurors, plaintiffs, defendants, law enforcement officers and numerous other people all had reasons to spend a good part of each day there. So why wasn't there a restaurant on or near the main street within walking distance of the county building?

When we inquired of a citizen about a place to eat, we learned that the only place downtown that served food at all was a pool hall, and its menu was limited to burgers. There were plenty of places to eat within the town environs, but they were all out at the edge of town in shopping strips or along the highway. They were all too far to walk to during an average lunch break, and were built in ways that discouraged foot traffic anyway — no sidewalks, wide roads without pedestrian crossings, big parking lots in front of the establishments, etc. All of that meant most people working downtown had to take to their cars at the noon hour to get to an eatery.

With the American love of the auto, I guess it shouldn't have surprised me. But until this trip, I had assumed that most communities with government offices and related services were still able to sustain sidewalk businesses. Now I realized some "downtowns" had picked up and moved to highways leading out of the city centers.

There were still some stores open on Lawrenceburg's main street, but I suspected they had a hard time competing with the similar establishments in the drive-up strips at town's edge. But it's an attractive town, complete with some magnificent old houses. I hope it can keep its original main street alive, for towns will have lost something when the only options are drive-in stores out on the highway.

After Lawrenceburg, 62 runs for some 20 miles before encountering another town large enough to have any businesses or even a post office. There were, however, three "congested areas": Fox Creek, (one long-closed store), Ashbrook and Johnsonville. Aside from a man mowing his lawn in one of these spots, we saw no one around in any of them.

The lack of activity and long empty stretches did make for good biking though. We had a few hours of scenic ridge-running through a landscape similar to what we'd seen the previous day, only with fewer tobacco barns. The low traffic count enabled us to ride two abreast, enjoying the views, the comfortable weather and conversation.

Eventually we came to Chaplin, a hamlet with a small grocery store, a hardware, a gas station, four churches and a handful of houses. We stopped at the grocery for a snack, and while eating it, we talked with a 70-ish man who had dropped in for an ice cream bar, which he devoured on the spot. He was a lifetime resident of Chaplin, and he worked spring through fall at a campground in Bardstown, about 16 miles further west on 62. Scott asked if he vacationed in the winter. "I've never taken a vacation," he said. "Never wanted one. I like it right here."

I asked him what made Chaplin special. "It's God's country," he said, but didn't elaborate. Then he called over to the middle-aged woman running the store, "This is God's country, right?"

"Sure is," she said.

"See?" he said. "God's country!"

And that seemed to settle it.

Cresting a small rise on the way out of town, a woman in a late model car came up behind us. I motioned to her to pass us, and she did. We soon lost sight of her on the undulating road ahead. About a mile later, we saw her again. Now her car was stopped skewed in a crossroad, and she was sprawled out on a lawn near the edge of the road. A pickup truck had come to rest in the field on the opposite side of the road. Obviously there'd been an accident, though neither vehicle looked badly damaged. Several people had gathered from nearby houses and one man was talking into a phone, so we didn't stop. Before we got to Bloomfield, four miles west of Chaplin, an ambulance and then a police car roared by us headed back the way we'd come.

Bloomfield was a little bigger than Chaplin, but apparently not large enough to handle the shopping needs of the area. The ice-cream-bar man in Chaplin had told us that people had to go to Bardstown for most shopping. "We used to have several stores here," he said. "But no more." He shook his head sadly. Apparently God's country had a few shortcomings.

As we pedaled out of Bloomfield, the ambulance came screaming past us headed toward Bardstown, with, we assumed, the injured woman inside.

Beyond Bloomfield, the land, though still rural, was in transition. Homes appeared more frequently and several looked to have been recently built, probably as outlying housing for Bardstown. The traffic was heavier, and we dropped into single file. We rolled into Bardstown, our destination for this segment of the trip, in time for supper, and then made our connections to return home.

Chapter 8

I returned to Bardstown alone very early on an August Sunday. Even at 6:15, the day was hot and the air cloying — "close" as old-timers used to call high-humidity days — and every movement caused me to sweat freely.

I found a restaurant open and ordered pancakes. When they were ready, the waitress plopped down with them three packets of something called "Table Syrup" and three single-serving containers of a brand-name spread. Now let me get this straight: Margarine was developed as a substitute for butter. And "spread" is a substitute for margarine. So that makes spread an imitation of an imitation, right?

In any case, I was hungry, so I slathered the stuff on the pancakes and then opened the first syrup container and anointed the whole mess. I took a bite and found it nearly tasteless. I grabbed the syrup container and read the ingredients printed on the tear-off cover. Sure enough, not only did the vile fluid contain no real maple syrup at all, it also didn't bother with any artificial maple flavoring. It was mainly corn syrup. I don't know what ingredients were used in the pancakes themselves, but even they were flat, and I don't mean that as a physical description. Slowly, and with little enjoyment, I chewed my way through the plastic breakfast, which at least proved filling.

Bardstown capitalizes on its history, so before leaving, I cycled to its east edge to see Federal Hill, a fine antebellum mansion built by Judge John Rowan between 1795 and 1818. The structure was immortalized by his songwriter cousin, Stephen Foster, as "My Old Kentucky Home." Now the centerpiece of a state park, the building would not open for a couple more hours, so I settled for a gander at the outside and a wander around the grounds. Nearby, I found the site of "Stephen Foster, The Musical" an outdoor stage production set in a natural amphitheater. All summer long, a drama troupe presents the life story of Foster, considered by many to be America's first great composer.

It would make a good — and believable — story to say that the "bard" in the town's name was none other than the songwriter himself, but actually the name predates him. Bard, or Baird, was one owner of the tract of land on which the community was laid out. The main street, however, on which 62 runs, does bear Foster's name.

The next street south is named John Fitch, and there's a monument to that man in Court Square. Fitch (1743-1798) was the probable inventor of the first American steamboat, although that achievement is often attributed to Robert Fulton. In 1787, Fitch conducted a successful trial of a 45-foot steam-powered craft on the Delaware River, and he later built at least two larger, paddle-wheeled steamboats; one of which was destroyed by a storm just before its launch date. Despite the success of his designs, he never was able to get enough financial backing to carry his invention into profitable production. Thus discouraged, he retreated to Bardstown where he owned land, only to find that overrun with squatters.

Finally, disillusioned and embittered, Fitch ended his life by swallowing poison, leaving the following note in his journal:

> *I know nothing so vexatious to a man of feelings as a turbulent wife and steamboat building. I experienced the former and quit in season and had I been in my right sense I should undoubtedly have treated the latter in the same manner, but for one man to be teased with both, he must be looked upon as the most unfortunate man of this world.*

Bardstown has done a good job of preserving some pre-Civil War buildings. It also offered a distillery tour and whiskey museum, though I didn't take advantage of them. I was surprised, however, that none of the brochures about the town mentioned the Wilderness Road. During the early settlement of Kentucky, the famous Wilderness Road ran through Bardstown on its way to its terminus at the Falls of the Ohio, as Louisville was then known.

This early road, an overblown term for what was little more than a footpath, had its beginnings in 1774 when a group of investors uniting as the Transylvania Company purchased a large block of what is now central Kentucky from the Cherokee Indians. The next year, the company employed Daniel Boone to mark a trail into the new land. Boone led a party of trailblazers from the western end of Virginia through the Cumberland Gap and then northward, incorporating existing Indian trails and buffalo traces plus cutting new path as needed. He halted upon reaching the Kentucky River, a few miles southeast of present day Lexington. Boonesboro was built where he stopped. Today U.S 25 and 25E follow that approximate route. By itself, that path became known as Boone's Trace or Boone's Road.

Later that same year, the Transylvania Company sent the first group of settlers into Kentucky over Boone's Road. Part way along, two members of the party decided to head out on their own. Benjamin Logan and William Gillespie, plus a black servant, left the main body about eight miles north of present-day London, Kentucky. There, at a point on Boone's Trace called Hazel Patch, they found a dim path branching off to the left. Known as Scaggs' Trace after three brothers who had hunted in the area, it led a few miles northwest to a natural crabapple grove, a spot eventually dubbed Crab Orchard. Logan and his two companions pushed on a little farther and established a homestead, the primitive beginning of the town of Stanford, but originally designated as Logan's Station. Later settlers who followed this western prong off of Boone's Road extended the trail to Harrodsville, Bardstown, Shepherdsville and on to Louisville.

Boone's Trace to Hazel Patch, coupled with this northwest branch from that point onward, eventually become known as the Wilderness Road, and over it thousands and thousands of settlers poured into Kentucky. The area became a state in 1792, and a few years after that, the Wilderness Road, still only wide enough for packhorses, was enlarged to accommodate wagons, and in places, it was re-routed. Later, after the National Road was built north of the Ohio River, that became the preferred immigration route and the Wilderness Road got little attention and deteriorated badly.

Actually, I wasn't surprised that Bardstown didn't trumpet its connection with the Wilderness Road. Over the years, sections of the trail were relocated, often with no records kept about where the original path ran, so absolute statements about the road's course are difficult to make. By the time the road linked to Bardstown, it was one of several paths branching off from Logan's Station, and some historians consider that settlement the terminus of the Wilderness Road per se. But several reports of the road name Louisville as its end point and at least one respected researcher traces its path through Bardstown on its way there.

By the early 20th century, the Good Roads movement had had its impact, and interest in the Wilderness Road revived. One result of the Good Roads agitation was that the Office of Public Roads decided to use its small budget to engineer some "object-lesson" road sections. The idea was to select small segments of road in various parts of the country. If local communities would provide the construction funds, the OPR would supply the engineering supervision to build short stretches of paved highway. Leaders in three Kentucky counties in the Cumberland region combined to take the OPR up on its offer, and in 1907-1908, a two-mile chunk of the old Wilderness Road in the Cumberland Gap received a 14-foot-wide macadam paving.

This reworked sector opened to a giant celebration, and as an object lesson, it accomplished its purpose. Soon afterward, several counties issued bonds to fund road building, and the modern road era in Kentucky began.

By 8 a.m. I was cycling westward out of Bardstown over steeply rolling hills, which were followed later in the morning by a flatter stretch, and then more hills. It was hot, drippy work.

Elizabethtown, the next community of any size (population 18,000) on my route, also makes hay on its history. Every Thursday evening during summer, a group of actors, dressed as 19th-century notables who once resided in the town, take to the streets to lead visitors on a "Historic Downtown Walking Tour." One of the notables portrayed is Sarah Lincoln. Thomas Lincoln, father of Abraham, worked as a carpenter in Elizabethtown, and then moved away following his marriage to Nancy Hanks. After her death, he returned to the community to marry Sarah Johnson, who became a beloved stepmother to the future president.

Since I was there on a Sunday and not a Thursday, instead of costumed actors, I saw local citizens walking into churches. I thought about going to a service myself, but knew I'd feel out of place garbed in my sweaty bike clothes, at least in the larger churches. But near the downtown, I spied a smaller church. I knew small congregations to be more comfortable with casual dress, and I noticed that not one of the men heading in sported a tie or jacket. I chained my bike to a tree out front, swapped my soaked muscle shirt for a dry T-shirt and sauntered in. Mercifully, the quiet interior was air-conditioned. I accepted a printed bulletin from an usher and slid as unobtrusively as possible into the back pew.

This was an Episcopal Church, and the service included the full trappings of high liturgy, though directed warmly and with enthusiasm by the middle-aged, bearded priest. Yet as an outsider, I found the service difficult to follow. In reporting that, I should tell you that I am an ordained United Methodist minister, and thus had a general sense of what was going on. I suspect someone with less church experience might have been bewildered.

There were two books in the pew rack in front of me, one a hymnal and the other *The Book of Common Prayer*. The printed order of worship I'd been handed had a list of numbers running down the left side, headed by the words "Prayer Book." Another list of numbers marched down the right margin, headed as "Hymnal." There was also an insert sheet in the bulletin containing some Scripture readings, fully printed out.

The first event in the order of worship was described as "Processional" and followed by the number "51" in the hymnal column. I turned to 51 in the hymnal, and when the singing started, discovered that the words and music being sung bore no correspondence to what was printed on page 51. I tried the other book, but it contained no music at all. The people around me were holding books with printed music, and singing lustily from them, but I couldn't find the song. About then, it ended anyway.

The next item was "Liturgy of the Word," proceeded by the number "355" in the prayer book column. I flipped to page 355 only to discover that the words printed there were not those being spoken from the pulpit and responded to from the pews. I just listened.

When we got to the "Lessons," I figured those must be the Scripture readings on the insert. I was right, and was relieved to find myself, literally and figuratively, on the same page as the other worshipers at last. This was followed by a "Sequence Hymn," whatever that was, and there, I had to skip over the one designated for the 9 a.m. service and try to find the one listed for 11 a.m., which was marked as being on the insert. There was no hymn on the insert, but I did finally find the one everyone else was now singing on a back page of the trifolded bulletin, and by the second verse, I was able to join in.

After that came the sermon, which at least required no printed instructions. Based on the gospel reading, it was presented with high energy and made an appropriate application for us listeners. The next items were from the prayer book, and now the numbers took me to the correct entries. We worked our way through several prayers in preparation for "The Holy Eucharist."

Before we got there, we came to an item called "The Peace." This was a disconcerting moment when the hitherto obedient congregation suddenly broke ranks, turned to one another, shook hands and mumbled something. Even the pastor came down from the pulpit to participate in this ritual. It seemed to me, however, that many people did this less than wholeheartedly. Eventually, a man in the row ahead of me turned around, presented his hand to me, and said, "The peace of the Lord be always with you."

"Thanks," I said, shaking his hand and noticing that he seemed a little surprised. After we all sat back down, I glanced at the prayer book. There I read that my response was supposed to be "And also with you."

From the bulletin, it appeared that we had only about 15 more minutes of service to go, but I was suddenly aware of a sense of uneasiness about lingering any longer. Being near the back door, I got up quietly and slipped out.

Pedaling out of town, I pondered my sudden impulse to depart. Despite my initial confusion, I had found the service respectfully worshipful and the sermon justly challenging. I had not been anticipating any awkwardness about shaking hands with the priest at the back door following the service. But then I realized the source of my disquiet. Sitting there in the refrigerated sanctuary, my will to ride in the humid, hot air outside had been slowly evaporating. I was beginning to get hungry, but by the time I piled a lunch stop on top of the worship hour, I would have stopped too long. I needed to make some more miles before I ate.

Actually, although I am in a religious profession, it's unusual for me to visit a church while long-distance cycling, generally because at the time of day most churches hold services, I find myself on the road between communities. After my cross-country ride, a man asked me if I'd had any "spiritual" experiences on the journey. Before I could even respond, he added, "Or was the whole thing spiritual?"

"Er, well, yes ... it was, sort of." I said.

I was able to go on to give a satisfactory — and true — answer, but later, I thought about why the question had taken me by surprise. I realized I knew the answer: Bicycling, especially of the long-distance kind, gives me a natural high that is more than a physical sensation. I'd go as far as to say it nourishes some inner part of me. But up until the moment of that question, I hadn't labeled it as "spiritual."

In my case, especially, I have a natural resistance to using religious jargon to "baptize" what is basically a profoundly satisfying human experience. Ironically, that's probably because I'm a minister. I'm proud to be in that profession, but I recognize that a wide range of claims, many of which I cannot support, get bandied about in the name of religion. And so despite being a member of the clergy, my book about the previous trip was not a "religious" volume. Nor is this one.

Having said that, however, I have to admit that yeah, bicycling sometimes is a spiritual experience. It's not just that some of my best sermon ideas have come while I'm on bicycle rides; it's also that I usually feel at peace and deeply content wheeling down a country road, and I know enough about spirituality to realize that those feelings are often a part of it. (I suspect this also has something to do with why I hate pedaling a stationary bike in my basement; it may exercise my body but it does nothing for my soul.)

Now that I think about it, the questioner had it right when he asked if my journey was a spiritual experience. It was, for spirituality — in

the sense that I recognize that there is that which is greater than I am —
is an integral part of my makeup. And I am grateful to my Creator for
the opportunity to pedal the byways of this good earth.

I pressed on from Elizabethtown through the steamy afternoon,
passing farms and woodlands, and zipping through the tiny settlements of Stephensburg, Summit, Big Clifty (it wasn't) and Clarkson.
Some of these were so small that I didn't realize I'd been in them
until I hit the sign for the next one. Between Summit and Big Clifty,
I crossed into the Central Time Zone.

In late afternoon, I began to feel nauseated, and I suspected I
was suffering from heat exhaustion. I labored for another 10 miles,
riding through a brief thunderstorm, and eventually came to
Leitchfield, having notched up 60 miles for the day. There I took a
motel room, showered quickly, slept for three hours, and then, feeling somewhat restored, emerged for a late supper.

Well, what do you do on a Sunday night in Leitchfield? It was no
problem for me, since more rest was high on my agenda, but what if
you are a teenager? Leitchfield is a small county-seat town and
limited in what it offers the young. The solution the kids themselves
figured out was the "cruise-in," and it was taking place that evening
in a parking lot just down the street from my motel. This activity, at
least as I witnessed it, involved a set protocol. One by one, cars full
of teenagers crept down the street, past the rendezvous, circled
through a paved parcel across the street, and then pulled into the
meeting lot, all parking their vehicles nose-in in a semicircle. Kids
sat on the car hoods and talked and laughed. Being together — and
not at home — I gathered, was the whole point.

The next morning as I chuffed out of town, a loaded school bus
passed me. Trapped inside, sad-faced teens stared mournfully at
me. Though it was only the second of August — midsummer for
kids elsewhere — here it was the first day of school. With my camping equipment on my bike, I must have represented the freedom they
were losing for another 10 months.

The temperature was slightly lower than the day before, but
more importantly, the humidity had dropped, and morning proved

a grand one for riding. From Leitchfield westward to Central City, Route 62 also carried the moniker "Blue Moon of Kentucky Highway." The terrain was rolling but not laborious, and I pedaled easily.

I wheeled through little Caneyville just as the local grade school was having its morning recess on this first day of school. Small children trooped out of the building, and like the older kids in the bus in Leitchfield, they stared at me. I waved, and several, ignoring the teachers trying to organize them, waved back. Cycling on, I had a brief impression of a short main street that crossed the Blue Moon of Kentucky at a right angle, but after only a few more revolutions of my pedals, the town was behind me.

Throughout the morning, I'd seen several small farms, some of which included fields of tobacco, though far fewer fields of the crop than I'd seen when riding with Scott below Maysville. These plantings made me think of something I'd learned about Eden, New York, after Dave, Mark and I cycled through there. That was in springtime, and the ground had been well watered, but with the advent of summer, a drought had settled over much of the United States. In late July, quite by chance, I'd met a farmer from Eden, and I asked him how the water shortage was affecting his crops.

"We irrigate and have the crop roots covered with plastic to conserve the water," he had explained, "so we're doing all right. We've had droughts before, so we were prepared. But this is the first year we've gone to the extra work and expense without having the prices we're paid for our vegetables hold up."

"Why is that?" I asked.

"New competition. With the growing strength of the antismoking forces, tobacco growers are being encouraged to plant less, so some are switching to vegetables."

Looking at the tobacco fields I now rode past, it was obvious that not all Kentucky growers had abandoned the crop. Still, I realized that I had not seen as much tobacco as I had expected. Later, while eating lunch in a diner in the nearby town of Beaver Dam, I asked two local men whether they had noticed a drop in the amount of tobacco being grown.

"Nah, it seems about the same," one said. "Most every farmer's got a field of it somewhere."

"But it's not doing very well this year," the other added. "It's been too dry. We really need some rain."

So what was the actual story? Was less tobacco being grown or not? I suspected the vegetable grower from Eden, watching the markets, was right. It may have been that this particular area around Beaver Dam had not switched crops but that other tobacco-growing areas had. Or perhaps the two men hadn't yet noticed a trend that was just beginning in their region. But I thought of the interrelatedness of American life. Declaring all public buildings in California smoke-free impacts Kentucky farmers whose crop switch drains income from a vegetable grower in New York.

Before getting to the town of Beaver Dam, I'd come to the small community of Rosine, little more than a collection of houses. A historical marker at the boundary informed me that the hamlet's post office had been established in 1872 as Pigeon Roost, but the name had been changed the next year to Rosine in honor of local resident Jennie Taylor McHenry (1832-1914) who wrote poems under the penname Rosine. Her claim to fame, according to the sign, was that "A collection of her poems was published." Evidently in those days, if the pond was small enough, you didn't have to be too big a frog to be the chief croaker.

It surprised me that the town had no marker for a more recent and far more famous citizen, Bill Monroe. Born in Rosine in 1911, Monroe, became known as "the father of bluegrass music." He wrote hundreds of songs, some of them inspired by his little hometown. "Going Up Caney" memorialized a nearby creek and "Jerusalem Ridge" was the name of the hill where he was born. His uncle, fiddler Pendleton Vandiver, was the subject of Monroe's song, "Uncle Pen." Monroe also authored Kentucky's Official Bluegrass Song "Blue Moon of Kentucky," which explains why the section of 62 running through Rosine bears that title. Monroe died in 1996 and is buried in the Rosine Cemetery near his Uncle Pen.

After Beaver Dam, 62 entered a hilly stretch and the day really heated up. By 2 p.m., I was looking for a place to get out of the sun, so when I rolled into Central City, I sought out the local library. As I'd hoped, it was air-conditioned. Gratefully, I scooted inside and sat down to read a newspaper, but I wound up talking to Ann Page, the librarian.

Founded in 1873 as a mining town, Central City sits in a basin among the hills. The mines are mostly gone now, which has had a negative impact on the town's economy. But according to Ann, most residents have chosen to stay put despite the downturn. "There is no hustle and bustle of big city life," Ann said. "Everyone is pretty laid back and mellow. We have big hearts and although we may not have a lot of money, we're willing to share. People feel comfortable here and tourists can sense it and feel at home too."

Riding into town, I'd seen a sign that proclaimed the portion of 62 within the city limits as "Everly Brothers Boulevard." Ann told me why. The family of the singing siblings had lived in Central City when the older brother was born. And though they'd moved elsewhere before the younger's birth, the brothers, Phil and Don, had been generous to the Kentucky community. A dozen years before my visit, when the local police station needed but could not afford a new radio system, Phil and Don somehow heard about it and donated the money to obtain it. To say thank you, the community had held a little party for the brothers, which in turn became an annual homecoming festival, the 12th of which was soon to take place on Labor Day weekend. In recent years, they'd had not only the Everlys, but also Billy Ray Cyrus, Chet Atkins and other stars of the music circuit. The event draws people from all over America and several other countries as well.

"I try to volunteer each year," Ann said, chuckling. "That way, I get to meet some pretty famous people first hand. Heck, I've been hugged by some of them."

Sitting in the library's cool air reading the local newspaper, I chanced onto the following item:

> *The Iranian city of Ramsar has banned women from riding bicycles, even if covered from head to toe as required by Iranian law. Conservatives fear that bicycles give women too much freedom to move about and hence will lead to promiscuity.*

Actually, if that's their concern, the men probably don't need to worry until the women start requesting bicycles built for two.

By 4 p.m., the temperature was still about as high as it had been, but the intensity of the sun had at least dropped a bit. I mounted up and rode toward Greenville. For part of the way, the road between the two communities has been rerouted from its original course, but along the old route, there was once a coal mine bearing the name Dovey. In 1881, a stranger showed up at Dovey Mine, ostensibly in search of employment. In casual conversation, he asked when the railroad pay train was to arrive in Central City. He was told that the train had chugged through earlier, and that William Dovey had gone for the money. Dovey was due back that night. The next morning, three men appeared at the mine. With cocked pistol, one demanded the contents of the safe, which he received. But because Dovey had been delayed in his return, all the men got was $13 and a gold watch bearing Dovey's name. About a year later, the infamous outlaw Jesse James was killed. Among his possessions was the Dovey watch.

The pay train doesn't run anymore. In fact, I wondered if any trains did in this region. For most of the day, 62 had been paralleled by railroad tracks, but not once had I seen a train. According to Ann, the librarian, up until the early 60s, the area had been serviced by two railroads, the Illinois Central and the Louisville & Nashville. She still saw occasional freight trains, now from CSX, on the line, though none now stopped in Central City. That was another reminder of how the closing of the mines had affected the area.

I cycled into Greenville, the seat of Muhlenberg County. 62 had already taken me through nearly two dozen county seats, and there were many more ahead. In fact, if one wanted to make a study of county courthouse architecture, following Route 62 would be an excellent way to do so. Just in Kentucky alone, Greenville was the 10th county seat on 62's path. Actually, this was not happenstance. In 1914, Kentucky's legislature authorized a system of roads specifically to connect the county seats, a practice followed by other states as well. Though the road system was more widely cast later, in many places, its real start involved county seats.

On the way into town, I passed several fast-food restaurants, but hoping for something other than fried vittles, I continued up the long hill to Greenville's center where I asked a police officer to recommend a place. He had no trouble doing that since there was only one restaurant there, an establishment specializing in barbecue, so barbecue it was.

After supper, I cycled several miles out of the city, found a small rural Baptist church along the side of the highway, and camped for the night behind it. I'd ridden 73 miles.

Chapter 9

"If idiots could fly, this place would be an airport."

That cheery observation greeted me from a wall sign as I landed at the Prairie Rose Café in White Plains the next morning.

While eating a bountiful breakfast, I meditated on the assorted Elvis Presley memorabilia festooned across one whole wall. The most garish of these was a clock, the face of which bore a likeness of the late rock-n-roller. Below that, Elvis' legs and hips swiveled back and forth constantly as the clock's pendulum.

Before taking off, I asked the waitress to put ice in my thermos. I'd not carried this item on previous bike journeys, but it would prove invaluable now. It was a wide-mouth, unbreakable model. Each morning and at least once more during the day, I filled this and one regular bike bottle with as much ice as I could fit in and then topped them off with water. My other two bottles got water only — being uninsulated, ice would be long gone by the time I got to them. During the first hour, I drank from the bottle with ice, all of which melted by the time I finished it. Next, I poured cold water from the thermos into the bottle, giving me a second helping of chilled liquid. At the same time, I poured water from my second bottle over the remaining ice in the thermos, which gave me a third bottle of cold water later. Sometimes the ice even lasted for a fourth bottle. In the even hotter days ahead, this system never failed to keep me supplied with chilled water.

At least once every day, some brave passenger in a passing vehicle would yell out the window at me, attempting to startle me. I'd gotten so used to it that I seldom even reacted. Twice within five minutes of leaving the Prairie Rose, however, drivers from vehicles going the opposite direction shouted something. They were moving so fast that all that reached me was an undecipherable fragment of sound. But my impression was that unlike those traveling my direction, these shouts were less to startle me than to tell me I didn't belong on their road. Certainly they were moving like they wanted it all to themselves. Tough luck, guys. I'm staying.

A couple of miles more took me through the edge of Nortonville, but didn't expose me to enough of the town to form an impression. But several miles of highway from there onward are memorable for the new challenge they presented me. Route 62 there is a two-lane road, of average width and with no useable shoulder — thanks to the endless rumble strip running on it. Riding on the road was okay except that every few minutes, coal trucks of the tractor-trailer type roared by at a high rate of speed. When there was no traffic in the oncoming lane, most moved over a little to pass me, but when that lane was busy, they kept coming anyway, refusing to wait for clear passage. Thus I repeatedly had to escape onto the rumble-stripped shoulder to let these charging behemoths have their way. The most nerve-racking moments were when coal trucks passed me in both directions at once.

After several miles of jockeying among these careless giants, I came to the crossroads community of St. Charles, the keystone of which seemed to be a small post office. Ready for a break, I cruised into the shade cast by the postal building and leaned my bike against the wall. I plundered some snacks from my saddlebags and refilled my water bottle from my thermos.

Just as I settled down with my back against the wall, the postmaster came out of the building and around the corner. He said hello and began asking me about my trip, my equipment and the gearing on the bike. He too was a cyclist, and he had dreams of riding long trips. He hoped to be able to do so after retiring, which he planned to do as early as possible.

I mentioned my ballet with the coal trucks, and the man said, "You've got to watch out for those. One of our patrons was killed by a coal truck right in front of here not too long ago. She'd just been in here to get her mail and was pulling out when a truck came over the hill. She never knew what hit her."

"I suppose they run as fast as they can because they are paid by the trip, not by the hour?"

"That's true, but there's even more danger because of who they get to drive. The drivers of the big semis you see elsewhere at least go to school to learn how to handle big trucks. With these coal buckets, a lot of the drivers have never been behind the wheel of a truck until they start here."

Despite this joyous news, I enjoyed talking to the postmaster, but I needed to get going, so I said goodbye.

"You be careful out there," he said.

A mile down the road, I passed a 55-mph speed limit sign. It had been battered and flattened by passing traffic.

I continued my pirouette with the coal trucks for a few more miles until I finally passed a side road where the trucks turned off. Wishing them adieu, I rode on into Dawson Springs, named for the mineral water wells in the area. During the late 1800s, its waters were thought to have curative qualities, and the town became a leading health resort. At its zenith, the community supported 17 hotels and numerous boarding houses, and water from the springs was shipped all over the country. Those days were long gone; I found a quiet, unhurried little town of 3,000.

I progressed on to Princeton, another county-seat town. Inquiring for a place to eat lunch, I was directed to a stylish eatery ensconced in a restored storefront and furnished with antiques. It was one of those places offering 18 varieties of flavored coffees and sandwiches on croissants and French rolls. The few customers were dressed casually so I clattered in wearing my full bike regalia, which didn't seem to raise anybody's eyebrows. The sandwich and salad I ordered proved to be both tasty and filling, and I was feeling quite good about the place as I went up to pay my bill. The woman working the register appeared to be either the owner or the manager. After settling up, I asked her if she could put some ice in my thermos. Although she said "All right," her movements suggested that she resented doing it — why, I don't know. She snatched the thermos, marched over to the dispenser and shoved a scoopful in. Suddenly my meal left a bad taste in my mouth.

The road from Princeton to Eddyville, yet another county seat, had been recently improved and widened, which was fine in itself, but part of such upgrades often include removing all the trees within several yards of the road on both sides. Thus, just after high noon, I found myself riding in blazing sunlight, with no tree near enough to cast a cooling shadow at that or any other time of day. This wholesale clearing also made the journey less interesting visually.

In the midst of the inferno afternoon, I entered the recreational region surrounding The Land Between the Lakes, a slice of real estate sandwiched between Lake Barkley and Kentucky Lake. Route 62 clips right above the top of this long park. The recreational area begins around Eddyville, although the part of that town seen from 62 gave me no sense of it as a community.

Route 62's passage through the area took me to a high metal bridge over Cook Creek. The steep approach and the bridge itself were just two lanes wide, with a shoulder of about 12 inches beyond that. Next to this narrow shoulder was a raised berm eight inches high and a foot wide. Since the traffic flow was steady and included the occasional speeding coal truck, I thought it unwise to take the lane. The shoulder and raised berm were too narrow to cycle, but offered another option. I lifted the bike onto the berm, and walking on the shoulder, I wheeled the bike across the bridge without impeding the flow of motorized vehicles.

Next I cycled through Lake City, of which 62 showed me a dusty gravel mine and widely spaced small businesses. The center of the community must have been to the left or right of the highway, but I saw nothing to give me any clear indication. Nor did anything in this weary stretch look like it would appeal to vacationers.

Nonetheless, a short while later, I came to the dam that forms Kentucky Lake. Route 62 cavorts right across the top of the dam itself, and I flowed over it with the rest of the traffic. Bypassing the resort and beach on the western shore, I continued on to a commercial campground right on 62 near Calvert City.

After checking in and setting up my tent, I swam in the campground pool to cool off, and then hit the showers. At 6:30 I walked to a nearby restaurant for supper, finding the day still so hot that I wondered how I had cycled in it.

The campground had its share of vacationers. Most pulled trailers or drove midsized motor homes, though one couple occupied a huge diesel-powered unit as large as a Greyhound bus. But a few residents were workmen living on the grounds temporarily while constructing a nearby plant. I discovered this when I asked one man about the large piece of machinery mounted in the bed of the truck in front of his trailer. It was welding equipment, he explained, and he used it on his construction job. I asked him how he liked living for weeks on end in his small unit, and he said it beat motel life. Later, as more workmen trickled into the park, I noticed that some returned to campers where wives and children awaited them.

By 9 p.m., the grounds were quiet and I was ready for bed, but the evening was still so warm that I knew I'd swelter in the tent. Anticipating no rain, I removed the rain fly, leaving just the mosquito-netting shell, but even this proved too warm for comfort. Because of bugs, sleeping outside of the tent was not a good option, so I lay miserably in the netting shell, sleeping fitfully until finally, sometime after midnight, the night cooled enough to make deeper slumber possible.

Shortly after daybreak, I joined the substantial stream of morning traffic moving down Route 62 toward Paducah. The forecast was for another very hot day, so I wanted to make as many miles as possible before the heat of midday.

For much of the way to Paducah, 62 is a four-lane highway, and where it is not, the houses and utility poles are set far enough back from the highway to allow for the eventual expansion to four lanes. In Paducah itself, Route 62 winds through the city, but misses the downtown area. Though I played in heavy traffic all morning, including the stretch through Paducah, I did not find the passage especially difficult. In the city, 62 took me past government offices, industrial areas, schools and some shopping districts.

Situated at the confluence of the Ohio and Tennessee Rivers, Paducah is the largest city in the western end of Kentucky. It was laid out as a village in 1827 by William Clark, half of the famous Lewis and Clark duo. Clark named the place for a Chickasaw friend, Chief Paduke. The place graduated to city status in 1856.

The way out of town changed abruptly from a wide urban street lined with businesses to a narrow suburban lane populated with high-priced housing. The character of this section was so different from what had preceded it that at first I thought I had missed a turn, but after a mile, the route opened onto a four-lane highway leading westward. This eventually became a narrow two-lane road, which sustained a moderate amount of traffic through open country.

I was aiming for Wickliffe, were 62 begins its run toward the Mississippi River. But nine miles west of Paducah, 62 jogs southward and begins a meander, eventually approaching Wickliffe, not from the east, but from the south. If my goal had been to reach Wickliffe as quickly as possible, I'd have continued straight ahead on Kentucky Route 286, which most of the traffic did. But I pursued my affair with 62, and after the routes separated, it became the road less traveled. I rolled along having the road to myself much of the time. I rattled through the small berg of Lovelaceville, passed some woods where kudzu had overrun all the greenery on several acres and about lunchtime, arrived in tiny Cunningham. This village was composed of some houses strung out along the highway, a bank, a store and a restaurant named simply "Cunningham Café." In this small cement-block building I had a lunch so good and served by a staff so friendly that it alone made the extra 15 miles of the meander worth it.

Continuing, I followed 62 as it nicked the corner of the countyseat town Bardwell, and then swung north toward Wickliffe. Here the roadbed was a built-up causeway running through a lowland forest, uninterrupted by signs of civilization. I couldn't see far into the surrounding woods, but what I could see appeared murky and dark. I was glad I was not traversing this area at night.

Nine miles of travel through this spooky forest eventually brought me to a long hill, which I climbed, along with semis exiting the paper mill at the bottom. After cresting the top, I encountered a giant metal cross on the edge of the hill, overlooking the confluence of the Ohio and Mississippi Rivers. The cross, several stories tall, appeared quite new, and the field in which it sat looked to have been cleared only recently.

I talked to a man repairing a barn nearby, and he explained that the cross had been built to honor those involved in the river industry. The immense cruciform commanded a great view of the confluence, and from the viewing deck in front of it, I looked upriver at the bridges I would be tooling over within the hour.

Wickliffe, seat of Ballard County, was laid out in 1880 and named for Colonel Charles A. Wickliffe, attorney, state legislator and former Confederate Officer. There is a museum called Wickcliffe Mounds near the town with the remains of an ancient buried city that had once occupied the site and apparently flourished there. This ceremonial and trade center had been in use for some 300 years by people of the Mississippian period, A.D. 800-1350.

Route 62 leaves town by means of a long, straight bridge, perhaps a half-mile long, stretched over river floodplain. At least I think it was floodplain; my crossing of the bridge was such a white-knuckle experience that I wasn't free to do much looking at what was under the bridge. Exactly two lanes wide, the bridge is the beginning of a six-mile approach to the Ohio/Mississippi River crossing. And it's a busy bridge because U.S Routes 62, 51 and 60, plus four state routes all converge in Wickcliffe for the final run toward the convergence of the two mighty rivers. A new bridge was under construction at the time of my visit, and I assume it will be wider, but it didn't help me then.

As I rolled toward the bridge, I was behind a semi. But trucks were required to enter an inspection station of some sort before crossing. So when the 18-wheeler pulled into the station, and, for the moment, there was no other traffic behind me, I figured it was my opportunity to scoot across the bridge.

I shot onto the span, but within seconds, heard the semi pulling in line behind me and roaring through his gears as he caught up. I shifted into my biggest chainring and pounded on for all I was worth, but seconds later, the big rig was snapping at my heels. As I fled onward, I heard the harmonic of the truck's engine change as the driver downshifted, but the sound drew closer. There was nowhere for me to go but forward, so I kept on. I figured I'd be okay as long as I kept moving, but I wondered what would happen if I blew a tire or my chain broke and I suddenly lost speed. The leviathan behind me was moving too fast not to roll over me if I had to stop abruptly. Pursued by the Peterbilt, I finally reached the far side, where the bridge emptied onto a levy. There was no paved shoulder, but I skidded to a stop on the grassy berm and let the truck, along with the string of other vehicles now in his wake, pass by. From one of these, a garbage scow, someone screamed something at me, which in my unnerved state of mind, startled me and caused me to jump, much to the screamer's delight.

The longer I stood there, though, the better I felt. I had ridden in the traffic stream, and though the truck driver may have wished me out of his way, he did not in fact run over me or try to squeeze by. In fact, I may have been reading too much into the sound of his gear changes. For all I know, he may not have been trying to rush me at all, but merely meant to keep moving forward as fast as he could under the circumstances.

During the next break in the traffic, I pulled back onto the highway, which continued on the top of the levy across the low, dark, wooded ground.

I hoped the bridges crossing the Ohio and Mississippi would be better. Actually, I was hoping they'd have a sidewalk so I could cross removed from the traffic stream — perhaps I could even stop in the middle and take some photos. Dream on, Stan.

After a few miles on 62, the road made a right turn and all at once there I was on the final approach to the bridge over the Ohio. The passage climbed upward rapidly, crested on the high steel bridge, and then shot down the other side. And the whole affair was, as the Wickliffe span had been, just wide enough to accommodate a semi in each direction. Dismayed that the steep approach would force me to move onto the bridge slowly, and worried that once I was over the top, overtaking traffic would not see me, I shifted gears and moved forward. Actually, there was no other choice. Now that I was unexpectedly on the bridge approach itself, there was no place to pull off to even consider options or to turn around.

As I puffed upward toward the high steel, overtaking traffic moved around me when breaks in the oncoming flow permitted it. The rest bunched up behind, and together we crested the rise high above the broad river and began the descent. Naturally, I could go faster downhill, so I popped my bike into high gear and was soon careening down at 35 mph, fast enough that the vehicles behind me were no longer crawling.

The bridge brought me to a narrow strip of Illinois, just south of Cairo. There, Route 62 makes a right turn, and immediately heads for the bridge over the Mississippi, which is the same width and configuration as the Ohio bridge. In a car, you'd spend no more than 45 seconds in Illinois. I made the turn and then pulled off the road to collect my wits.

As it happened, two men on the roadside were hooking a pickup truck to a large piece of farm machinery and a moment later, they pulled out onto the bridge approach with this huge implement in tow. One man spoke into a two-way radio, and I realized what was going on. They were preparing to tow this wide machine over the bridge and no doubt had someone on the far side holding traffic. The man must have grasped my dilemma as well, for he waved me in front of him.

Gratefully, I leaped on my bike, and of course, with my first stroke, the chain jumped off and jammed between the derailleur and the chainring. Not wanting to lose my protected passage across the river, I jumped off and began tugging furiously at the chain, which did not budge. Disappointedly, I called to the man in the pickup, telling him he better go ahead. "I can wait a minute," he said, so I turned back to my bike, gave the chain another yank and got it re-railed. I climbed back on, pulled ahead of the pickup, and with him behind me, blocking both lanes of traffic with his huge towed machine, I rode merrily across the Mississippi.

On the Missouri side, a long line of traffic waited to make the eastbound crossing, and a collection of large farm implements, including combines and other machines I did not recognize, sat on the roadside, apparently having already been shuttled across. I waved my thanks to my protector, and sailed out westbound following 62 across the top of a long levee between crop fields on the flood plains below.

Geologically speaking, the region was part of the "Mississippi Alluvial Plain." It was once a swampy wilderness but had now been drained, providing flat, fertile cropland, stretching out for miles and unrelieved by high ground.

It was also a land of economic and social contrasts. Wilson City, the first community I encountered, bore the bleak look of poverty.

The people I saw were black, though I don't know if that describes the whole population of the town. An economic development agency for the delta area was housed in a school building along 62. Charleston, a county seat town just seven miles further on, looked more prosperous and had a lush golf course. Most of the people I saw there were white, but again, whether that defined the town's population, I don't know.

Continuing westward, I ambled through Bertrand, a small, agreeable-looking community and then on toward Minor. For several miles approaching Minor, a railroad track paralleled 62, about 25 yards north of the road. While some of this land between highway and tracks was a kind of no-man's land, in one section, someone had established a slender, linear ranch, with horses corralled in long, narrow stable yards. Nearer town, light industry and farm implement dealers lined both sides of the highway.

Minor squats at the junction of U.S. 62 and I-55. Consisting largely of motels and campgrounds, the community appears to exist primarily for tourism. The attractions? A factory outlet mall and a restaurant called Lambert's, the "Home of Throwed Rolls." That means just what it says — they throw their rolls to you instead of serving them in the usual manner. And people drive from all over to be on the receiving end of those throws. Apparently the food there is good, though delivered to the table in a more traditional fashion.

The outlet mall is pretty much like outlet malls elsewhere, but busloads of people arrive daily to wander its stores. Both the mall and the restaurant have large parking lots especially to accommodate buses and RVs.

Although it was now 7 p.m., the temperature was still above 90, and neither of the campgrounds offered much in the way of shade, so I acquired a room at one of the motels. I had racked up 88 miles for the day.

Minor wasn't established until 1951, but it sits cheek and jowl with the larger community of Sikeston, founded 1860. Sikeston works hard to paint itself as a tourist attraction. In glowing terms, a promotional brochure describes the city's "historic" downtown with "century-old structures" and the city's oldest park. Since many communities have century-old buildings and long-established parks, I looked for something that made Sikeston's special. Beyond the burnishing they got from the advertising copy, I couldn't find any. A major attraction over which the brochure waxed eloquent — I kid you not — was six pillars remaining from an old Methodist church that burned in 1968. The brochure also included headings such as "So Much Heritage," "So Much to See," "So Much to Do" and so forth, but when I finished reading it and tried to recall what made the place unique, nothing came to mind. The brochure reminded me of the old fable about "The Emperor's New Clothes." Nonetheless, the Sikeston/Minor Convention and Visitors Bureau, the publisher of the pamphlet, deserves credit for doing "So Much From So Common a Place" with its sell job. In reality, the town looks like an ordinary, decent place to live and work — no more and no less — enough to ask from any community.

Was I judging the place too harshly? Was I overlooking something that makes the city stand out over your hometown or mine? To check, I talked to the young cashier in the grocery store where I purchased some food that evening. "I see a lot of visitors here," I said. "What's the big draw to this area?

"Well, people like that restaurant down the street, Lambert's," she said.

"That's all?"

"Oh, well, there's the outlet mall. A lot of people go there."

"Anything else?"

"No, not that I can think of. That's about it."

Actually, there were a couple of other things. For one, the town puts on a four-day rodeo once a year, one of the largest in the Midwest. There's also a Cotton Festival of the Arts and a Cotton Carnival each September. But then, other towns have their festivals as well.

One thing that caught my attention was that U.S. Route 61, which runs north-south through Sikeston and concurrent with 62 briefly, was laid out in 1789 during the time when the region was controlled by Spain. The Spanish king ordered the overland route for connecting the cities of St. Louis with New Orleans. The road, which bore the name El Camino Real, or King's Highway, includes Sikeston's main street.

This royal road wasn't the only one known as El Camino Real, however. Another existed as an early California road, running north from San Diego to Sonoma to connect the Franciscan missions. Today U.S. 101 closely follows that old road's course. El Camino Real was also the name of the first road built by Europeans in what is now the United States. But you'll have to wait awhile for that story, until 62 takes us to El Paso.

Chapter 10

Route 62, which had been flowing westward, turned abruptly southward in Sikeston, joining Route 61. The two ran together for about 20 miles to New Madrid, where 62 again turned west. My morning ride along this path found me on a wide, straight and flat road, the modern successor to the King's Highway. For mile after mile, the road was lined with crop-heavy fields, and on several of these, irrigation was taking place, either in the form of a series of mobile towers rotating around a central point or as trickle irrigation piped to the crop rows themselves.

There were crops I recognized easily — corn and soybeans — since they also grow in my home state. I also saw milo, a grain used in animal feed, which I learned to identify while cycling in Kansas on my transcontinental ride. But a fourth crop was new to me. It was about as high as the soybeans and had leaves similar in shape to those on a maple tree. It also had pink blossoms. I hoped for an opportunity to ask someone to identify that crop.

After miles of remarkably similar scenery, I came to the town of New Madrid, right at the top of Missouri's Boot Heel region — so named because that's exactly what the extreme southeast corner of the state looks like. Sitting right on the outside of a 360-degree bend of the Mississippi River, New Madrid can boast some remarkable history, although it does so with more humility than Sikeston. Route 62 merely breezes through the upper edge of the community, but I decided to head into the small downtown, about a mile off-route. There, on the levy, I found an observation deck that offered me a sweeping view of Old Man River. On street level, right below the levy, an old river tavern housed a modest museum. The building was a "historic" edifice but that fact was understated in the community brochure rather than trumpeted.

In addition to serving as port for the river trade, New Madrid is notable for two events, the first being a series of earthquakes centered there beginning in December 1811 and continuing almost daily for nearly two years. The main shock was the most violent known to have occurred in North America. Because the area was sparsely settled, the first earthquake caused only slight damage to manmade structures in the epicenter, though the shaking was strong enough to alarm the population over an area of 1.5 million square miles. Cabins fell down as far away as Cincinnati.

It was another story with natural surroundings. The ground rose and fell, hillsides slid and the contours of the land were drastically changed. On the river, huge waves overwhelmed many boats and washed others high onto the shore. Whole islands disappeared. Large waves moving upstream made people think the river had reversed its direction of flow. More than 200 moderate to large earthquakes occurred on the New Madrid fault between December 16, 1811, and March 15, 1812, and many smaller ones in the months following. Though seismic recorders didn't exist in the 1800s, the reports of damage and the area affected have led seismologists to estimate that the worst of the New Madrid quakes was 10 times larger than the 1906 San Francisco quake (which was a 7.9-magnitude shocker), and five of them were of 8.0 magnitude or higher. For more recent comparison, the 1999 quake that devastated a large area of Turkey and took thousands of lives just a couple of weeks after my sojourn in New Madrid, measured 7.8 on the Richter scale.

Many seismologists believe that there will be another significant quake somewhere along the New Madrid fault within the next 40 years. Some of the utility companies even have emergency plans in place for dealing with the disruption such an occurrence would entail.

The other major event was an 1862 Civil War battle involving Island No. 10, a few miles downriver from New Madrid. Confederate forces had occupied both the town and the island as strongholds for defending the Mississippi River. After Union forces laid siege to the city, the Confederates decided that defending New Madrid was impracticable, and evacuated their troops to Island No. 10. A U.S. Navy flotilla then converged on the island, with the Union ironclad

Carondelet taking on the Rebel batteries and guns. With the southerners thus occupied, Yankee troops crossed the river and blocked the Confederate escape route. On April 8, the Rebels surrendered the island, leaving the Mississippi open down to Fort Pillow, Tennessee.

From the observation deck, I could clearly see a large island, and assuming it to be Island No. 10, I snapped a couple of pictures. When I later mentioned something about it to the museum curator, she said that the island I'd seen was New Madrid Island. Number 10 no longer existed because of the way in which the river had moved over time. She showed me a chart that indicated half of the old island was now one with the shore and the other half was submerged in the river. But then she chuckled and said, "A lot of people think the island you saw out there is No. 10. We had one man here who had taken several pictures of it. After I told him it wasn't 10, he said he'd just tell his friends it was so as not to waste his photos."

Leaving New Madrid, I cycled out into the flat countryside, rolling over miles of cropland and landing at lunchtime in Risco, a hamlet of a few houses and store/café combination. Inside, while munching on a hamburger, I fell into conversation with four men at the next table. Two of them, in their early 20s, were dressed in farm clothes and were dusty from working in the fields. Like me, they were enjoying a lunch break in the relative cool provided by the building's overworked air-conditioning unit.

As an opening gambit, I asked about the crop I hadn't recognized, describing it for them.

"That's cotton," said the young man in bib overalls. "Where are you from?"

"Ohio."

"That's why you haven't seen it before. This area is about as far north in America that cotton is grown." (That explained the reason behind Sikeston's cotton festival.)

They then asked about my trip, and I described it for them.

The man about my age wore a cap with the name of a seed company on it. He said, "We had a guy come through here who'd been trying to ride a horse across country. But he gave up right here. He came here looking for me to buy his horse — I raise horses. He wanted to sell everything — horse, saddle, camping gear, the works."

"Why'd he quit?" I asked.

"He found it was a lot harder than he expected. Every night before he could take care of himself, he had to find somewhere for his horse and make sure it was fed and housed for the night. He found lots of places for himself, but not so many for his horse. He got tired of the hassle. I bought his horse and then drove him to town to catch a bus home."

The fourth man was the proprietor of the store. He said, "We also had a guy come through here on foot dragging a cross — like Jesus. He was planning to go clear across America. I guess he made it."

"Didn't he have wheels on the bottom of that thing?" the seed-cap man asked. "That seems like cheatin'."

"Yeah, but he said he'd already worn the bottom off one cross draggin' it like that," the proprietor said.

Returning to the subject of crops, the bib-overall man asked me if I'd noticed the rice growing in the fields. "It's the one that looks like a field of very green grass," he said. When I indicated I hadn't, he told me that I'd be running into a lot of it as I proceeded westward, especially in eastern Arkansas, which he explained was a major rice-growing region. "That grows in fields of water, so you'll want to be careful camping near it. The mosquitoes breed in the water and after dark they are fierce."

The proprietor spoke up, "Let me ask you something. Do you carry a gun?" When I said I didn't, he added, "I wouldn't try going out like you are without a gun. It's dangerous out there. Too many crazies."

I explained that I'd never had any trouble, and he seemed surprised. "Well, that's good," he said.

At that point, the two young men had to get back to work. They pulled on sweat-rimed straw hats, wished me well and headed out. Moments later, I rose to leave and the two remaining men both offered a friendly goodbye. "I enjoyed talking to ya," the seed-cap man said.

I wheeled through the hot afternoon in brilliant sunshine, following a relatively empty 62 westward, touching the town of Malden, rolling through Campbell and finally crossing into Arkansas on a concrete bridge over the St. Francis River at the community of St. Francis. This town had once boomed from the timber industry. Lumbermen labored all week amid swarming mosquitoes and mud, and on Saturday nights, celebrated riotously in a saloon at the Missouri end of the bridge. The lumber industry had long since declined, and the bar was gone as well.

Despite being in a new state, the character of the land — flat, rich crop ground — continued as far as Piggot. The temperature had soared, causing the tar on the paved shoulder to become soft and sticky, making riding on it difficult. I moved to the traffic lane, which being of a different substance, let me roll freely.

At some point during that afternoon — and I failed to note whether it was before or after Piggot — I rolled past a homestead that gave me an uneasy feeling. The house sat in the center of a rectangular grassy lawn. The place was not fenced, but on each of the four corners, cement-block walls had been erected, bracketing the site. A painting of the Confederate battle flag was displayed on the house itself and on each of the four corner enclosures, giving the place the distinctly unwelcoming look of a compound.

I am aware of the argument that the flag of the Confederacy is simply a symbol from the historical war over states rights and that its use by neo-Nazis and other hate groups is an unjustified usurpation of the flag. Be that as it may, some appropriations — or misappropriations — are so successful that hanging on to them for legitimate uses may not be worth the cost. When I saw this house, I did not think "the home of a southern history buff," but "the home of a racist who's proud of it." That characterization may have been unfair, but unfortunately, that's the kind of freight the Southern Cross bears.

I had set Corning as my goal for the day, so I lingered in Piggot just long enough to buy a cold drink and refill my thermos with ice. Piggot and Corning, though both county seats, are a bit unusual in that they both serve the same county, a practice followed in some other places in Arkansas as well. When the state legislature established the county boundaries, it did not consider the natural barrier created by the hills and especially the Black River bottom, which at times was nearly impassable. So Piggot became the eastern county seat of Clay County and Corning the western one. Better roads and high-water bridges eventually overcame the transportation problem, but the dual seat arrangement, by then entrenched, remained.

I soon experienced the first of these barriers when I launched myself up the hilly ridge beyond Piggot, the first climbing I'd done since leaving Kentucky. After several miles of ups and downs, I dropped down to flat plain again. Before the days of good roads, this bottomland harbored a nearly impenetrable jungle, making farming and everyday commerce impossible. After 1910, some hardy souls began burning off the ground cover and digging drainage ditches. Today, the moist land lends itself to rice growing, and I saw field after field of it, just as my lunch companions back in Risco had predicted.

I met my supper companions in an unexpected manner. I was lost in thought when a loud wolf whistle cut through my reverie. (As I said, I have great legs, but I suspect the whistler hadn't really noticed.) An old pickup trundled by, and as I looked up, a young man in the passenger seat was just drawing his head back inside the cab. The truck pulled ahead of me, and I saw that its bed was full of scrap metal. I continued riding without making any response.

About 10 miles later, I arrived in tiny McDougal looking for somewhere to eat. The only choice — indeed, the only business of any sort — was a small, ragged store. In front dozed the beat-up old pickup.

I lumbered in to discover that a small selection of hot food was available, cooked on an electric skillet by a young woman behind the delicatessen counter. I ordered a sandwich and then wandered the aisles while waiting for it to cook. The shelves were jammed with an assortment of foodstuffs, hardware, auto supplies, notions and other sundries. Near the back, at an ordinary kitchen table, sat two young men dressed in oil-stained clothing. One of the pair, beefy but muscular, weighed at least 300 pounds. I recognized the other — who was half the size of the first — as the one who had issued the wolf call. The only remaining place to sit was across from this pair.

When my sandwich was ready, I clattered over to the table and slid into a seat. "You the guys that whistled at me?" I asked.

The big guy stopped eating and looked wary. His partner immediately blushed and said, "Oh ... yeah ... ah ... We used to do that in high school." It came out sounding like an embarrassed apology so I decided to let him off the hook.

"Good." I said. "I thought I was losing my touch. Nobody's whistled at me in a long time." They both laughed, and I could sense the tension evaporating.

As we all ate, I asked the pair about the load in their truck. The big man, clearly the spokesman for the duo, explained that they were self-employed scrap haulers. The pickup outside was their smaller vehicle. They also ran a larger truck when loads warranted it. He went on to tell me that the scrap yards in some distant cities paid more than some nearer ones, but it required a pretty substantial load to balance the cost of running the truck over the greater distance. I listened, asking a few questions, which he answered in a straightforward manner. He then inquired about my trip, and I told my story. By the time we were done eating, there was a companionable feeling at the table. When the pair rose to leave, the big guy wished me a safe journey, and it sounded sincere.

His partner, the whistler, waved and added, "Me too."

I rode the final 14 miles to Corning. My odometer rolled over to 101 miles as I hit the center of town, where I inquired about a place to camp. Finding none, I opted for a room in a low-grade but clean motel run by a Pakistani woman who, after learning about my endeavor, promised to pray for my safety.

Following a refreshing shower and a change into my evening duds, I set out to explore the city on foot. The motel was located on an entry road into town, adjacent to a shopping center and some fast-food joints. Seeing nothing around that resembled a true downtown, I asked a roving teenager where it was. "Right here," he said. "This is where all the stores are."

I tried a different tact in the grocery store where I purchased fruit for a bedtime snack. I asked the cashier where the courthouse and business district could be found. She scrunched her forehead as though thinking hard, and finally, in a tentative tone, named a street, pointing vaguely over her shoulder. But then she added, "This is where everybody shops, out here."

I was too hot to wander further, and the light was rapidly fading anyway, so I ambled back to the motel to soak in the refrigerated air of my room. Riding in the sun for hours, I ended each day feeling as if I were being broiled for someone's dinner. My arms, exposed from the shoulders down, were now a deep brown, as were my legs between shorts and socks, and my neck ran toward red (no comments necessary, thank you) but when I removed my shirt, my chest was a stark white. My hands too, encased in riding gloves all day, looked ridiculously pale attached to my bronzed arms. I wore a biking helmet with a sun visor, which did shade my face and some of my bald head, but the large air vents on top let sunlight reach my scalp in checkerboard fashion, so each day I applied a layer of sunscreen to my pate. But with all this baked area on my flesh, it was hard to get cool enough at night to sleep. The air-conditioning helped.

Wheeling out of Corning under clear morning skies, I recalled a comment by George Featherstone, an English geologist, who passed through the area in 1834 and found a perplexing maze of roads. Apparently, several residents were unhappy with the route of the main path and so cut their own roads, blazed them to look like the official course, and routed these past their own cabins. Featherstone wrote, in droll understatement that, "in consequence of this we got out of our way."

Those route disputes having long been put to rest, I rolled along the well-marked and decently paved 62, passing a small airstrip with a single-engine two-seater plane parked near the highway. Minutes later, the same plane — or one identical to it — came streaming through the sky above. For the next several minutes as I continued on my way, the plane provided me with a private air show as it performed loops, twirls, figure-eights and other joyful maneuvers. It was a perfect morning for flying, and not a half-bad one for cycling either, though I suspected the cooler temperature was not going to last the day.

The ride from Corning to Pocahontas, yet another county seat, proceeded along straight highways over flat terrain, the last of both I would see in Arkansas. That was because my encounter with the Ozarks started at Pocahontas. As mountains, the Ozarks cannot claim the elevation of either the Appalachians or the Rockies. The tallest of the Ozarks rises only to the height of 2,560 feet and that mountain was not on my route. But plenty of others were. The Ozark Plateau stretches from eastern Oklahoma to southern Missouri to northern Arkansas. Covering 60,000 square miles, it's the largest area of highlands between the Appalachians and the Rockies, consisting of steep hills, low mountains and rugged terrain, eroded by springs and rivers flowing to the Mississippi River.

From a cyclist's perspective, distance above sea level doesn't mean that much, unless it's so high as to make the air thin. What does matter is the length of the hill and its rate of incline. I've previously ridden in both the Rockies and the Appalachians, and the former soar to much greater elevations than the latter. But the climbs in the Rockies are often long and steady, and even though they may go to 11,000 feet or more, you may already be at 9,000 feet when you encounter the upslope. The Appalachians, seldom rising above 6,000 feet, offer steeper, more abrupt climbs beginning farther down.

All of this is by way of saying that cycling up the Ozarks, though relatively low mountains, was still hard work.

I breezed through Pocahontas and puffed up the mountain wall, which started before I left the city limits.

Once well up, I stopped in the shade of trees in a church cemetery near Birdell to cool off. Sitting with my back against a tree and sipping from my water bottle, I gazed at the tombstones. One of the closest bore the words, "John Wayne Hawks 1960-1970." Ten years old at time of death. I wondered what tragedy had ended the dreams of the parents who'd named their son after the legendary movie star, but of course received no answers.

In Imboden, U.S. Route 63 joins 62, and they romp together from there to Hardy. Route 63 has long been a truck route, moving traffic and cargo from Memphis, Tennessee, northward into Missouri where 63 makes connections to Springfield and Kansas City. During the entire stretch where 62 and 63 followed the same course, I shared the highway with fast-moving semis — not day-haulers, but the long-distance big boys. Although there were a lot of them on the curving road, they drove with more care than the coal truckers of Kentucky and never made me feel uneasy as they passed. Actually, because the Ozarks are a vacation region, I felt more at risk from the RVs driven by shaky old guys and the trailers towed by young fathers dealing with minivans full of buoyant kids.

I've previously described how cyclists and later automobile drivers played important roles in the good roads movement. In time, truckers joined the outcry for dependable roads, and especially for highways that linked across state and local boundaries. Although the previously mentioned Federal Aid Road Act of 1916 was landmark legislation in the development of the highway system, it had several shortcomings, not the least of which was its failure to specify that roads on which federal aid was spent had to *connect* across jurisdictions, and especially state lines. I once saw a 1916 highway map of the southwest corner of Massachusetts and adjoining slices of New York and Connecticut. It showed several highways, but all except one ended without ceremony at the state borders. Even many of the roads within the states didn't connect.

But when America went to war against Germany in April 1917, the urgencies of that effort exposed the continuing weaknesses in the country's transportation systems. In the end, highways benefited from what the country learned.

Until that time, railroads had been the prime mover of the nation's freight. But when called upon to move the greatly increased amounts of materials needed for both the war effort and the nation's industries, the railroads fumbled badly. With long-haul freight bottlenecking the terminals, many railroads stopped accepting short-haul shipments, including foodstuffs, and the food distribution system faltered. Faced with little other choice, farmers and food wholesalers began using their own trucks for direct delivery or pick up of the necessary items. In doing so, they made a portentous discovery: Using trucks was no more expensive than using trains, and there was less delay. In that single fact lay the beginning of trucking as the dominant force in the freight-hauling business.

This increased use of trucks in turn had a major impact on the highway system. Not more than five months after America's declaration of war, so much cargo had been diverted to trucks that road breakup became common. Lots of roads were still unpaved, or surfaced with only stone, shell or planks, but even those with tar-bound macadam proved too thin to withstand the pounding from heavy trucks.

Naturally, this increased the need for highway maintenance, but the same railroad problems that forced the nation to turn to trucks to begin with also made it difficult to get stone and bituminous ingredients for road repair, so those materials had to be hauled by truck as well. This, in turn, beat up the roads even more. America's transportation system in all its forms now experienced high stress.

Meanwhile, the Allies needed trucks for military operations in France, and in September 1917, the Army ordered 30,000 of them. Given the sorry state of the trains, shipping such huge numbers by rail was clearly impossible. So it was decided that the trucks should be driven from the factories to the ports of embarkation. Although this is perfectly feasible today, it was a bold proposal then, and a trail-blazing group had to be sent out in advance to find a route that would give the trucks a reasonable chance of making it. The first route selected ran from factories in Toledo, Ohio, to the port at Philadelphia. That's at most a two-day trip by auto today, but in the winter of 1917-1918, it took the trucks three weeks, with 29 of the 30 trucks on that first caravan completing the run. The trip occurred in the midst of a particularly severe winter and the route crossed the Allegheny Mountains, so the Pennsylvania Highway Department had to put forth heroic efforts to keep the mountain passes open, and they succeeded. With the roads made passable for the military trucks, private vehicles used the roads as well.

In the end, this mission proved both the feasibility of long-distance travel by motor vehicle and the possibility of keeping highways open in even extreme weather.

As trucking continued through the following spring, roads which when frozen had handled trucks reasonably well, broke up badly. But at the same time, suppliers found that shipping by truck was no longer just cost competitive with shipping by rail, but was becoming considerably cheaper. The trucking industry was here to stay.

All of this — the need for movement of military materials, the proven performance of trucking, the value to the public of year-round roads, as well as the earlier accepted need of rural mail delivery — lay behind the Congressional highway act of 1921. That bill provided matching funds to the states for seven percent of the roads in each state to be designated as federally supported highways. It also corrected the defects of the 1916 act. Among those corrections were specifications for durable surfaces, ample lane widths and this little item: "That in approving projects to receive Federal aid ... the Secretary of Agriculture shall give preference to such projects as will expedite the completion of an adequate and *connected system of highways, interstate in character*" [Italic mine].

The mountain country I now entered consisted of forests and pastureland, with a few houses scattered here and there. It did not appear to be a highly developed region, but was apparently alive with forest creatures. Earlier in the day, I had noticed a dead armadillo on the road. This came as a surprise, since I didn't think the armored mammals ranged this far north. Apparently they did, however, for from that point on, armadillos were the most frequent roadkill I saw. It was not uncommon to see one every mile or so.

Shortly after lunch in Ravenden, I climbed the biggest hill I'd encountered so far in Arkansas, and though I was cycling well, I seemed to be noticing the heat more than I had any day so far, and wondered why. I drank bottle after bottle of water, refilling them and my thermos of ice at a roadside store. Pumping on, I rolled into Hardy, a small town thriving on tourism, and noticed that the digital sign outside the bank read 98 degrees. No wonder I was hot!

The main attraction in Hardy is its two-block-long shopping district on its narrow main street. There, more than four-dozen shops packed into turn-of-the-century buildings, entice visitors to browse and buy. The entire downtown is listed on the National Historic Register, so the more modern-looking businesses have been placed at the ends of the town, leaving the center as a historic preserve. Hardy claims to be Arkansas's "smallest Main Street city," and at least during my brief sojourn, it was crowded with pedestrians.

The town also features a vintage motorcar museum, a military museum and a clock museum. Set on the banks of the Spring

River, the town draws tourists for camping, canoeing and fishing. It was founded in 1883, thanks to the newly built railroad. Established to service locomotives and to provide food and lodging for rail passengers and housing for employees, the town was named for James A. Hardy, Jr., a 25-year-old trackage subcontractor who saved his boss' life.

Looking for a place to get out of the heat, I wandered into the Chamber of Commerce, which advertised visitor information. Inside, thankfully air-conditioned, I talked with Ann Raheem, who represents the Chamber in Hardy. She asked me about my experience with the trucks. Although I'd not had any problem, Ann, as a resident of the area, knew how frequently there'd been truck-caused accidents on 62/63. "They happen a lot," Ann said, "often because of trucks trying to pass when there really isn't room for them to do so." She went on to tell me that there'd been two area people who lost their left arms, which they'd had resting on the window ledge of their vehicles, as trucks forced their way past and came too close.

Since there was no bypass around Hardy, the trucks have to drive right down the town's narrow main street. Ann said, "Recently during a celebration downtown, we suddenly heard a crash. A truck had gotten too close to something and it tore his mirrors off."

Actually, given the almost constant truck traffic, I suppose the percent of accidents caused by the big rigs was small, but several of those that Ann described where bad enough to mark the passage as a dangerous one. I was grateful that my run through the area had been without incident and that here at Hardy, 63 split off from 62, taking most of the trucks with it.

The town was visually attractive, and I could see what drew visitors to the place. But I asked Ann what the residents liked about the town. In reply, she used herself as an example, explaining that she first came to Hardy as a tourist. Then her parents retired in the community, and Ann and her family came to visit. "The attraction was how peaceful it felt to sit on the front porch swing and visit with family or neighbors or just admire the scenery. It reminded me to be thankful for what this life means. I can't say that it does all that for everyone, but I think it connects with those who are tired of high crime areas and the city rush — or who miss the slower times and want their children to have that."

"What's the downside?" I asked.

"Jobs are fewer and wages are lower. I guess you have to take the good with the bad. But land and housing is much cheaper. There must be some truth to what this place makes me feel because in the past six years, I've seen younger people moving in."

From Hardy to Ash Flat, 10 miles further on, 62 runs as a four-lane highway, with several businesses, shops and offices strung out along its length. The road climbs immediately as it leaves Hardy, and as I labored up this incline, I shifted as usual down to my smallest chainring, the "granny" gear, for creeping up the hill. This time, however, the chain jumped off the ring, sending my feet abruptly spinning around ineffectively while the bike rolled to a halt. I jumped off just before the bike would have fallen over and gave the chainring a cursory examination. Seeing nothing out of the ordinary, I placed the chain back on the ring with my fingers, remounted and continued up the hill.

It's not all that uncommon for a chain to jump off a ring occasionally, especially when shifting quickly under load, such as when climbing a steep hill. But my setup had been shifting erratically all day, and I now wondered if it needed more lubrication. Although oil will work, it leaves the chain messy, transferring an oily smear to riders' legs and everything else that happens to touch the chain. So like many cyclists, I use one of the dry lubes — in my case a paraffin-based product — to lubricate my chain. Unfortunately, that product is found only in bike shops, and I'd used the last I had with me back in Kentucky. I'd been hoping to find a bike shop and pick up more, but so far hadn't seen one.

When I reached the top of the hill, I pulled into the lot of an insurance company and checked the chain. It didn't feel like it needed more lubricant, but then with a dry lube, the feel-test isn't the most reliable. I decided I'd better find a lubricant of some sort — even household oil — and douse the chain.

With all the stores along this route, that sounded like a simple task, but proved harder than I expected. I saw no bike shop, but stopped in a farm-supply store. The clerk claimed to have seen a chain lube somewhere, but though he walked me all over the large store, and even consulted with another store employee, he couldn't find anything. Next I tried a Wal-Mart, where I did find household oil, but in a giant can that I had no intention of carting along.

The Wal-Mart also included a grocery store, and since I needed some laundry detergent for washing out a few things, I checked the soap aisle. There again, I found the right product, but only in a huge box.

What do single people do? More and more, I see products packaged only in sizes that require a person to either waste and throw away some of it, or keep it and try to remember where it is if the need for it ever arises again. This is especially frustrating with something like household oil, which the average person would use only for the occasional squeaking door hinge.

I finally found a small container of oil in an auto parts store and lubricated the chain, which functioned okay as I pushed on. Route 62, true to its love affair with county seats, touched Ash Flat before heading off toward Salem, both county government towns.

Ash Flat, in Sharp County, was not the original seat. As with Clay County, Sharp initially had two seats. Hardy served the county's northern district and Evening Shade, 22 miles below Hardy, the southern. The two government units were combined in 1967 and transplanted to Ash Flat, situated halfway between the two.

Other than the stores along the highway, however, I never really saw Ash Flat, as 62 just caressed its edge before loping toward Salem, 14 miles away. But judging from the number of stores along 62, it appeared that most of the business district really lived out on the highway anyway. Clearly these stores did not expect pedestrian traffic.

During the few minutes I spent in the auto parts store, the sky changed from blue to a roiling gray. As I rode toward Salem, I expected to be whumped with a downpour at any moment. But because the dark sky provided relief from the intense sun, I accepted the likelihood of rain gratefully. Anyway, the entire area was in drought, and the residents would welcome any precipitation.

Despite the threatening sky, the rain never materialized. I cycled through what I'd come to call "Ozark scenery": forests, rough pastures, a sprinkling of homes and at least one squashed armadillo per mile, all set on steeply rolling terrain. Arriving in Salem, I found a recently opened campground — so recent in fact that they had not yet received their permit for showers and restrooms, so the owners had designated their park for self-contained RV units only. On learning that I'd ridden 90 miles to get there, however, the couple who owned the camp welcomed me to stay free. I'd have to use the restroom in the convenience store across the street, but that was okay with me.

Learning that I camped in a tent, the woman said, "You do know we have poisonous snakes in Arkansas, don't you?" Actually I hadn't given them much thought. "I don't know if I'd want to sleep out there," she said. "You be careful." On that comforting thought, I selected a site and erected my tent.

I washed up in the convenience store restroom and changed to clean clothes. A few stray drops of rain, barely a mist, fell for about three minutes during the twilight hour, but by the time I retired, the stars were twinkling and the sky was clear. Because it was still uncomfortably warm, I left my rain fly off the tent, leaving it where I could pull it on quickly if rain should hit during the night, and slept inside the screened mesh.

I lay awake for a long time, troubled not by the thought of snakes, but by the oppressive heat. It was turning my journey into an ordeal, and for the first time, I began to doubt I'd be able to ride in it much longer.

Chapter 11

The oil I'd searched so long for the previous day did not solve my chain problem. I discovered that after riding less than five muggy, hot miles the next morning. Seconds into my first serious climb of the day — and my first use of the granny ring — my chain jumped off. Thinking dark thoughts about my bike, I pulled to the side of the road. I put the chain back on the small chainring and started out again, but with the first pedal stroke, off it came. I repeated the procedure with the same result, so this time, I inspected the chainring closely. With the chain off the ring, I turned the pedals slowly by hand. Within one revolution, I spied the problem. The granny ring had warped, with one section bent outward toward the next largest chainring. There was no hope of keeping the chain on the ring, and that meant that my lowest gears, the ones I relied on for climbing steep grades, were unavailable.

I'd encountered this problem once before, also while climbing mountains, but that had been on a tandem bike I was riding with my daughter. In that case, I'd assumed that the stress of two sets of legs pounding on the pedals had bent the ring, but now I concluded that the sheer force of downshifting under load was rough on the mechanisms, and decided that in the future, I'd carry a spare granny ring.

That didn't help me at the moment, however. I had tools with me to remove the ring, and I considered trying to straighten it, but as it was now weakened, I doubted it would remain usable, even if I succeeded in repairing it. I still had the gears in my two higher ranges, so one option was to ride as much as I could in those, and when the grades got too steep, simply walk the bike uphill.

I limped on that way for another seven miles, trudging up the hills on foot and whizzing down mounted. Plodding on in this fashion, I entered the precincts of Viola, marked by a cluster of houses.

In the early third of the 20th century, Viola was the location of an annual singing festival, held each April, and drawing as many as 3,500 people. Unlike today's music gatherings where people come to be spectators for performers, this earlier type invited people to attend as participants. Everyone came to sing. A few amateur groups vocalized, and some sheet-music publishers sent performers, but much of the singing during the two-day event involved the entire audience, usually singing hymns together. There was no charge and no prizes, and people loved it. The event belonged to the pre-television era, but in the vicinity of Viola, I came to a house with a sign out front that advertised a singing fest, scheduled for a date in the near future and marked as "Open to All."

I soon concluded that the walking-riding combination wasn't going to get me very far very fast. The area was so hilly that I had to do way too much walking. The bike was an efficient pack horse when I was mounted on it, but it made a lousy wheelbarrow. So I formulated Plan B: I would hitchhike. I pushed my mount to a stretch of road where passing drivers could see me well in advance. I stood by the bike, a lugubrious soul with my thumb stuck out, as numerous vehicles sped by me without hesitation. I could imagine them thinking "That fool should have known it was too hot to ride today, and now he's expecting someone to rescue him." I wished I had a sign saying "Mechanical problems," so they wouldn't assume I was wimping out. But then, so what if they did?

After about 10 minutes, a large pickup truck driven by a gray-haired woman stopped. I quickly explained my problem, and she waited while I hefted my loaded bike into the truck bed and then climbed appreciatively into the air-conditioned cab, sharing the front seat with the woman's tiny Chihuahua.

"I don't usually pick up hitchhikers," the woman said, "but you looked like you needed help."

I thanked her sincerely for stopping for me. She drove us on toward Mountain Home, the first community down the line large enough to have a bike shop — at least I hoped it did.

When I asked if she were a native of the area, the woman, who introduced herself as Mallie, explained that she hailed from Nevada, but now that her husband had died, she had moved to Mountain Home to be near her brother. "Only he recently got married, so now I hardly see him either," she said.

We talked of the heat. I said, "I guess this wasn't my finest bit of planning to ride across Arkansas in August."

"Oh, I don't know. Sometimes you just have to go when you can," she said. "Later on we get lots of rain around here, so that might have not been so good either." She went on to tell me that some of her ancestors had been on the Trail of Tears, the forced removal of Cherokees from the South to Oklahoma in 1838. "I've been thinking of following that route myself," she said.

When I had dumped my bike into the back of her truck, I'd noticed a "fifth-wheel" apparatus mounted on the bed floor, so I asked if she towed a camper.

"Yes. That's what made it so easy to pick up and move up here. My husband's work took us over six states, so I really wasn't attached anywhere. Sometimes it's good to be able to move on."

The land we drove through looked similar to the area I'd ridden through the last two days — rolling hills with woods, pastures and occasional houses. But as we drew nearer to our destination, homes appeared with greater frequency, and the region took on a vacationland look, with signs advertising area attractions. Shortly after I spotted a large body of water in the valley below, we plunged downhill to the shore level, where we passed a harbor with numerous pontoon boats bobbing at dockside. The blue, clear water, sparkling under the bright sun, was Norfork Lake. I'd noticed it previously on my map. Shaped like a gnarled branch of a dogwood tree, this long, lean reservoir stretched perhaps 40 miles from end to end, rising from rivers in Missouri and twisting down to Ozark National Forest, some 15 miles south of Mountain Home.

We climbed away from the lake and minutes later came to Mountain Home, which, need I say it, was a county seat. Mallie pulled into a gas station and suggested I inquire inside about a bike shop. The clerk didn't think there was one, but I used his phone book and found one listed. Mallie drove me on to the shop, letting me out right by the door. I thanked her again, unloaded my bike and lumbered inside.

The shop owner, a middle-aged man, grasped my dilemma immediately, and soon produced a new chainring. The only problem was that the only small ring he had in stock was a 26-tooth ring. Mine was a 24. I'll bypass a boring discussion of gear ratios simply to explain that the fewer the teeth on a chainring, the lower the gears it produces. The 26-toother would work fine on my bike, but my resulting low range would be slightly higher than the one I'd had with the 24-tooth ring. Still, that was a whole lot better than not having the low range at all, so I purchased the ring and installed it right away.

By that point, I'd explained my journey to the shop owner, and he'd thought of a problem. There was major work being done on 62 west of town, with the highway reduced to barely two lanes for several miles. He said I'd have real difficulty getting through. As I've mentioned, I've learned to discount a lot of the road advice I receive from nonriders, but I've never gotten a bum steer from a bike shop, so I listened carefully.

"I'd drive you through it myself," he said, "but I can't leave the shop." I asked if he knew anyone who might be available and indicated I'd be willing to pay a driver. I confessed I was beginning to feel the effects of the heat, and wouldn't mind getting a few extra miles down the road anyway to take the pressure off reaching the day's goal. He thought a few minutes and then made a phone call. After he hung up, he told me his father-in-law would come by, and he suggested I have him drive me to Yellville (the next county seat, of course), 22 miles farther on. This would not only get me clear of the construction area, but would put me back on schedule for the day's ride.

Minutes later, a small, soft-spoken man arrived in a pickup truck, introduced himself as Joe, and helped me load my bike. As he drove me through the construction area, I saw immediately that I'd been advised correctly. Apparently the highway was being expanded from two lanes to four, but it was early in the project. The area to the right of the existing westbound lane had been excavated to make room for a road base, and in the process, the shoulder of the existing highway had been chiseled away as well. To keep vehicles away from the deep drop-off, orange barrels had been placed *inside* the westbound lanes, narrowing it to little more than vehicle width, and continuing that way for miles. Traffic flowed steadily in both directions, so if I'd entered the highway on my bike, I'd have had to take the lane, and keep the westbound traffic behind me for a long time — not a good idea.

I told Joe about the chainring problem that had brought me to his son-in-law's shop, and the toll the mountains were taking on me due to the heat. Joe agreed the heat was bad but gave me some perspective on the mountains. He said, "They're just hills, to my way of thinking. Folks around here think of Mountain Home as high, but it's only 800 feet. I'm from Memphis, where the altitude is 100 feet, so this isn't that much higher. These are just hills around here."

As we drove on, Joe told me about his family. He had moved to Mountain Home because a couple of his children had migrated there. He also told me about his late wife, how they had enjoyed trailer camping together and about her eventual death. Joe had cared for her through her final illness, and now he clearly missed her.

Deep in a valley to my left I could see two bridges, which I assumed to be over the White River. According to my map, this flowed southward out of Bull Shoals Lake, an even larger body of water than Norfork Lake. Both were created by the Corps of Engineers and each eventually connected with the White River, which carries their waters downstate to empty into the Mississippi River. Bracketed as it was by the two lakes, Mountain Home was a popular vacation area.

We arrived in Yellville where I suggested Joe let me out at a store where I could get lunch. With all my fiddling with the bike, the morning was well gone. I pulled out some money and extended it to Joe. "Nope," he said. "I don't want it. Maybe you'll need it somewhere else down the road. I'm glad to do this."

After he left and I was eating my lunch, it occurred to me that Mallie and Joe should meet. Both had lost their spouses and seemed to miss them a lot. I wondered if there were some way to introduce them. (Later, when I got home, I wrote a thank-you note to both. In Mallie's, I asked if I could give her name to Joe. She wrote back, agreeing to that. I then phoned Joe and told him about Mallie. He took her name and number, and said he'd like to think about it. But he asked enough questions that I gathered he might call her. I left it at that.)

Originally called Shawneetown after an Indian village that had occupied the site, Yellville got its current name from Colonel Archibald Yell, who was elected governor of Arkansas in 1840. Four years later, while running for Congress, he visited Shawneetown and paid the residents $50 to rename the settlement for him, proving that seeking instant fame for political purposes was not a modern invention. Colonel Yell was later killed while leading an Arkansas cavalry unit in the Mexican War.

The only way out of Yellville, both in the colonel's day and now, was up. I crawled up the steep hill under the blazing afternoon sun, drenched with sweat. The air, registering 99 degrees, felt as if it were emanating from a blast furnace, and I baked in misery. My mechanical problem was solved but the heat and humidity had become the overpowering theme of the trip, realities I could not escape and which exacted a high price from me. Because of the discomfort they caused, I was becoming increasingly focused on just getting to my daily destination and was paying less attention to the regions I cycled through. The enjoyment had evaporated from the journey and the road ahead, instead of enticing me, had become an obstacle to be overcome.

I plowed on, up hill and down, gulping water copiously and popping salt tablets. The miles passed very slowly.

At about 2:30, I started up another long hill, feeling nauseous. I suspected I was falling victim to heat exhaustion and knew I had to get out of the sun. The map said I was approaching Pyatt, which appeared to be little more than a roadside hesitation, but I struggled upward toward it and found at hilltop a convenience store with gas pumps in front. Plopping the bike against the wall, I staggered in.

Marshaled in a row along the windows were three tables with benches. From a fountain, I filled a glass with pop and carried it toward this area. In the first booth a weathered-looking man of about 70 sat, wearing a cap with a heavy-equipment brand name on it and smoking a cigarette. I nodded to him as I approached. Waving the hand that clenched his cigarette between two nicotine-stained fingers, he motioned toward the bench across his table, and invited me to have a seat.

Glad for a reason to stay indoors, I dropped onto the bench. "Been ridin' far in this heat?" he asked, and I told him my story. He listened quietly, finishing his cigarette and lighting a new one a moment later. I sensed he wasn't so much interested in my trip as he was just glad to have someone to pass the time with. He wasn't overly talkative, but answered my questions. And since I lingered in the store for nearly 90 minutes, I eventually learned a few things about him and the area.

He told me that the mountainous region was lousy for crop farming but did support chicken-raising and some timbering, though the latter had declined a lot in recent years.

Regarding his own history, he explained that after serving in the Navy during World War II, he'd operated an asphalt business on the West Coast, but eventually gave it to his son and retired to Arkansas where he'd been raised. There was no wife now, though I never learned if she had died or they'd divorced. He was sharing his home with his teenage granddaughter whose mother couldn't handle her, though he wasn't finding parenting easy either. I gathered that they coexisted reasonably well because he didn't demand anything of her. That afternoon, she was in Harrison with a neighbor lady shopping.

Aside from lighting one cigarette after another, he moved very little, smoking his way through the hot afternoon with the air of a man who had nothing to do and who expected little to happen. As he talked, the expression on his heavily lined face changed little, moving neither toward smile nor despair, but set — at least so it seemed to me — with a kind of grim acceptance of the disappointments of life.

His right eyebrow arched permanently higher than his left one, and when our conversation wandered to something about doctors, he mentioned that the surgeon who'd removed a skin cancer from the side of his face near his eye had cut a nerve to his face, causing the distortion. A scab about the size of a nickel marred the side of his nose, and I wondered if he'd had skin cancer there as well.

Finally, he rose to leave, and I decided that I had better move on too, though I felt only slightly revived. But I still had 13 miles to go, which in my exhausted state, sounded like 100.

It was 4 p.m. and not perceptibly cooler, though the sun wasn't quite as high. There were still plenty more hills, and I concentrated on creeping up them as slowly as possible to keep my body temperature from soaring. I stopped often, gulping water heavily.

A mile short of my destination, I found a diner, where I ate a good supper. Afterward, though, I felt as if it were not going to stay down. Very slowly, I cranked on to a commercial campground in Bellefonte.

It seemed fitting that I should camp there, for in Arkansas' early years, Bellefonte was a camping stop for drivers who hauled freight in ox-drawn wagons to and from Springfield, Missouri. Oxen were preferred over the faster mules because the bovines were less likely to bog down in the muddy quagmires on the miserable roads.

The modern campground for my stopover was a tidy, well-run place where even the restrooms were air-conditioned. Unfortunately, that didn't help me in my tent. I'd been assigned to a shady spot, but as daylight faded, the problem was no longer the blaze of the sun but the temperature of the air itself, which stubbornly refused to cool down. As with the previous night, I left the rain fly off the tent and lay down inside the mesh shell. Even that screening retained too much heat, so I moved outside, but the bugs soon found me, and I returned to the tent. Inside, wearing nothing but shorts, I lay miserably on top of my sleeping bag, waiting for the air to cool as nightfall deepened. Each of the nights I'd camped on this leg of my trip had started warm and then, sometime after midnight, cooled enough to make comfortable sleeping possible, so I expected the same thing to happen this night. But after a couple of restless hours in the tent, the air seemed as warm as it had been. Finally, seeing no other alternative, I rummaged in my kit for a sleeping pill and gulped it down. A fitful sleep finally descended.

It never did cool off during the night. I awoke before 6 to find that I hadn't even pulled the sleeping bag over me, and I was as hot as when I first lay down. This did not bode well for the day ahead. Nonetheless, I packed up, pedaled the handful of miles from Bellefonte to Harrison, yet another county-seat town. It carried the title, "Crossroads of the Ozarks," due to its location in the resort area of the Crooked Creek valley. State Route 7, running south from Harrison, crosses two national forests, and, according to my Auto Club guidebook, "is popular for scenic drives and photographic opportunities."

This guidebook acclamation of the area surprised me because all the tourist literature I saw both at the Bellefonte campground and in Harrison itself talked not about the local area, but about Branson, Missouri, the country-music resort town 35 miles to the north. To judge by the brochures and flyers, Harrison and Bellefonte had settled for being bedroom towns for visitors to Branson.

In 1873, Bellefonte and Harrison were both contenders in a hotly fought election to be the seat of Boone County. In the end, Harrison won by 18 votes after distributing watermelons to the voters.

To me that morning, Harrison primarily represented breakfast. After eating in a fast-food place, I filled my thermos with ice and my bottles with water and set forth.

Approaching a traffic light at the outskirts of town, a young man on a Harley-Davidson rumbled by, his long blond hair flowing from beneath the bandana he had tied around his head. The light changed to red, and he braked to a stop. Seconds later, I rolled up beside him. As we waited side-by-side for the light to change, he leaned toward me and asked were I was headed. When I told him, he said, "Well, you're going to get a lot more workout than I will on this," indicating his motorcycle.

"But you'll at least have a good breeze."

"Yes, that's true. This heat is bad." Just then the light turned green, and he added, "God bless you."

Until my cross-country bicycle trip, I'd never thought much about motorcycles. When I had, images of Hells Angels came to mind. But on that trip, I'd found that unlike most drivers, passing motor-cyclists often waved. At restaurants, they'd suggest good items on the menu. When I was struggling with hills or running before storms, they'd give me a thumbs-up as encouragement. I finally concluded that they recognized some kinship with me, perhaps because, like them, I was on two wheels, exposed to the elements and not relying on a car, which I learned some bikers call a "cage." I'd come to feel a bit of that kinship myself.

In fact, in Darwinian fashion, motorcycles and bicycles share a common ancestor, the "Safety" bicycle. Though not introduced in America until 1892, it was developed in England in 1885. Unlike the "penny-farthing" bikes, so called because of their huge front wheel and tiny rear one, the Safety bicycle had two wheels of equal size and was chain driven.

When the automobile was first introduced, it was slow and expensive, and worse, not widely available. And America's roads had not yet been improved either. Some of the inventors of that era envisioned a motorized bicycle — or "motorcycle" -- as a solution: reliable transportation for common people that could navigate the rutted and broken paths that could only be called roads in the most generous use of the term. William Harley and Arthur Davidson, motorcycle pioneers, began by developing a small gasoline engine, not for motorcycles, but for a boat, but eventually saw its potential as auxiliary power for bicycles.

The idea of motorcycles as the poor man's Ford soon faded after highways were improved and Henry Ford's mass-production methods brought the price of his Model-T car within reach of the masses. But initially, the motorcycle was intended as simply a logical step beyond the bicycle. Even some of the first motorcycle dealers started as bicycle shops.

Route 62 and Route 65 run together as an improved highway to a few miles northwest of Harrison, where 65 plows more directly north heading for Branson and 62 turns west. Following my chosen highway, I found the road under construction, being widened from two lanes to four. The old road, still in place, sustained the current traffic and apparently was to be retained as the westbound lanes. The new road would become the eastbound lanes, with a grassy strip between old and new. Clearly, the new portion was being built to newer standards than the original road, and I soon came to a spot where the difference was obvious. From the bottom of a hill, I could see the old road climbing its way upward in irregular fashion, humping over the contours of the land. The new lanes, however, climbed steadily because the irregularities had been scraped and filled. Also, the modern lanes didn't have to go as high because the very top of the hill had been lopped off. A biblical passage from Isaiah 40, which could almost be the instructions in a highway engineer's manual, leapt to mind:

Every valley shall be lifted up, and every mountain and
hill be made low; the uneven ground shall become level,
and the rough places a plain.

A few miles later, I rolled into Alpena and into the horns of a dilemma. Up to this point in Arkansas, 62 had been flowing in a wandering but essentially westward course. At Alpena, however, it canters decidedly northwest, heading toward the recreation area around Eureka Springs near the top of the state. A short distance beyond Eureka Springs, 62 wanders within a mile of the Arkansas-Missouri border and then plunges straight south to Fayetteville before finally turning west again.

Adding up the point-to-point mileages on the map, I calculated this to be a ride of at least a day and a half, and more likely two. Moreover, the route between Alpena and the northernmost point of this meander appeared on the map as a writhing line, which boded a more hilly stretch than any I'd encountered so far. Actually, I'd been climbing ever since Pocahontas, which sat at 310 feet above sea level. Hardy was 362 feet, Salem 664, Mountain Home 799, Yellville 860 and Harrison 1,049. By Alpena, I'd climbed to 1,135 and would go to 1,463 if I proceeded to Eureka Springs. Three different Arkansans I talked to in the last couple of days had spoken of the hills in that area and advised me that the numerous twists on that section's narrow highway rendered it too dangerous for cycling. Since none of the three were cyclists, I didn't buy that line, but I now knew firsthand what the high heat combined with the hills could do to me. I was already feeling crummy, and it hadn't reached high noon yet.

The map showed another route, 412, which would take me more directly to Fayetteville and let me reach it by evening. Of course, that meant abandoning 62, which wasn't acceptable in terms of the trip's purpose. But I had to face facts. The last two days had been terrible. Survival had replaced enjoyment as a journey goal. The weather reports predicted no relief for days, and I'd soon be in Oklahoma, where everything I read and heard said the temperature was three- to five-degrees hotter.

My end point for this leg of the journey was Oklahoma City, a reasonable destination for the days I had remaining if the temperature were 15 degrees cooler. But it was not. So what to do?

In the end, I decided to head immediately for Fayetteville and fly home from there instead. I would return at some cooler time and resume the trip from Alpena. Since 412 is not the concern of this narrative, I won't spend time describing that trek other than to say it too demanded a lot of climbing, though over fewer miles. I drank 12 bottles of water during the day, and covered 80 miles by evening. I was nauseous for the last 10 miles. On arrival in Fayetteville, I immediately consumed a quart of orange juice and later a quart of milk, and still felt dry. I checked into a motel and spent the night trotting between the bed and the bathroom.

In other words, I had made the right decision not to push on at that time.

During the following days, back home in Ohio, I watched the national weather report. Every day that week the temperature in Oklahoma hit triple digits.

Chapter 12

I resumed my trek on Route 62 eight months later, arriving back in the Fayetteville area late on Easter Sunday. Springtime, I assumed, would offer more bearable temperatures.

My flight touched down at the Northwest Arkansas Regional Airport, and I headed for a car rental desk where I'd arranged to have a vehicle waiting. I would use it to get back to Alpena, and then drive the 86-mile portion of Route 62 between Alpena and the airport. The car was a concession to the realities of my schedule, for I had only two weeks to cover the remaining distance to El Paso.

In my fantasies about bike trips, I always picture myself with unlimited time, so that when I roll into a new community, I can linger and get a feel for the place. When I'm tired or facing bad weather, I can take a day off of riding. When I meet intriguing people, I can visit long enough to start friendships.

I've never had such a trip. My coast-to-coast odyssey, thrilling as it was, had been a time-pressured affair nonetheless. I'd done it in three separate time blocks, and even at that, I'd had to leave a couple of gaps unridden. In my book about that trip, I characterized it as "a piecemeal journey."

As I began planning my return to Route 62, calculating mileages and eyeing the responsibilities on my calendar, I realized that I needed to slice a day of riding out of the remaining distance to avoid a panicked rush at the end. I considered simply skipping the backtrack to Alpena and commencing my present ride directly from the airport, but didn't like leaving a hole in my route.

I settled for the rental car. My plan was to drive the Alpena-Fayetteville section in the morning, and be on my bike and heading into fresh territory by early afternoon.

The car didn't fit with my ideal of pedaling the entire distance, but from the start I knew compromises might be necessary. Though in one sense, I was footloose while on the road, in reality I still moved within the confines of calendar and commitments. I've suffered wanderlust as long as I can remember, but I've chosen to have a family and a career, and thus could not give free reign to the wayfarer within me. For me, that's been the right thing to do, for without relationships, wandering doesn't have much meaning. But as I've grown older, I've felt compelled to give that wayfarer a longer leash.

In pouring rain, I shoved my boxed-up bike into the car's back seat and then drove out into the darkness. Recalling no lodgings in Alpena, I drove only as far as Eureka Springs, a town swelling with motels, where I got a room for the night. Once settled, I pulled the bike out of the packing box and reassembled it.

Come morning, I parked at a roadside café for breakfast. The eatery, perched in front of a rustic motel, was of log-cabin construction outside, with knotty-pine paneling within. I was the first customer of the morning, and was given a cheerful "good morning" by the 40-ish waitress as I slid onto a counter seat.

I love eating in establishments such as this one. The food is plain, hearty and tasty, and the serving staff moves with a practiced efficiency. That was the case with this waitress. She responded to my questions about the area freely, but never stopped moving, filling sugar shakers, wiping off counters and wrapping silverware sets in napkins. She was clearly a professional in her field and seemed to actually relish her work. Her conversation, while friendly, gave no personal information about herself and asked none of me.

Through the serving window behind her, I could see the cook, a women in her 60s, at work. She too, had the quiet efficiency of someone who knows what she's doing. With minimal movements she soon had my breakfast platter set on the window ledge, from which the waitress almost immediately delivered it to me.

I asked about the attractions of Eureka Springs.

"Most people come for the Passion play," the waitress said, referring to an outdoor drama about Jesus' final week, held nightly throughout the tourist season. "We've also got a couple of musical shows, the Hoedown and the Jamboree."

Did those feature country music stars? I inquired.

"Not big names, like Branson does," she said. "Just local talent. But they're pretty good. This is also a nice outdoor recreation area."

I mentioned my surprise at the number of motels in the tiny mountaintop town.

"Yes," she said, "someone counted, and including the bed-and-breakfasts, there are 64 restaurants here, and several thousand hotel rooms. But they get filled. People come from all over to see the play."

Afterward, I drove the remaining distance to Alpena, population 319. Though it had been eight months since my last time in the town, little had changed except the temperature. This time, the air was not only chilly, but the sky was also gray.

There was little open in what was once Alpena's two-block-long business district, and the town appeared impoverished. The old stone buildings still stand, however, and the town has an Old West, though seedy, look.

I paused at the very spot where I'd abandoned 62 the previous year and felt glad to have returned, even if by auto. The visit gave both a visual connection and a sense of continuity to my trip that I would not have had if I'd settled for merely starting this leg from the airport.

Having tied the loose ends of my journey together, I turned the car around and started back toward the airport on 62.

In the next miles, the highway bounded over steep hills, surrounded by woods and pastures on which were small herds of cattle. Viewing the convoluted terrain, I knew my judgment the previous August was correct: Continuing on 62 in the humidity and heat would have been torture and probably detrimental to my health. But now, feeling fit and with the advantage of cooler weather, I felt disappointed not to be addressing this portion on two wheels.

I continued, passing through Hough, a berg whose commercial district consisted entirely of two gas stations and a convenience store bearing the name "Quicker Liquors," and then on to Green Forest, with its posted population of 2,050. This community was tidy and seemed modestly prosperous. Although the downtown contained some empty stores, the place did not have the abandoned appearance of Alpena's main street.

The apparent upward movement in prosperity continued in Berryville. Housing more than 3,000 souls, Berryville featured thriving stores on its hilltop square. The square was neatly dissected on an east-west axis by highway 62.

The surroundings became more mountainous as I plowed back toward Eureka Springs, where I'd spent the night. If I'd had any doubt where I was, that was immediately dispelled by the clutter of billboards as I neared the mountain hamlet. These variously touted the steam train, the Passion play, numerous motels (several boasting of their proximity to the amphitheater), country shows and other tourist lures.

Coming to a sign pointing up a side road to the Passion play, I made the turn, and within a mile found myself at a complex of structures built to look like ancient Palestinian architecture. Two of these housed, respectively, a Bible museum and a sacred arts center. Near the buildings was the outdoor hillside amphitheater (seating 4,100!), which featured a permanent stage down front, set to represent a variety of locations in first-century Jerusalem. The two buildings immediately adjacent to the amphitheater were both gift shops. This, of course, lent a further air of authenticity to the whole business: There were moneychangers around the temple in Jesus' day as well.

Continuing on the road beyond the amphitheater, I came to a kind of prayer garden, dominated by a 67-foot-high statue of Jesus, with outstretched arms. This "Christ of the Ozarks" faces a deep valley and the town of Eureka Springs beyond. Though I've never been much moved by iconography, especially of the stylistic stick-figure type such as this sculpture was, I did find the quiet of the well-groomed grounds meditative. And thinking about the piety that must have driven someone to fund the massive work seemed to add a sense of sincerity to the site.

Returning to 62, I found buildings of all sorts within the town limits — from the rustic to the regal. One of the grander ones announced itself as a wedding chapel ("Walk-ins Welcome"). The town, with only 1,900 year-round residents, has capitalized admirably on its scenic location, its historicity and even the devoutness — or perhaps curiosity — of its visitors. All in all, I found no fault with it.

As I drove out of town, a roadside sign warned "Rugged and steep, next 2½ miles." Next to that a downhill-truck sign admonished big vehicles to use lower gears. The winding and hilly route that followed would have required extra caution on a bike, including a willingness to pull completely off the blacktop from time to time to let following traffic pass. But it would have been doable.

The road caressed mountain curves for several miles. Once away from Eureka Springs, roadside development was replaced by forested mountain scenery interlaced occasionally with scenic vistas of the rural valley below.

Finally, motoring through tiny Gateway, population 65, I left the mountains behind and entered a more prosaic, flattening landscape.

From Gateway to Fayetteville, Route 62 overlays the path of two historic journeys. One is the Trail of Tears, whose route Mallie, my Mountain Home rescuer, hoped to follow. The other was the course used by the Butterfield Stage on its run with mail and passengers from Tipton, Missouri, to San Francisco.

The first of these journeys resulted from one of the most shameful episodes in America history. Before the European settlement of America, the Cherokees had ranged over a large area of the American south. But in the face of the colonists' advance, the Cherokee gradually ceded more and more territory in 28 treaties, all of which were eventually abrogated by the colonial government or its U.S. successor. By 1819, the remaining Cherokee domain lay mostly in Georgia. Significantly, the Cherokee became a civilized and peaceful people, adopting the dress, lifestyle, education, commerce, land ownership and agriculture methods of their white neighbors. Some embraced Christianity. They established their own government, set up to be similar to that of the surrounding states, complete with a constitution and a legislative body. Many Cherokees and whites intermarried.

In drawing up the state boundaries, however, the states disregarded the Cherokee borders, and the federal government, in accepting these boundaries, ensured that white settlers would covet the remaining Cherokee land. Even though the tribe successfully appealed to the U.S. Supreme Court to have the latest treaty enforced, President Andrew Jackson defied the court and set forces in motion to relocate the Cherokee to "Indian Territory" — Oklahoma.

The actual move began in 1838 and continued through the winter into 1839. Under military guard and against their will, the entire Cherokee nation was forced to migrate. Some were taken by steamboats and barges by way of the Tennessee, Mississippi and Arkansas Rivers, but most ended up going overland through Tennessee, Kentucky, Illinois and Missouri before entering Arkansas at Gateway and then following the path of present day 62 to Fort Gibson, Oklahoma.

During the roundup and forced march, so many of the Cherokee died of exposure, illness and deprivation — some 4,000 of them — that the trek became known as the Trail of Tears.

Although the Cherokee story is the best known and most tragic of the Indian removals to Oklahoma, it was neither the first nor the only one. The Choctaws, living in Mississippi, were forced to relocate to Oklahoma in 1831, and dozens of other removals followed, continuing until the 1890s.

The Butterfield Stage operation is a happier story. The stage line was established in 1858 after Congress voted to subsidize overland mail service between St. Louis and San Francisco on a semi-weekly basis. John Butterfield, a former New York stage driver and entrepreneur who had helped found the America Express Company, set up his Overland Mail Company and won a six-year contract. While the mail subsidy was vital, he counted on making his profit from the passengers ($150 each, one way), newspapers and parcels his stages also carried. Trains carried the mail to Tipton, Missouri, so Butterfield began his route there.

Butterfield used existing roads, though many were in bad shape, and he had additional ones built. From Tipton, his stages trundled southward through Springfield and on into Arkansas at Gateway, proceeding from there on the path of what is now Route 62 as far as Fayetteville. Route 62 turns west there, but Butterfield's coaches continued south to Fort Smith, at which point they lurched on a southwest trajectory through Oklahoma and Texas.

The stage line intersected with today's 62 again in Texas at Guadalupe Pass and at El Paso before continuing west, ending at San Francisco, a journey of nearly 2,800 miles. Each trip took about 21 days. The service sent two coaches a week in each direction and continued until the Civil War forced its suspension.

To make the trip feasible and speedy, Butterfield set up numerous stops where tired teams of horses, usually run at full tilt, were exchanged for fresh ones. The whole operation required 700 horses and some 2,000 employees. Of the passage through the Ozarks, a passenger from Connecticut wrote that "Connecticut hills and roads are mere pimples and sandpaper compared with the Ozark ranges." After my ride over them, I agree with that assessment.

Missouri's first telegraph line, run in 1860 and connected to St. Louis, followed the Butterfield route as far as Fayetteville.

After traveling so much of 62 by bicycle, it seemed odd to be whizzing along it now in a car. Compared to the bike, which often invited conversation, the auto was an isolation cage that made me merely another anonymous blip on the highway. I felt less connected to the people I saw and places I passed through. I looked forward to being back on the bicycle later in the day.

In Garfield, Pea Ridge National Military Park sits beside Route 62. Site of the 1862 Civil War battle of Pea Ridge, which saved Missouri for the Union, the park touts itself as the most well preserved Civil War battlefield in the United States. A highway marker in front of the park dubs 62 the "Blue Star Memorial Highway, a tribute to the armed forces who have defended the United States of America."

At Rogers, I re-entered urban life. A city of nearly 40,000, Rogers is the northernmost of a string of cities that thrive beside Federal Highway 71, an Interstate clone. Fayetteville anchors the southern end of the string. This corner of Arkansas is a growth area for the state, thanks in no small part to being the headquarters of Wal-Mart and Tyson Foods. Wal-Mart founder Sam Walton opened his first store in Rogers in 1962. Today, the Wal-Mart Visitors' Center is a fixture on Route 62.

I stopped at a McDonald's to use the restroom, and while there, in came an embarrassed-looking man shepherding two small girls toward a stall. I could tell from his red face that he hadn't had much experience with this sort of thing. The three of them crowded into the stall and the man hastily shut the door. The last thing I heard before leaving was a childish voice saying, "Help me, Daddy. My zipper's stuck."

Ah, how well I remember those days. My daughter is now grown, but it wasn't so long ago that taking her out without my wife made me uneasy. It was always a question of when — not if — Becky would say, "Daddy, I have to go to the potty, right now!"

Malls were the worst. Those shopping havens, of course, are designed to delight the consumer. Typically they are surrounded by several thousand parking places and inside boast a temperature-controlled environment featuring 125 stores, including two book nooks, eight shoe stores, three eyeglass labs, 12 places to eat, three large department stores, a wide variety of specialty shops, and two — count them, two — public restrooms. And these conveniences are always located at the most distant point possible from where we happen to be when the call of nature strikes. This explains why you will occasionally see a grown man running through the mall like a madman with a little girl in his arms.

It's not hard to distinguish those fathers who are with their second or third daughter from those with their first. The former lead their little girls into the men's room without the slightest hesitation. They are able to do this because they've taken time in advance to explain why men don't sit down every time and what those strange looking porcelain fixtures are that the child didn't see when mommy took her to the ladies' room. The neophyte fathers are obvious; in addition to their red faces, they are the ones saying, "Don't point, Sweetheart. I'll tell you later."

Although it may not be obvious to the bystander, one mark of the seasoned dad is that even if he takes his child into a mall where he's never been before, the man quickly notes the location of all men's rooms as soon as he arrives and is constantly aware of the quickest route back to one. Also, he soon determines if there are any one-holer restrooms. These are the easiest to use with small children since they guarantee no smirking audience.

Once in the coveted privacy of a stall, the pro knows to place the child on the seat sideways; the novice holds onto the girl anxiously, having visions of the child suddenly folding in half and dropping into the waiting abyss, tiny bottom first.

Those who provide public comfort stations are at last taking notice of the increased number of men who shop alone with their children. Several men's rooms now have "changing stations," set-ups for diapering babies.

Still, there will probably always be some chagrin whenever men have to take little girls to public toilets. For men who care about image, such activities are not exactly macho. Nor are they especially dignified. But we are better men in the long run for being willing to help our little ones with this most basic of human needs.

Originally, Route 62 ran north-south through the Rogers-Fayetteville area on what is now a busy commercial strip, but 62 has since been rerouted to run concurrent with 71, which prohibits bicycles. Though I was still in the car, I elected instead to take Arkansas highway 112, which offered a reasonable alternative for bikes.

This route also brought me near the regional airport from which I'd embarked the previous evening. I drove back to it now and turned in the car. I hoisted the reassembled bike from the trunk, attached my gear, and wheeled out of the airport.

The business of transporting a bicycle by plane is a sore point with me. Airlines insist that the bike be disassembled and boxed, and then charge a hefty fee to include the box as part of your luggage, even if you have no other pieces. This trip, they added injury to insult. When I began pedaling the bike, I discovered that the large chainring, despite the ample packaging protecting it, had gotten bent in transport. With my pliers, I was able to straighten it sufficiently to ride away from the airport, but I couldn't leave matters in that condition.

Fortunately, one of Fayetteville's bike shops was just a short jaunt off of 112, and I was able to get a replacement chainring there. But the whole business set me back a couple of hours, and I ended

up leaving Fayetteville, heading west on 62, during the evening rush
hour. Traffic sailed carelessly past me, with vehicles jockeying for
positions that would get them home a minute sooner. The day had
turned warm and I was thirsty, but such was the surge of traffic that
I dared not take even one hand off the handlebars long enough to
snatch up a water bottle from its cage on the bike frame.

After an hour or so, the traffic flow calmed, and I arrived in the
small community of Prairie Grove, home of another Civil War battlefield preserved as a park. The Battle of Prairie Grove took place
December 7, 1862, with the Union Army as victor.

I ate supper in a hamburger joint in Prairie Grove, then rode on
to Lincoln. There, a sign informed me that Lincoln possessed the
"Largest Apple Orchard in Arkansas."

It was late in the day, and I started looking for a place to camp.
Glancing up a Lincoln side street, I spotted a church steeple and
pedaled toward it. The building belonged to a congregation of my
own denomination, United Methodist, and inquiries in the neighborhood led me to the parsonage, directly across the street from the
church.

Removing my sunglasses to look less sinister, I rang the bell,
and soon found myself talking with Scott and Polly Shafer. Scott
was the pastor, and Polly, a seminary-trained education director,
was also employed by the church. When I identified myself as an
Ohio UM pastor, Polly mentioned that they had attended seminary
in my state. When she named the school, we discovered it was my
alma mater as well, although they had entered the school several
years after I had graduated.

This struck Scott as a unique coincidence, especially since he
and Polly were the only graduates of that seminary in the entire
Arkansas branch of United Methodism. Of all the churches I could
have picked by chance, I had stumbled to their door.

This common ground bridged whatever hesitancy the couple may
have had about welcoming a stranger. They not only granted my
request to pitch my tent in the church yard, but also invited me in to
spend the evening in their home with their family, which included
two daughters, Sophie, 8, and Zoe, 5.

We traded seminary and church "war stories," talked about their community and my trip. After I learned from Zoe that she attended kindergarten, Scott told me a tale from his daughter's class of political correctness gone mad. The teacher had recently been disciplined by the school authorities for handing out an alphabet sheet to the children. Since a few students already knew their ABCs, some parents — presumably of the kids who did not yet know the alphabet — complained that distributing the paper injured the self-esteem of the unlettered children. Scheezzz.

At their invitation, I had breakfast with the Shafers the next morning. Polly anticipated that riding was hungry work, and had prepared a feast of eggs, meats and breads. Afterward, I said goodbye, waddled out and mounted up.

Eight miles down the road, I entered Oklahoma.

Although riding in April dodged the high temperatures of summer, springtime on the southern plains boded possible weather problems of its own, and I rode into the new state with a recent warning resounding in my head. My aunt Rozelle was raised in southern Oklahoma, and she and my uncle Hal now lived in Texas. They had cautioned me that in both states, spring is tornado season. That wasn't news to me, of course, as spring tornadoes on the plains make national headlines many years. But detecting the level of concern in my uncle's carefully worded letters intensified my sense of vulnerability on the road. They'd also mentioned severe hailstorms, miles of sparsely and uninhabited space, speeding traffic, shortages of potable water and rattlesnakes.

Well, at least I couldn't say I wasn't forewarned.

Actually, frightening as those things can be — and I'd encountered all of them but full-blown tornadoes and rattlesnakes while bicycling across America — they seemed acceptable risks. It was the alternative, staying put, that I found unacceptable.

Oklahoma surprised me by being greener than expected. Because during the 1800s, Oklahoma territory had been designated as the dumping ground for numerous Indian tribes forced out of more desirable land, I'd assumed that Oklahoma was primarily waste land. But clearly that was not the case. Although I didn't see a lot of farming, there were green pastures, and cattle grazed in several fields.

I rode through a string of four small towns, the third of which was Proctor, site of the first murder trial in the state. In fact, the accused was the man for whom the town is named, Ezekiel Proctor. In 1872, he killed the wife of the miller, though he meant the shot for the miller himself. Proctor was a Cherokee, and faced trial at the tribal court. When federal authorities attempted as well to arrest Proctor, the Indians resisted, and a battle followed during which several people were killed and Proctor was wounded. When it all later shook out, federal officials dismissed their indictments and Proctor recovered, later to become a sheriff in the Cherokee nation.

During my visit to Proctor, I saw nothing there to commemorate this dubious distinction. In fact, I saw not much at all there. Proctor today is a tiny spot with only a few houses, a post office and a one-pump gas station/grocery. I entered this establishment to refill my water bottle.

It's odd what people will talk about with strangers. Inside, I found a woman clerking the store and another woman who was a customer. The two obviously knew each other. When I requested water, the clerk willingly filled my bottle, and the two asked a few questions about my trip. Somehow the discussion migrated from there to the fact that both women had recently stopped smoking. And they went on to tell me of their struggles to accomplish that. (Later, in Texas, a shopkeeper I'd just met regaled me with tales of his chronic illness and the fact that he was born with oversized lungs.)

Fortified with this new bit of information about the women, I resumed my journey on 62, which in this part of Oklahoma, was not heavily traveled and seemed like a country road.

I had planned to eat lunch in Tahlequah, but while still a half-hour from there, I began feeling very hungry, not a good condition to leave unaddressed while cycle-touring. So, coming to a small grocery, I purchased a loaf of bread, and from my supplies, created a couple of peanut butter and jelly sandwiches. It was hardly the lunch I had envisioned, but my cardinal rule of long-distance biking is "A mediocre sandwich in the hand is worth a steak in a town I haven't yet reached."

Eventually I came to Tahlequah, which on a sign at its boundary announced itself as the "Best Small Town in Oklahoma, 55th Best

Small Town in America." I assume the latter rating came from one of those periodic studies that rank small towns according to an established set of criteria, but if my town came in at only 55th, I don't think I'd brag about it.

A few miles before Tahlequah, 62 had become a four-lane expressway and lost its rural feel. At town's edge, it darted onto a four-lane bypass, but I continued into town, following 62's earlier path. Tahlequah is the capital of the Cherokee nation, and I wanted to see how this played out in the community.

On the main street, I found a courthouse-like structure ensconced in the middle of a park. A sign in front proclaimed the building "Cherokee Nation Judicial Branch, Cherokee Capital Square." Not surprisingly, the ground included monuments to notable tribe members, including General Stand Watie, the only full-blooded Cherokee brigadier general in the Confederate Army, and John Ross, principle chief of the Cherokee nation 1828-1866. Ross long resisted efforts to move his people from their southeastern lands and abridge the sovereignty of their nation, but he was finally compelled to accept the Trail of Tears evacuation.

In light of that forced uprooting, one item on the square seemed especially ironic. It was a small replica of the Statue of Liberty, inscribed beneath with these words: "With the faith and courage of their forefathers who made possible the freedom of the United States, the Boy Scouts of America dedicate this replica of the statue of liberty as a pledge of everlasting fidelity and loyalty."

There were people in the town of various colors. In addition to whites and blacks, some residents appeared to be Indians, and others perhaps Mexican or of mixed ancestry. But everyone seemed integrated into the mainstream of community life. People dressed like Americans everywhere, worked in the usual sorts of jobs, drove cars, shopped in the stores, ate fast food. Except for the heavier concentration of brown skin tones, Tahlequah was an average American small town.

Rejoining 62, I continued my trek. For 26 unremarkable miles, from Tahlequah to Muskogee, 62 runs as expressway, bypassing Fort Gibson on the way. The shoulder, a lane wide and well paved, made cycling easy but boring. The problem with restricted highways seems to be the same for motorists and cyclists alike. The unrelieved sameness mile after mile invites a longing to be done with the journey.

Finally arriving in Muskogee, I found a busy, sizable city. My only previous acquaintance with the place was from Merle Haggard's country song, "Okie from Muskogee," the lyrics of which led me to picture a smaller, less sophisticated community than what Muskogee actually was. The song was born after Haggard and his band saw a sign for Muskogee while on tour. One of the band members mused that the people of Muskogee probably didn't smoke marijuana, and Haggard and the band's drummer, started fooling with the line. According to Haggard, the whole thing started as a joke, but they quickly realized its potential. It then took only 20 minutes to finish the song, which went on to be number one in the country charts in November 1969.

Because the song was seen as an attack on the hippie culture of the late 60s, Haggard was asked to endorse ultra-conservative George Wallace's run for president, but Haggard refused. The following year, the Youngbloods recorded an answer song called "Hippie From Olema."

In the fast-food place where I ate supper, I inquired of an older man about camping areas along my path. There were none he knew of, but he moved to my table and spent a few minutes looking at my map, suggesting places like the local hospital that had lawns where I might get permission to camp. None of them were really suitable, being too much in the center of population to offer either privacy or security. And some would likely invite attention by either the local police or a private guard service. But more importantly, I didn't feel like stopping yet. I wanted to ride. So I wheeled out of town, confident I'd eventually find someplace to camp when I was ready.

A few miles out of town, I noticed a sign pointing to a small community a couple miles north of the highway, Taft. It was an all-black town, one created after the Civil War when many southern blacks migrated to Oklahoma.

I rode for a couple more hours, but by the time the daylight began to fade, my confidence level had dropped. Out on the highway, I had yet to find a church or public building where I might pitch my tent. There were homes along the road, and I wasn't above asking for permission to camp on private property, but unlike in the previous states, most of these houses were surrounded by chain-link fences and many were posted with signs reading "Beware of the Dog." Those that weren't posted didn't need to be — the dog was already bounding at the fence and barking sternly.

Finally, near the junction where 62 joins State Route 72, I spotted a small white-frame Baptist church. I swung in, and, in the last glimmer of light, set up camp behind it. This day I'd ridden 84 miles, and felt good.

Remember that story I told you about me being compulsive? This time when I camped, my compulsiveness failed me. In the semi-darkness, I reached for my flashlight in the saddlebag pocket where I always keep it, and did not find it. A search through all my stuff didn't turn it up either. I had to set up my tent by feeling my way along.

The next morning, while packing up, my "lost" flashlight turned up — stuck inside a tennis shoe. Of course, once I found it, I instantly remembered dropping it in there while in my tent behind the Lincoln church. But why I put it in the shoe to start with, I couldn't say.

Chapter 13

I was awakened sometime during the night by pain in my intestines and an upset stomach. I toughed out the night, but by morning I still felt lousy. I was up at first light.

Seeking relief, I pulled out my stove and brewed a cup of tea. I had not carried a stove on the previous legs of the 62 trip. Though many cross-country riders use one regularly, I prefer to eat in the diners, cafés and convenience stores I find along the way, enjoying conversation with staff and fellow customers and soaking in a little of the local color. Cooking out and cleaning up afterward consume energy I'd rather devote to riding. On my coast-to-coast ride, I'd gone the entire distance without cooking, though occasionally I had to settle for some meals of severely limited menu.

Two things had persuaded me to add the stove this time. One, a trend I'd been noticing on recent bike travels, was the increasing number of small communities where restaurants and even small groceries no longer survive, victims of the car culture. It's just too easy to drive to the fast-food place down the road. The other was the long stretches on the map, especially in west Texas, that were uninterrupted by communities of any sort. There *might* be places to eat there, but I just didn't know.

I still planned to eat in restaurants when possible, but my saddlebags now included a cooking pot, the stove, a stove fuel bottle and the makings of a full meal. When I'd consumed that one, I'd buy more. The cooking gear and meal fixings also added flexibility to the journey. Now, if I came upon a camping ground or national park where I wanted to stay for the night, I didn't have to go out of my way to first locate a place to get supper.

The tea helped a little, and afterward I munched on a piece of bread while striking camp and loading the bike. Then, though feeling weak, I mounted up and began slowly pedaling toward Boynton, the next town on 62.

Shortly, I became aware of an annoying "tick" sound coming from my chain with each revolution of the pedals, and it finally dawned on me that the chain probably needed fresh lubrication. With the type of lube I use, it's helpful to use a rag when applying it. I'd forgotten to bring one, but that didn't worry me. From previous rides, I knew I'd soon have one.

As a cyclist, I know that America's roadsides, besides being almost nonstop littered with cans, bottles and other trash, are also the final resting place of more discarded cloth than you'd ever suspect from whizzing by in a car. At least once every couple of miles I'd see a handkerchief, T-shirt, washcloth, cleaning rag, trousers, underpants, blanket or some similar item. Needing a rag now, I began scanning the roadside. Sure enough, within a half-mile, I found two perfectly good hand towels lying side by side in the grass. Both were damp from the dew, but appeared clean otherwise. I tore a strip off one and proceeded to lubricate my chain, which, as I'd hoped, eliminated the ticking.

Other common roadside items, by the way, include scraps of blown tires, sections of rope and tie-down cords, as well as enough bolts to outfit a hardware store. There must be an awful lot of unsecured stuff jiggling along on America's roadways.

I came eventually to tiny Boynton, which appeared far from prosperous. It had a post office and a convenience store — convenient no doubt because without it, there'd be no business district at all.

Feeling a little better, I entered the store in hopes of finding a more substantial breakfast than what I'd eaten thus far. While I munched an egg and sausage sandwich from the store's hot-food case, I questioned the clerk, a middle-aged woman, about the town. How do people there make a living, I asked.

"The farms are pretty well gone," she said, "but there is some ranching. And some people have oil. But most folks here drive to either Tulsa or Muskogee to work." Then she asked about my trip, and I explained it. "How far do you ride a day?" she asked.

"I try to do at least 70 miles. I need to do that much in order to finish in the time I have."

"Then you'll be in Oklahoma City by tonight," she said.

I knew that wasn't feasible because the map showed Oklahoma City to be twice that far, but I saw no point in debating her conclusion. But then a customer who'd been listening to our conversation responded to the clerk. "No, he won't make it by tonight. It's farther than you think."

"Oh, I guess I was thinking how quick I can get there in the car," the clerk said.

I'd gotten used to local people misjudging things about their own area. A couple of years earlier, my daughter Becky and I had ridden a tour of the Outer Banks of North Carolina, starting on the mainland. At one point, we'd have to pedal a three-mile bridge at Kitty Hawk to get out to the slender barrier islands, and we received our first warning about the bridge when it was still 60 miles distant. It was unsolicited advice at that.

The warning came from a man where we'd left the car. "The bridge has got no shoulder," he said, "and the traffic is heavy this time of year. You should try to cross it in the early morning." Great. I calculated that we'd probably arrive at the bridge about noon the following day.

The second warning came the next morning from a man at the campground. When he mentioned the bridge, I said, "We've been told we should try to cross it in the morning."

"It wouldn't make much difference," the camper replied. "The traffic is nonstop all day long. But I think there's a wide shoulder."

"A shoulder?" laughed our third advisor two hours later. "Maybe this much." The young man held his hands about 14 inches apart. Once again, the advice had come unbidden. This time, however, I was inclined to put a little more stock in the report, since the chap giving it was mounted on an old, single-speed bicycle and claimed to have personally ridden the bridge one time. Still, some of his stories seemed exaggerated — preening tales designed, I assumed, to impress my 17-year-old daughter. Clearly, she was not buying his line, but like me, she was now concerned about the bridge.

Another opinion came from a man in a store where we used the restrooms. "There's a wide shoulder," he said. "Nothing to worry about."

The reports were now two against two, and the deadlock was not broken by the data supplied later when we stopped to refill our water bottles. "There's actually two bridges, one for each direction," a lady said. "I drive across them every day, but I can't recall if there's a bike lane or not."

When we actually got to the bridge, we found the explanation for the conflicting reports. There were two side-by-side spans. Both directions offered two transit lanes, but only the return link, which was the newer of the two, had a wide berm. The shoulder of the older bridge, the one we needed to use, was barely a foot wide.

Becky said, "Oh well," and started across. I fell in directly behind her. The traffic was unrelenting and moving quickly, but most drivers veered partially into the passing lane to give us a wider berth, and we crossed okay.

I'm not from North Carolina, but that, my friends, is the accurate information about the Kitty Hawk bridge.

Beyond Boynton, I saw a field of wheat, the first crop I'd noticed since entering Oklahoma. The clerk was right about the scarcity of farms. There was a lot of open country, but not a lot of crops growing on it.

Morris, the next small town on 62, looked like it was prospering better than Boynton. Though my stomach was still uneasy, I was moving well, so I didn't stop, but something about the pleasant little village reminded me of an Ohio small town where I used to live. It was a similarly attractive little place, but I was surprised by how some residents badmouthed it. According to those folks, the town's newspaper was a joke, the shopping second-rate, the school district behind the times, the bank's staff unfriendly and the police "yokels." Maybe it was because I came there from a larger community, but I found none of those things to be true. Sure, there may have been a few slip-ups now and then, but generally the town's organizations and services were doing pretty well. As one exasperated citizen put it to me, "People here have a maddening habit of ignoring facts in favor of some negative perception that has been handed down through the years." In contrast, I like the comment of an elderly woman from an Iowa small town who explained why she stayed there all her life. "It was enough," she said simply.

I hoped the people of Morris felt that way.

Route 62 next took me to Okmulgee, which is the capital of the Creek Nation, another tribe forced to relocate to Oklahoma in the 19th century. Today the tribe has a modern headquarters north of town, but the 1878 tribal council house, a stately two-story building with a cupola on top, remains on a square in the center of the community. It's maintained as a museum, and I decided to look around. Inside, I found tasteful exhibits depicting various periods from Creek history and displays about the ceremonial, religious and artistic aspects of the Creek culture.

In Okmulgee, I sought routing advice. Route 62 flowed to Dewar, the next town, as a busy expressway. Once it got there, 62 dropped onto an Interstate highway for about 13 miles. My map showed no alternative path for the bike. In my pre-trip attempt to plot a way around the Interstate stretch, I had written to Oklahoma's official bike coordinator, but what I received in reply was a general packet of "bicycling in Oklahoma" material that focused on highway safety and left my question unanswered. Now, however, an Okmulgee man confirmed that there was a way — actually old 62 — but that the pavement was in bad shape. Nonetheless, it was passable, he said. He further recommended that I take an alternate route starting right from Okmulgee. It would bypass Dewar, but would bring me into Henryetta, the town on 62 beyond Dewar. I'd still have the broken pavement of old 62 to contend with from there to the following community, but the road he proposed was good until Henryetta, he said. I decided to take his advice.

His suggested route to Henryetta was a quiet country road, a good route for the bike. But because it meandered, it added mileage to my day's ride. I was still off my feed, and felt weak, making the long ride through the country seem interminable. I was dragging by the time the detour finally delivered me to Henryetta. Had I not had a schedule, I'd have stopped there.

The problem was, I intended to spend the next evening with my aunt's relatives in Oklahoma City, and quitting today in Henryetta would leave too much ground to cover the next day. So, after a rest stop and a cold drink in a Henryetta shop, I started pedaling old 62 toward Okemah.

Over the next several miles, I saw a number of hand-painted "NO PRISON!" signs. Apparently one had been proposed for the community, and the signs were the work of those opposed to the idea. It was a classic case of NIMBY (Not In My Back Yard).

The man who had directed me on this course had not overstated the condition of old 62. Between Henryetta and Okemah, it was terrible. Originally paved with concrete, the highway had not had attention in years. The pavement edges at the seams between concrete sections had broken away in chunks, allowing the seams to become gaping chasms. I had to keep my eyes glued to the road immediately in front of my bike to constantly dodge wheel-killing potholes. Even with my attention riveted on that task, it was impossible to miss them all and I flinched each time I hit one. I had high-quality tires on my bike (they cost half as much as the ones on my car) and was thankful now for the way they absorbed shock and protected the wheels. A few cars and trucks also used this road, and I often thought I saw the drivers mouthing curses as they jounced along.

After picking my way for several miles, I finally reached better pavement when I neared Okemah, but I was ready to stop. In a restaurant, I discovered some vestige of what had ailed me during the night remained. The idea of dinner sounded good, and the food was decent, but when I tucked into it, I wasn't able to eat a lot. I left hoping for a better appetite in the morning.

Since I had camped out the previous two nights, I was ready for a shower. There was a motel across the street, part of a national chain, but I'd noticed a sign for a locally owned motel a few blocks away, so I headed for it. A citizen of Okemah told me it wasn't much of a motel, but that only encouraged me. I figured it would be cheaper. I've got nothing against nice motels, but I have an aversion to paying big dollars for what is basically just a place to sleep, something I can do for nothing in my tent. And in practice, I've found most inexpensive motels provide adequate lodging.

This one proved no exception. For $25, I got a small but clean room, a comfortable bed with mismatched but clean sheets, and a hot shower. The easy chair was broken down and should have been thrown out, and there would be no mints on the pillow at bedtime, but next to camping out, it was a palace.

After I was showered and settled, I stepped outside to enjoy the cool evening air. The motel had only 10 rooms, and the owner, a man in his 40s, was working in one of them. I asked him if the motel was full most of the time.

"We rent a lot of rooms in the summer," he said, "but I couldn't make it just on what this place brings in. I also work as a corrections officer at Boley Prison." He referred to a facility a few miles away. "But we've got four events throughout the summer that bring in a lot of people, so I get filled up here, especially on weekends."

I had noticed a carnival in operation near the downtown and asked if that was one of the events.

"Yes, that's part of Pioneer Days. It's going on right now. It's really a kind of homecoming event. After that there's the Boley Rodeo. It's the only all-black rodeo in the country. Later in the summer we have the annual Woody Guthrie Festival. He was born here, you know. We get a lot of performers in town for that. His son Arlo's been here lots of times. And finally, in the fall, there's the Indian Stomp. That's a dance thing."

He went on to tell me that the town was working hard to keep things alive there, and these events all contributed to the vitality. "We recently started an industrial park, and we've got some businesses moving in."

Finally I asked what the separate Indian government meant for the area.

"Mostly it has to do with law enforcement. When crimes happen on Indian-owned land, there used to be conflict about what police force responded. The Indians have their own force, the Light Horsemen. When there's a problem, the local police can respond, but they usually try to work with the Indian police."

I wandered downtown to have a look around. There was a long, wide main street, running downhill from the residential section. Like many prairie towns I would see, it had a number of empty stores. The homes I saw were all modest, middle-class houses. If the town had any modern or wealthy neighborhoods, I didn't see them. This was a workaday town, with a mixed population: native, black, white.

The folk singer Woody Guthrie had been born in Okemah in 1912, and he once described the town as "one of the singingest, square dancingest, drinkingest, yellingest, preachingest, walkingest, talkingest, laughingest, cryingest, shootingest, fist fightingest, bleedingest, gamblingest, gun, club, razor carryingest of our ranch and farm towns, because it blossomed out into one of our first oil boom towns." In even earlier days, when the area was still open range, the Okemah citizens had completely enclosed the town with a barbed-wire fence as protection against the thousands of longhorn cattle that roamed the prairie.

It stormed during the night, so I was glad to be under a solid roof, but by morning, the sky had cleared. The way the town was laid out, I had to backtrack about a mile to get breakfast, so I left my gear in the motel room and rode my bike unloaded toward the restaurant. Part way down the main street, a passing motorist in a minivan tooted enthusiastically and motioned toward the curb. I pulled over, and so did he. As he parked, I noticed a bike rack on the back of his vehicle.

The driver was about my age, and looked physically fit. "Are you from around here?" he asked.

After I explained that I was a pilgrim, the man introduced himself as Ron Breedlove. He had grown up in Okemah, but now lived in Kansas City where, until his recent retirement, he'd been a police officer. He was back in Okemah on family business and had brought his bike along to ride in case he had time.

"You're the first adult I've seen in town riding a bike," he said. "That's why I had to find out if you're from here." He was on an errand, but asked if he could drive me to the restaurant so we could continue our conversation. I hung my bike on his rack.

Naturally he wanted to know about my trip, and in return, told me about how he had reluctantly begun cycling at his wife's urging, and to his surprise, had fallen in love with it. I invited him to join me for breakfast, but his immediate obligations prevented his accepting. We said goodbye and I headed inside.

I should have been hungry, but apparently whatever sickened me the previous day was still with me. I ordered pancakes and ate about half of the serving, but more because I knew I needed the carbs than because food appealed to me.

Afterward, I returned to the motel, packed up and hit the road. About two miles out of town, Ron pulled up behind me in his van, his bike hanging from the rack. I stopped, and he got out and walked to me. "There's a little spot called Castle up ahead a short way," he said. "I can leave my vehicle there. Would it be all right with you if I rode with you for a little while?"

I was glad for the company. He drove to Castle and I continued riding. Shortly, Ron came cycling toward me, then swung across the road to my side. The highway there offered a lane-wide shoulder, and we continued side by side.

We rode together as far as Boley. Like Taft, Boley is an all-black community, but unlike Taft, the ethnic solidarity was intentional at Boley. During the Reconstruction era in the South, many freed slaves moved from there to Oklahoma, then called Indian Territory, drawn by the congressional decree that barred whites from living there. In addition, many blacks were already in the territory, having been slaves to Indian owners. When the tribal governments were liquidated following the war, the black freedmen shared equally with the Indians in the land allotments. Thus, by 1890, Oklahoma had 28 all-black towns, but that was a fact of settlement patterns rather than intention. Towns such as Taft were all black because large numbers of African Americans migrated there.

Boley, in contrast, was established in 1903, well after the territory had been opened to white settlement. It was set up at the urging of a white roadmaster who convinced the railroad that blacks could govern themselves (a fact, which, ironically, blacks had already proven by governing themselves just fine for years before white settlers arrived in the territory). Within a short time, Boley had 4,200 citizens.

In 1905, Booker T. Washington visited Oklahoma, and after a stop in Boley, wrote that while there were a number of small communities (including Taft) that were known as "colored" towns, only Boley was intentionally black. He described it as "the most enterprising and in many ways the most interesting of the negro (sic) towns in the United States" and called it "a rude, bustling, western town." Washington further observed that Boley was the town, "where, it is said, no white man has ever let the sun go down upon him."

For a time, some residents of Boley hoped the town would become the spiritual center of a national black separatist movement, or at least the seat of an all-black county. That dream was squelched when white Democrats realized that blacks tended to vote as a bloc, usually for the Republicans, the party that had liberated them. Before long, the election commissioners instituted measures to disfranchise the blacks, and Boley's hope of political power sank into the dust of its streets.

The town continued, but today, just like in other small towns across America, the population has dwindled considerably.

Ron and I stopped at the historical marker at the edge of Boley, and as traffic rumbled by on 62, he told me about growing up as a white person with segregation. "I can remember when I was a kid in Okemah, blacks used to come into town on Saturday night. There was only one theater they were allowed to attend, and they had to sit in the balcony. As a kid, I didn't think anything about that; it was just the way things were. But as I got older, I began to see things differently. And by the time I was in college, I realized that segregation — well, that wasn't right at all."

What about living with Indians? I asked. Did segregation apply there too?

"Not really. Around here at least, we thought of Indians as pretty much the same as us. I dated Indians. Farther west in the state they were sometimes treated differently, but not here."

I'd enjoyed talking and riding with Ron and was sorry that he was unable to continue with me. Evidently he felt the same, for his last words were, "Darn, I wish I could go with you." We shook hands and he turned his bike back in the direction we'd come.

A few miles down the road, I suddenly realized that I no longer had my sweatband. I recalled that back at the Boley marker, I had removed my helmet and hung the sweatband from my handlebars. Apparently it had blown off while Ron and I talked, and I hadn't missed it when I put the helmet back on. The loss was no major problem, and certainly not worth pedaling back to search for it. I had a couple more sweatbands with me. But the matter of losing things while touring always concerned me. Not everything could be as easily replaced.

The sweatband was loss number two for this leg of my trip. Because of the longer distances between communities, I had started with an extra water bottle. My two usual ones fit in cages on the bike frame, but my stove fuel bottle occupied the third cage. I had tucked the extra bottle under the bungee cords that secured my sleeping bag to the rear rack. Somewhere before Okmulgee it had slipped out. I'd replaced it with a sports drink bottle, which I refilled with water after consuming the drink. Before the trip was over, I'd also leave a small bottle of shampoo in a shower stall. Fortunately, my wallet never went astray.

A few miles later I came to Paden. Route 62 unrolled down its short main street, and halfway through town stood a small, unnamed café attached to a gas station. Seeing it, I decided to make a second attempt at breakfast. I swung in and parked my bike in front of the large window. Inside, in obedience to a sign, I placed my order at the counter. Then I slid into a booth to await my meal. There were four booths in all, with a gap between the third and fourth ones. An overstuffed easy chair occupied that spot. An older man sat in the chair reading a newspaper. "It looks like that chair was put there just for you," I said as I sat down.

"Yes," said the man, not looking up. "I'm the resident know-it-all. Every town's got to have one, so this is where I sit." Then he looked up and told me that a pair of British cyclists had come through the town on a tandem bike a couple of years before during bad weather. He had housed them at his home for the night.

Apparently I had unknowingly planted myself in the middle of the area where a local gaggle of old men gather in midmorning for coffee, and during the next few minutes, five or six of them wandered in. I gathered that I was in a "reserved" seat when one of them, who appeared to be about 85, dropped onto the bench across the table from me without either asking to share my booth or saying good morning. Others sidled into booths all around us, coffee cups in hand. One, smoking a cigarette, remained standing. My presence seemed neither to excite nor annoy anyone, and for the next half hour, I was included in the conversation to the degree I choose to be.

Two things quickly became evident: First, both Mr. Know-It-All and my table companion were former sailors. In fact, the man across from me wore a hat with the name of a military vessel on it. Second, these two were respected by the others as the knowledgeable ones.

The topic that soon emerged was the New York Senatorial race, where the wife of the U.S. president was running against the mayor of New York City. His Honor had just revealed that he had cancer, and the men discussed the ramifications.

At this point, a monologue, oddly disconnected to the rest of the conversation, began. The smoker, hearing the president's wife mentioned, took that as a cue to blast the president for favoring gun control. "He better not come here and try to take away our guns," the smoker said. He paused as though waiting for others to agree, but no one responded at all. They simply continued the conversation at hand. I suspected they'd heard it all before.

The man tried again. "Guns don't kill people! People kill people!" No response. The group conversation moved on, the men talking in pairs on topics of their own choice, while every once in a while, the smoker floated another gun-lobby slogan in an attempt to divert the discussion.

If being ignored bothered him, he gave no sign. I wondered if that might not be his customary role in the group — the ignored one. It may have felt perfectly normal to him. "It's the moral decline of our country that's the problem!" he uttered. He might as well have been talking to the wall.

Using his Navy connection as an opening, I began talking to the man in my booth about his military service. He had served in WW II, he explained, and had later gone back for a second hitch. After that he went to college. Before his retirement, he had been the school superintendent for the district that included Paden. He liked the community so well that he had stayed on after retirement. At that point, Mr. Know-It-All passed a newspaper clipping to my table mate, who looked it over and then passed it to me. It showed a young man from Paden, currently serving on a Navy aircraft carrier, receiving a commendation.

Eventually, as I finished my meal, the men asked the usual questions about my trip, and most agreed they'd prefer to do it on a motorcycle. As I rose to leave, they all, one by one, wished me well.

"So long."

"Good luck!"

"Yeah, take care."

"Be careful out there."

"If you criminalize guns, only criminals will have guns!"

A sign at the next county line informed me that I was entering the Sax and Fox Nation reservation. Indian land it might be, but the first town I came to was Prague (rhymes with "egg"), which had been established as a Czechoslovakian settlement. The population base had broadened since, but another sign announced the upcoming Kolache Festival, an annual event in the community. The town stretched over some hills and had a tidy, healthy look that reminded me of the Amish towns I'd ridden through in Ohio. Only here, the animals grazing on the hillsides were beef cattle instead of diary cows.

One more sign declared Prague the birthplace of Jim Thorpe, the member of the Sac and Fox tribe who became one of the most famous American athletes of the 20th century. In the 1912 Olympics, Thorpe was the first and only person to win both the Pentathlon and Decathlon. He was also the first American to simultaneously play professional baseball and football; and he became the first president of the National Football League.

As a Route 62 note, he twice played for the Bulldogs of Canton, Ohio, another Route 62 town. Thorpe is also enshrined in Canton's Football Hall of Fame as well as in the National Indian Hall of Fame (on 62 in Anadarko, Oklahoma), the National Track and Field Hall of Fame, and the Pennsylvania and Oklahoma Halls of Fame.

In the end, he was buried in a town where he'd never lived or even visited. After he died in 1953, his wife attempted to get Oklahoma to build a memorial to him, but the state declined. Then she heard about the efforts of two adjacent Pennsylvania towns, Mauch Chunk and East Mauch Chunk, to recover economically after the decline of coal mining. She visited the towns and made an offer that motivated the two municipalities to come together as one community, name the new town in honor of her husband and build a memorial to him. In February 1954, Thorpe's body was transferred to its final resting place in the town that now bore his name, Jim Thorpe, Pennsylvania.

Much later, Oklahoma finally came around. In 1998, January 30 was proclaimed Jim Thorpe Day in his home state.

The ride to Oklahoma City proved especially tiring. The edge I'd had from my winter spinning classes when I'd flown into Fayetteville was used up, probably in part by whatever had upset my digestive system. But the terrain also demanded more from me than I'd expected. While not once that day did I climb a hill steep enough or long enough to be memorable, the route humped over ridge after ridge after ridge. I had the sensation that I was pedaling across a giant swatch of corduroy. And on top of that, I had a headwind. It wasn't terribly strong, but enough to knock three or four miles an hour off my progress. By the time I finally arrived at the home of Ray and Dixie Fallis on the edge of the city, I was deeply exhausted.

I had never met Ray and Dixie, but Ray was my Aunt Rozelle's brother, and the invitation had been extended for me through her. The Fallises live in a mobile home park they own in Midwest City, an Oklahoma City suburb, and they had been dealers in manufactured housing for years.

Earlier in the day, I had phoned Ray to confirm that I would arrive that evening, and I'd given him an estimated time-of-arrival. In my growing weariness, I'd missed that projection by a good hour. Now as I pedaled slowly down the last few blocks to their home, I saw a car coming toward me. When the man and woman inside spotted me, they turned the car around and followed me into the park. It was Ray and Dixie, coming out to look for me.

A great evening followed. Within minutes, I felt as if Ray, Dixie and I were old friends. They housed me in a mobile home they kept as a guest unit, complete with shower and laundry facilities. After I'd cleaned up, Dixie prepared an excellent meal, but I was so exhausted and my stomach so unsettled that I could barely eat it. I felt bad about that after the work Dixie had gone to in preparing it, but she immediately put me at ease about it. "If you can't eat, you can't eat," she said kindly. "Don't worry about it."

During dinner I asked about whether 62 would take me past the site of the former Alfred P. Murrah Federal Building, which in 1995 had been blown up in the deadliest act of internal terrorism ever against America. That single act of infamy killed 168 people, several of them children, and injured 850 more. Just days before my arrival in Oklahoma, the site had been opened as a memorial park.

Ray said that 62 did not pass the site, but he suggested that he drive me to it to have a look. It was after dark when we arrived, but the memorial was lit well, and there were hundreds of people roaming the grounds. There was no convenient parking, so we settled for driving around the parameter of the park a couple of times. Even from the car, I could see the special 168 chairs, illuminated against the night to represent those killed in the bombing, and I experienced a wave of sadness at the memory they evoked.

A few days later national news reported that more than 100,000 people had visited the site during the first three weeks it was open. The sheer crush of people had practically obliterated the grass, and the authorities were having to plant a hardier variety. Even more troublesome were the coins thrown into the reflecting pool by visitors. Each week, the park service cleaned money out of the water by the bucketful.

Ensconced in the plush seat of Ray's large Lincoln with the air conditioning washing over me, I began to feel better than I had in the last two days. Tomorrow, I felt certain, would be a fresh start.

Chapter 14

I awoke feeling good and knew at once that I was recovered. Dixie prepared pancakes and sausage, and I did full justice to the meal. As we ate, Ray and Dixie's two grown sons, Randy and Tony, stopped in. Together with their parents, the brothers operate the park, maintain the grounds, and refurbish used mobile homes they purchase as rental units for the park.

Randy's 11-year-old son, Ryan, was also on hand. This sharp, inquisitive boy obviously enjoyed being with the adults, and asked lots of questions about my trip. I could tell by the way he quizzed me that he was a thinker. I suspect he will do well in whatever he chooses to do when he grows up.

Ray, who had lived in Oklahoma City for 31 years, was stumped about how to help me get out of town. In the city, 62 dropped onto an Interstate. He could think of several ways around that would get me to the Canadian River at the southern edge of the city, but there all the routes came to the same obstacle. There were just two bridges across the river, and both carried Interstates that forbid bicycles on them. Finally Ray concluded that the best plan was for someone to drive me through the city, across one of the bridges and deposit me in Newcastle, the community on 62 just beyond the bridge.

One connection Route 62 does make in Oklahoma City is with the path once used by Route 66, the most famous of the U.S. numbered highways. On 23rd Street, between Lincoln Boulevard and Western Avenue, 62 briefly overlays 66's course.

Although decommissioned in 1984, Route 66 remains the quintessential symbol of the open road. Stretching from Chicago to Los Angeles, 66 was, from the 1920s into the 1950s, the primary corridor for reaching southern California.

Most of the roads that became federal numbered highways in

1926 were already in use; the numbering simply made them "official" routes eligible for federal funding. But the highway that became 66 did not exist beforehand. When established, it used sections of old trails at its eastern and western ends, but most of its midsection was built as entirely new road. That this happened was largely because of one man, Cyrus Avery, the State Highway Commissioner of Oklahoma. Avery also served on the national board charged with assigning the route numbers of the National Highway System. Not only did he push to have this new road built and included in the numbered system, but he also helped to organize a Route 66 Association to promote the use of the highway.

Wisely, Avery sensed that highways and tourism were twin motors to drive road construction. The more tourists who drove the roads, the greater the demand for improved highways. And the more the highways were improved, the more tourists who took to the roads.

Avery put this principle into operation through the Route 66 Association. He proposed dubbing 66 "The Main Street of America," an idea that helped travelers view driving as a legitimate form of vacation and 66 as a destination in itself. And as the tourists came through the towns along 66, the highway spawned hundreds of motels, gas stations, diners and tourist attractions.

During America's Great Depression, thousands of families, whose Midwest farms were ruined by drought and winds that blew their topsoil away, migrated to California over 66, looking for new lives. In his classic novel about the Dust Bowl migrants, *The Grapes of Wrath*, John Steinbeck, called 66 "The Mother Road." The migrants he described viewed the road as a pathway to better times. The road gained further fame from Bobby Troup's classic jazz song, "Get your kicks on Route 66" and the 1960s TV series *Route 66*.

With the advent of the Interstates, Route 66 was gradually bypassed. Beginning in the late 1950s, section after section was replaced by Interstate superslabs, gradually rendering the old road superfluous. But the 66 mystique remains, and in many places, pieces of the old highway survive, marked with signage as "Historic Route 66." In fact, about 85 percent of the old route can still be driven.

In one way, Route 62 benefited from Avery's persistence in getting the path of 66 designated. As originally conceived, all of the federal highways were to run north-south or east-west. But 66 trundled across the country in a bow-shaped path from Chicago in the north to Los Angeles in the west. In prevailing with 66, Avery set a precedent that made 62's diagonal cross-country course acceptable. A 1926 report filed by the Joint Board responsible for setting up the Numbered Highway System, stated, "Diagonal routes have been introduced which follow the prevailing flow of traffic and recognize actually existing demands from the traveling public."

Shortly after breakfast, Randy, accompanied by Ryan, shuttled me to Newcastle in his pickup. As I unloaded the bike, Randy commented that today, the wind would be pushing me. And he was right. With the boost of the tailwind, I sailed down the highway, the joy of cycling reborn.

I really wasn't surprised. From experience on the road, I've come to expect rebirth days to follow tough ones, for inevitably, that's what happens. I've learned never to judge a journey solely on the tough days.

Route 62 runs southwest on good highway to Blanchard, an agreeable small town, but beyond there, the road shrinks to one of its narrowest sections on the entire length of the route, and offers no shoulder. This 13-mile segment is as heavily traveled as the good road preceding it, and is used by semis, so I had to exercise a lot of caution. But it was also a scenic sector, and for the first time the views offered sweeps of land that reminded me of cowboy movies.

A few miles before Chickasha, the road improved, and I whizzed energetically along, anticipating a good lunch when I got there.

I wasn't disappointed. I found a diner right on 62, just a block from the boxy looking courthouse, and went in for a hot meal, glad my appetite was back to normal. On my way inside, I noticed a "Help Wanted" sign in the window, and part way through my lunch, a young, blond-haired man exploded into the restaurant to inquire about it. "What's the job you need help for?" he asked the waitress loudly.

Clearly she didn't like his boisterous manner. "I don't know," she said curtly. "You'll have to ask the owner."

He continued just as loudly. "Well, is she here? Is the job dishwashing?"

At that moment, a woman appeared at the serving window, and the waitress indicated that she was the boss. The young man turned his attention to her, asking about the job.

She apparently didn't care for him either. "I don't have a job," she said. "I'm not looking for anyone."

The young man, looking angry, turned to leave. As he got to the door he shouted back, "You shouldn't put a sign up if you don't need help." When the woman didn't respond, he shouted it again, and stormed out.

From mumbled conversation between the owner and the waitress that I half overheard, I gathered that neither of them knew the man, but both had him pegged as trouble from the minute he erupted into the diner. It was a case study in how not to apply for a job.

After lunch, I took a few minutes to look around the town. I found a busy, substantial main street as well as a long strip of businesses and retail stores tailing out to a shopping center. That strip was U.S. Route 81, which runs north-south through Chickasha. As it unwinds in both directions, it follows the approximate path of the old Chisholm Trail, over which Texas cattlemen once drove their stock northward to railheads in Kansas for shipment to eastern markets.

At the end of the Civil War, at least five million longhorn cattle roamed Texas, but there was no way to get them to the East, where the price for beef was high. But in 1867, Joseph G. McCoy, a Chicago cattle dealer, arrived at Abilene, Kansas, the end of the Union Pacific rail line, with a plan. He intended to take advantage of a trail that had been established by Jesse Chisholm, a Cherokee trader. Chisholm had nothing to do with cattle, but had marked the route southward from Kansas though Oklahoma for his trading wagons. McCoy built stockyards in Abilene, and advertised widely throughout Texas that he would buy cattle there for shipment to the East.

Texans soon organized trail drives, some starting as far south as San Antonio and even Brownsville, and drove cattle northward at about 12 miles a day. By 1871, so many drovers were arriving in Abilene that as many as 5,000 were often paid off during a single day. After the deprivations of trail life, many of these cowboys went looking for excitement, and Abilene became known as one of the roughest towns in the West.

As the railroads kept building, they reached farther south, shortening the distance the cattlemen had to drive their cows. Within Kansas, the trail terminus shifted successively from Abilene to Newton to Wichita to Caldwell, which was just north of the Oklahoma line. By then the region north of Caldwell was closed to cattle drives by barbwire and quarantine laws. After 1880, when railroads reached Texas, cattle could be shipped directly and the long trail drives became unnecessary. But in the 13 years from 1867 to 1880, at least 10 million longhorns were driven up the trail, the largest migration of domestic animals ever.

Of course, that generation of cowboys has long since passed on to the great trail ride in the sky, but I imagine some of them must have had difficulty adjusting to life that no longer required their drover skills. As I pedaled out of Chickasha, I wheeled passed a building marked "Chisholm Trail Counseling Center." And walking into the building — I am not making this up — was a cowboy: ten-gallon hat, cowhide vest, jeans and boots.

I pressed on, still riding high, rolling through Verden, which seemed to consist mostly of a public school. In 1865, it had been the site of a council between Union forces and several Oklahoma Indian tribes. During the Civil War, the "Five Civilized Tribes" — the Choctaws, Cherokees, Chickashaws, Creeks and Seminoles — had sided with the Confederacy, and now that the North had won the war, accommodation had to be made with the Union forces. Several of the Plains Indian tribes were also present, and one significant result of the council was that all the tribes together pledged to establish peace among themselves, realizing that they needed unity among their peoples to resist white aggression against their lands. They agreed that to survive, "an Indian shall not spill an Indian's blood."

Peace among themselves was especially important over the next few decades, for the federal government used the Indians' wartime loyalty as an excuse to gradually take back Oklahoma lands that had been granted to the tribes during the earlier Indian removals.

This set the stage for the series of land rushes in the territory that brought in thousands of white settlers.

Next I came to Anadarko, "Indian Capital of the Nation." The town was founded in 1901 when the surrounding Indian reservations were opened to white settlement. More than a third of the town's 6,500 people are Native Americans, and the community offers several attractions based on Native American culture. These include Indian City, USA (includes replicas of seven Indian villages), Riverside Indian School, Bureau of Indian Affairs offices, American Indian Exposition, the National Hall of Fame for Famous American Indians, and the Southern Plains Indian Museum.

Both of the last two are situated on Route 62 within the city boundaries, and I took the time to visit the Southern Plains Indian Museum. Inside, I found displays of some historical materials, but mostly stunning art and crafts, including contemporary works, from Kiowa, Comanche, Apache, Cheyenne, Arapaho, Wichita, Caddo and Delaware peoples.

Another 18 miles of riding brought me to the little town of Apache, an aptly named place, for a couple miles north of town, I passed a modern brick building identified as the tribal headquarters of the Fort Sill Apache. The town itself is notable architecturally for two buildings where 62 and the town's main street cross. They occupy respectively the southeast and southwest corners of the intersection and are memorable because each has a tall turret on its corner.

It was suppertime, and I was hungry for spaghetti. Hoping to find some, I swung in front of a pizza shop just as two teenage boys came out. I asked them about the menu, and they referred me to a restaurant across the street. "This place only sells pizza," one said. "And you probably can't get it across the street either, but at least you'll have a larger selection."

They went on to inquire about my trip, and after I described it, one boy said, "I wish we could do something like that. This is the most boring town in Oklahoma." Then they told me that if I was looking for a place to camp, I should talk to the pastor of a church around the corner. "You can't miss the church. It's got a tepee in front."

The restaurant they directed me to had an American-Chinese

menu. No spaghetti, but chicken lo mein at least included pasta noodles, so I settled for that.

While I waited for my food to arrive, a man seated nearby with his wife asked about my trip. As I began to explain, the couple, who were in my generation, invited me to join them at their table. They introduced themselves as Coy and Gail Bush, and I learned they were from Chickasha, where I'd eaten lunch. They were in Apache because they maintained a small weekend retreat home near the town. And this being the start of the weekend, they were en route. After they apparently decided I was not a roving axe murderer, Coy offered me a spot in his garage for the night. He even had a rollaway bed out there, he explained. They didn't look like axe murderers either, so I accepted. Their place was just a few miles further along on 62. Did I feel I had to ride every mile? Coy asked. They were driving a pickup truck. Would I accept a ride that far? I would.

As we rose to leave, Gail snatched up my bill and insisted on paying for my dinner.

Riding in the truck to their place, I began to learn about my hosts. Gail operated a machine quilting business in Chickasha, and Coy was a plumbing contractor, much in demand. In fact, he had crews operating in several counties. "We don't advertise," he said. "I don't even have a business card. We get all of our business by word-of-mouth referrals."

"You must have a good reputation then," I said.

"I guess we do. It takes a long time to build a good reputation, but it can be destroyed overnight. That's why we try to stay on top of everything."

As I got to know the pair better, I discovered Coy did not let his trade define his life. He was a Renaissance man with multiple hobbies, wide interests and an insatiable curiosity about life. Gail said he was a high-energy guy, sleeping only a few hours each night. He stayed up late to pursue his interests or to read. His hobbies ranged from creating welded furniture to artistic machine embroidery. The latter hobby involved using the needle as a paintbrush, and creating, freehand, portraits and landscapes. Coy even made his own patterns. Gail also practiced machine embroidery, and the pair had previously taught the skill up and down the California coast.

At their small, tidy cottage, my hosts gave me the use of the shower, which I appreciated. Then, sitting on their deck, we talked through the evening. Coy was filled with knowledge about Oklahoma and its people. "We didn't become a state until 1907, a lot later than the eastern states, and in some ways we're not as far along or as sophisticated. Most people around here have some Indian blood and the state's not that heavily populated. There are more people in the Dallas-Fort Worth area than there are in all of Oklahoma. And a lot of us are independent thinkers out here."

When Gail and Coy addressed each other, I noticed that they often used the term "baby" as a term of endearment, much as couples elsewhere use "honey." I had heard Ray and Dixie address each other that way too, so perhaps the usage is a regional mannerism. In the local speech, the word is gentle on the ear, not the hard BAY-bee, BAY-bee of pop and rock music with its sexual overtones, but a soft unaccented beb-bee, with tender connotations. It was pleasant to hear spouses address each other that way, and made me yearn for home.

Before I headed for bed, Coy and Gail solved a couple problems for me. The first was my next routing dilemma. Lawton, one of Oklahoma's larger cities, lay just ahead on 62, but before I would get to it, I'd have to traverse Fort Sill Military Reservation, a facility that occupied land several times the size of the city. The problem was, the path of 62 through both the military base and the city lay on Interstate highway. Clearly I'd have to depart from 62 to get through the area.

Coy proposed an L-shaped bypass, skirting the region on the north and west, passing through tiny Meers and the Wichita Mountains Wildlife Refuge. "We're going to take you to breakfast that way anyway, and if you don't mind, we'll drive you around to the other side of Lawton." Not only did I not mind, but I also realized that that would solve my other problem, the one of time pressure. Even with the rental car I'd used in Arkansas, I still was hard pressed to make El Paso in my allotted time. But this, coupled with the time I'd gained from Randy's shuttle out of Oklahoma City, would put me on a more comfortable schedule, easing things for me down the line.

As it turned out, the Bushes inadvertently spared me a third problem as well — rain. It began falling during the night, and at dawn it continued sporadically. But by the time we'd eaten breakfast at a café and they'd driven me beyond Lawton, the rain had stopped.

Coy's bypass route was beautiful. Driving through the Wichita Mountains area, we had several views of Mount Scott, a peak over 2,400 feet high that looms over the area. And in the Wildlife Refuge, I saw herds of buffalo and elk, grazing on prairie grassland in front of rocky outcrops hundreds of feet tall. The park is also home to deer and Texas longhorn cattle, as well as the location of some of the last untilled native prairie land in America. Had it not been for the rain, the route through the area would have been a great bike ride. The 60,000-acre refuge is the oldest managed unit in the Wildlife Refuge System.

At the hinge-point of the "L" where we made a 90-degree turn to the south sat Meers, an old mining town founded during Wichita's gold rush days just after the turn of the last century. Actually, what occupies the site now is the last remnant of the town, a rambling old store building that's been reborn as a popular restaurant specializing in longhorn burgers and steaks. The building incorporates a post office and, surprisingly to me, a geological survey station complete with a seismograph (installed to monitor the Meers fault, a nearby crack in the earth). The instrument sits in the lobby of the restaurant, and Coy and I went in to have a look at it. The Meers seismograph has recorded earthquakes as far away as the Indian Ocean and nuclear tests in the former Soviet Union. A 1997 magnitude-2 quake in Oklahoma itself was close enough to break the pin on the instrument.

Before leaving the refuge, Coy and Gail showed me a location known as "The Holy City." It's another outdoor Passion play, but unlike the one at Eureka Springs, this one is not a commercial venture. Placed in a natural setting not unlike the rugged hills of Judea, this Oklahoma version is centered on 20 native granite structures built to resemble places in Jesus' itinerary. They are set in a wide, natural amphitheater. And rather than running all through any sort of "tourist season" with high-priced seating, this one offers just two performances, one on each of the two Saturdays before Easter. Spectators provide their own seating and are asked for a mere dollar each as a donation. Though I looked, I could not find even one gift shop. This annual pageant about Jesus began as a Sunday school Easter drama and has been taking place since 1926. It now draws about 20,000 visitors each year.

Eventually the delightful time with the Bush's came to an end when they deposited me on the Highway 62 shoulder beyond Lawton. The rain had stopped and the sky was clearing.

The evening before, Coy had mentioned that many towns in Oklahoma are about 10 miles apart because that's how far a horse and wagon could travel in a day. The string of towns stretching westward from Lawton — Cashe, Indiahoma, Snyder, Headrick, Altus, Victory, Duke, McQueen, Gould and Hollis — were all spaced approximately on that scale. Route 62, running as expressway for more than 30 miles, bypassed Indiahoma, Snyder and Headrick, though each sat within view of the highway.

Actually, it may have been the towns rather than the highway that moved, for this corridor had a reputation for natural disasters. Snyder had been almost completely demolished by a 1905 tornado. Headrick had suffered both a tornado and several fires. The original townsite of Altus flooded out and had been rebuilt on higher ground.

If 62 was disaster alley for the towns, it was smooth sailing for me. From my first pedal stroke, I benefited from a splendid tailwind that shoved me forward with even more vigor than the breeze I'd had behind me the day before. I shot forward, sometimes hitting 25 mph on the straightaways.

I arrived in Altus in midmorning. A historical marker at the edge of town marked Altus as a stop on the Great Western Cattle Trail, a 1,000 mile route that, like the Chisholm Trail, was used to drive cattle to northern railheads. The trail had functioned from 1876 to 1895.

There were families in the parking lot beside the marker, watching the sky intently. The community is the home of Altus Air Force Base, and on this day, there was an air show in progress. As I looked up, several parachutists waving smoke streamers came floating toward the earth. A man there with his family told me that an entire day of festivities and aerial acrobats was planned, with the finale being a routine by the Thunderbirds, a crack air squadron from the Air Force.

Altus, though not huge, was the largest community I'd encountered since Anadarko. It offered a good selection of eating places, businesses and retail shops, including a bicycle shop, something that's a rarity in small towns.

Beyond Altus, the land became even more prairie-like, reminding me of western Kansas. The next towns — Duke, McQueen and Gould — were tiny and looked like they were struggling to stay alive. West of Duke, I saw some irrigated fields. Some others that were not irrigated had winter wheat, a dry-land crop, growing on them.

The temperature had been rising all day, and now, in midafternoon, it was well into the 80s, making it the warmest day so far on this leg of my journey. The air felt good, especially with the cooling breeze at my back, but the sun broiled my skin. I stopped and smeared on sunblock, but by day's end, my ears, nose and the newly exposed flesh above my socks were very red.

With plenty of empty highway between towns, I thought about the road that made my trip possible, and how finding directions had been so simple with the well-marked route.

Before investigating the origins of the U.S. Numbered Highway System, I had assumed that the orderly numbering scheme was the work of some agency in Washington — the Federal Highway Administration, perhaps. At the very least, I figured some national bureau oversaw the sewing together of previously separate segments into continuous routes. My assumption was wrong.

As I mentioned earlier, the highway act of 1921 stipulated that states should coordinate with each other so that the roads of each jurisdiction would connect at the boundaries. Before this, many roads ended abruptly at state or even county lines.

This mandated coordination, as well as the actual selection of routes and assigning of route numbers, was done by the American Association of State Highway Officials (AASHO) — one of the most important but least known groups in the country.

The idea for numbered highways initially came from a Wisconsin highway engineer, A.R. Hirst, in 1917, and the next year, his state became the first to introduce numbered roads. In the early 20s, AASHO, with Hirst as its president, requested the Secretary of

Agriculture to establish a committee to plan for a national system of numbered highways, which was to include a standard signage scheme. The Secretary not only agreed, but also turned the assignment over to AASHO itself, appointing a Joint Board of officials from the Bureau of Public Roads and the various state highway departments to prepare the plan.

Founded in 1914 as the move for good roads heated up, AASHO became so influential that its agreement was necessary before any practical national highway policy could be enacted. One reason for AASHO's ascendancy was the old idea that the federal government could not infringe on the sovereignty of states. The 1921 act extended the federal primary-aid system that had been kicked off in the 1916 act and specifically earmarked money for U.S. routes. But in keeping with the principle of state jurisdictions, it was left to state officials to designate which roads in their respective states would become federal routes.

Specifically, officers in each state were given the prerogative to pick up to seven percent of their state's highway system to receive federal funding. Naturally, to accomplish U.S. routes that would connect across state lines, the highway officials of the respective states had to work and plan together. Thus their organization became the ruling body for road policy almost by default. Even the setting of highway standards, originally granted to the Secretary of Agriculture by the 1916 act, eventually fell to AASHO.

What is remarkable about the Numbered Highway System that resulted was that participation in it by the various states was purely voluntary. Within about a year's time, states that did not have highway departments established them. Where the existing state laws worked against participation in the system, legislatures changed them.

Of course, the motivation for this cooperation was obvious: More and more people in every state were becoming car owners, and as people took to the highways, the shortcomings of the entire system, including both road surfaces and signage, was plainly evident. Drivers were frequently put to extra expense and inconvenience because of the unnecessary mileage caused by misdirection and lack of signs.

The Joint Board did its work promptly, considering the requests of more than 100 existing trail associations, numerous chambers of commerce, automobile clubs, boards of trade, civic organizations and even individuals, all lobbying to have their communities and existing routes included on a numbered highway. AASHO monitored all of this work, and many of its meetings were devoted exclusively to reconciling these entreaties. In the end, the Joint Board had to deny many of them, sticking to its mandate to select transcontinental and major state-to-state routes on their merits. The final report of the Board was presented November 11, 1926, with a numbered network of 96,626 miles. This figure grew in succeeding years as additional routes were added or existing ones extended, so that by 1951, there were nearly 164,000 miles on the numbered system. This growth continued for another decade or so until, with improved routings, shortenings and even decommissionings of routes, the mileage figure began shrinking. Its last reported length, in 1989, was 157,724.

When the system was introduced, a few critics argued that switching from named highways to numbered routes would take the passion out of driving. But they were wrong. The numbered routes soon took on a romance of their own. Highways like 66, 2, 101, 20, 50 and others became symbolic of the freedom of the open road.

Only after AASHO and the Joint Board had done its work was the federal highway signage mounted along the agreed-upon routes. The U.S. shield sign marked not federal ownership or selection of the road, but federal support in its construction.

More importantly, the standardized signs and highway numbers marked a shift from focusing just on specific routes to considering the entire highway system, the system of a nation firmly established on its land. The pioneer era was closed; the modern era was upon us.

AASHO also established the comprehensive plan for other traffic signage, such as the cross for railroad intersections and the octagon stop sign. In addition, they set standards for two other matters important to cyclists: the width of traffic lanes and the size of highway shoulders.

Now renamed the American Association of Highway and Transportation Officials (AASHTO), this nonprofit group remains highly influential in highway decisions and now handles all applications for changes not only to the U.S Numbered Highway System but also to the Interstate Highway System and the U.S. Bicycle Route Systems.

About 4 p.m., I rolled into Oklahoma's final town on 62. Hollis is the seat of Harmon, the most southwestern county in the state. But though it was the center of the county, Hollis was an empty place. The entire eastern end of town appeared abandoned. Beyond that was a downtown a couple of blocks long, but it was now a mausoleum of empty stores. The only places that seemed to have much going on were a grocery store and a small café. There were two other restaurant buildings near by, both fast-food chain outlets, but neither were in operation. Large sections of roofing materials were missing from the top of one.

The next community showing on my map was Childress, 36 miles away in the Texas panhandle. I inquired in the Hollis grocery if there were any place to eat in between. There was *nothing* in between I was told. Even though I wasn't really hungry yet, I decided I'd better eat supper in the café at hand.

As I walked my bike toward the eatery, a grandmotherly woman pulled over in her car and asked me about my trip. She mentioned she had passed me on the highway earlier in the day. I supplied the usual answers and thought no more about it. But after eating supper, when I was about to mount up and head west, the woman appeared again, still in her car. "Are you going to Childress tonight?" she asked.

When I told her I was, she said, "You've got to watch for storms out here. They come up fast. There's supposed to be one coming later tonight." She went on to tell me the location of a culvert approximately halfway to Childress where, if need be, I could take shelter. Finally, she gave me her address and made me promise to write her and tell her whether I completed my trip safely. All of this coming from someone who lived daily in the region of my pilgrimage did little to bolster my confidence, but I headed out anyway.

As I left, she asked one more question. "Why are you doing this?" I explained my love of cycling and travel, but she drove off shaking her head.

Chapter 15

With minor exceptions, the ride from where the Bushes had dropped me off to the Texas line had been flat, but almost as soon as I entered the new state, there began to be a little rise and fall to the land. And, as if to welcome me to Texas, a tumbleweed rolled across the road not more than five minutes into the Lone Star state.

Coming from "back East," my mental image of Texas consisted of "wide, open spaces," which was approximately what I found as I pedaled into the state. I say "approximately," for while the land around me was certainly spacious and wide, it could not exactly be described as "open." That's because no matter how unusable the land appeared, barbwire fencing sealed it off on both sides of the road, broken only by a very occasional gated drive heading off into the hinterland. I'd already seen a good bit of roadside fencing in previous states, but from here to the end of my ride, it was almost nonstop.

That the fences continued without interruption soon became obvious when I came all at once upon a dark-brown calf at the roadside, on my side of the fence. He was about the size of a large dog, but more hefty. How he'd gotten there I could only guess, but he appeared to be tying to get through the fence, perhaps to rejoin his mamma somewhere deep in the sagebrush.

In any case, when he saw me, the young animal spooked and set off running along the fenceline, heading west, as I was. Periodically he'd turn toward the fence, as though searching for a way to get through, but no opening presented itself. He raced along in a panic, running from the hombre in spandex on the strange-looking horse behind him.

Finally, he turned toward the fence, bulled between two strands of barbwire and, in what must have been a painful effort, kicked his way to the other side.

Of course, the West was not always fenced, and, as I later learned, open range was the standard until the 1880s. But, fencing, which began on a large scale in the early years of that decade, had pretty well shut down the open-range cattle industry by 1890.

In part, the very success of open-range cattle-raising set the stage for its demise. Because of the huge profits possible from selling western beef, a number of eastern and even European capitalists began to invest in the business. These investors had the funds to buy lands and fence them, an important move as the ranges became crowded and more and more beeves competed for the available grass. Cattlemen eventually realized that fencing was the only logical way to stabilize the cattle industry.

Another reason the late 1800s saw the closing of the range was because barbwire, invented in 1873, was just making its way onto the market, and it provided a cost-effective way to enclose lands.

Not that it happened without resistance. Since the first lands to be fenced were those that included a water supply, those who owned waterless tracts opposed fencing. Fencing made theft of stock more difficult, so rustlers opposed it. With fences, herds could be managed with fewer men, and many cowboys had to seek other employment. But the most resistance arose simply because the largest fenced landholdings usually belonged to eastern capitalists, people Texans viewed as absentee barons denying land to poorer residents.

So, for a time, fence cutting was widespread, with local lawmen unable to do much to stop it. Finally, an 1884 Texas law made fence cutting a felony. However, the same legislation required that gates be installed every three miles along a fence and outlawed the enclosure of land not owned or leased. Following this act, the fence wars subsided.

About 10 miles in, 62 suddenly ends its long westward run and makes a 90-degree turn to the south, joining U.S. 83. I'd ridden 77 miles since morning, all with a tailwind propelling me. Now, after I made the turn, the same strong wind that had been a blessing became a curse, and for the next 17 miles I labored against a crosswind so fierce that it cut my speed to a third of what it had been.

Still, the ride was interesting, and the helping wind earlier had left me with enough energy to slog happily along. En route, I crossed the Red River, though the water level was so low that what I mostly saw was red mud.

The wind slowed me so much that dark was falling when I finally hit the outskirts of Childress. That was no problem, but about the same time the sky changed and angry clouds gathered — the storm the Altus woman warned about, no doubt. Childress had several motels. I picked out one with "budget" in its name and made a beeline for it. Heavy rain started falling moments after I checked in.

It rained all night. In the morning I flipped on the Weather Channel on the motel TV. It was filled with dire reports for the area around Childress, warning of a miserable day with no promise of improvement the next day either. With my schedule, I couldn't really afford to layover. But then it came to me that if the storm was going to hang around Childress, my best move might be to get out of the area as soon as possible. So I packed up, layered on my bad weather clothes, and fled southward toward Paducah, 30 miles away.

Within a few miles, it seemed my plan had worked. After several minutes of brief showers, the rain stopped. Although the sky remained overcast and the air stayed cool enough that I was not tempted to shed any layers of clothing, I seemed to have dodged the storm, so I congratulated myself on my wise decision — a premature compliment, as it turned out.

For the most part, the land south of Childress was more of the same — prairie and sagebrush — though it did temporarily change character after I pedaled up a long ridge. After that, there were a few miles of gullies, washes and arroyos, very much western-looking land. Eventually, however, I finished crossing the ridge and returned to prairie.

Through this segment, 62 continued to be united with 83, and that route, a roadside plaque told me, was the Texas Viet Nam Veterans Memorial Highway, selected because it ran from the southernmost tip of Texas to its northernmost point.

As I ground on toward Paducah, I contemplated the distance between Texas towns. Thirty empty miles was par for the course. Clearly a different standard than how far a wagon could travel in a day had been used in this state. (I later learned that it was the location of water and the huge amount of land needed to support each cow, due to the scarcity of grass for grazing.)

Toward noon, I pedaled into Paducah. Its courthouse, built to resemble an Egyptian temple, stood in the center of the town square, but nearly every building on the four sides facing the square was abandoned. And this being Sunday, no one was around. I had the sensation of having ridden into a set for a Twilight Zone episode. The vacant stores puzzled me. Paducah was the only community in a 30-mile radius, so I expected its businesses to be thriving just because there was no competition nearby. But apparently that was not the case.

Just beyond the square, 62 made a right turn and headed west again, and when I turned that corner, the Twilight Zone feeling was dispelled by the number of people I saw moving in and out of a busy family-style restaurant. Most were dressed in their Sunday best. Despite my lack of similar attire, I joined the crowd and ate Sunday dinner.

By the time I finished my meal, the sun had broken through and the day had warmed up considerably. As I exited the restaurant, a man also heading out advised me that I'd have good riding now. "The storms are over and we've got sunshine for the rest of the day." I assumed he'd heard a weather report, and I was heartened by his words. The air had warmed so much that I stripped down to my short-sleeve jersey and bike shorts.

A couple in their 60s came out of the restaurant. Spotting the bike, they ambled over and asked where I was headed. After giving them my standard spiel, I inquired about the empty stores on the square. "That's been done deliberately," the man said. When I looked surprised, he added, "That's the way they want it."

"Who is 'they'?" I asked.

"The government," he said with passion. "They want to empty all these little towns out here." At that point, I noticed his wife wander off. She'd heard all this before, I suspected, but I was interested in where he was going with this and urged him to continue.

"They've purposely made it so people can't make a living out here." He went on to mention the large number of ranches the county had once supported and how few remained. "When kids graduate from high school, they leave here and never come back. There's no way for them to make a living here now."

"What's happened to the ranches?"

"The government has kept prices ranchers get for their products so low that people just can't make it. They'd rather loan money to poor countries to produce what we used to grow ourselves so as to keep those countries in debt to us. They want an economy based on debt instead of new wealth."

When I looked uncomprehending, he explained, "There are only four sources of new wealth: the harvest of the ocean, timber from the forests, minerals from the earth and agriculture. You don't create those things; God gives them to you. But if you can't use them, then you are forced into debt, and that's the way they want it."

I thanked him for explaining his view and we shook hands. He said, "You won't usually hear things explained this way, but that's what's going on." He added, "You have a good trip and be careful out there."

As I rode out of town, I mulled his words. I was frankly skeptical of the broad-based conspiracy at the root of his theory, but he did not impress me as a kook or as someone just parroting a screwball idea he'd heard somewhere. He seemed to have thought out his conclusion thoroughly. Even if his hypothesis was wrong, it did show how the changing economy of the plains affected one's view of life.

As to the validity of what he had to say apart from the underlying conspiracy, I'm the wrong one to ask. I've never been strong on economic theory. In the publishing business where I work, I stay on top of editorial matters but my eyes glaze over when the financial reports are passed around. I've tried hard to get interested in the numbers side of business, but it just isn't in me. I'd rather cycle through a storm than work a spreadsheet.

Actually, I was about to put that statement to the test. Within minutes of leaving town, the air all at once became oppressively humid, a situation that continued for about 10 minutes. Then, as the sky ahead began changing from clear blue to a roiling dark gray, the mugginess was driven off by a freshening wind that propelled me forward vigorously — but toward what fate?

Out there alone on the treeless prairie with a seething sky flowing toward me, I suddenly felt extremely vulnerable. Clearly, I was
in for trouble, with no shelter in sight.

I was already 10 miles out from Paducah and there was no time
to turn back. I'd never make it against that powerful wind even if I
were closer. Nor did I have time to don my bad-weather clothes
again. In the last seconds before the rain began, I shoved my watch
and notebook in the waterproof bag with my camera, and braced for
the blow.

First came a heavy veil of rain, driven by wind that had suddenly
reversed and pushed the precipitation almost horizontally, reducing
visibility to less than 10 feet. This was soon joined by golfball-sized
hail that made me thankful for my bike helmet even as the frozen pel-
lets stung my shoulders and arms. Seeing some shrubbery nearby, I
laid my bike on the highway shoulder and ran behind the bush. It af-
forded a modicum of protection, but after a few minutes, I heard something that drove me out of its meager refuge — the crack of thunder,
and it sounded close. Huddled behind a lone bush was no place to be
when lightning was hitting, but what was the alternative?

I decided that since I was going to be at risk no matter what I
did, my best course was to try to ride out of the storm. I pulled my
bike upright, turned on the flashing taillight so passing vehicles would
see me, and mounted. The storm seemed to be driving toward
Paducah so I rode into the wind, continuing my westward journey.
Hail beat my hands where they gripped the handlebars, and I flinched
each time lightning pounced nearby, but I kept going. Occasionally
a car or truck passed, and one even slowed as though contemplating
whether to stop and offer assistance, but then apparently the driver
thought better of it and drove off.

After about 20 minutes of anxious pedaling, I finally emerged
from the curtain of the storm. The sky remained gray and the wind
erratic, but I was thankful to be alive. The air was chilly, but although I was soaked, the space-age fabric of my cycling jersey and
shorts kept some warmth in my body anyway. I cycled harder to
raise my internal temperature.

Moments later, a string of vehicles, some sprouting antennas
and other instruments, rushed by me heading in the opposite direc-

tion. Glancing at the logos on their doors, I realized these were storm-chasers, meteorologists on wheels seeking data on the tempest I just escaped.

When I'd left Childress that morning, I'd set Floydada, 95 miles away, as my destination for the day. With towns averaging 30 miles apart, my stopping-place choices were limited unless I wanted to camp in the open beside the road. But now I knew I couldn't go that far, and decided to pull up at the next town, Matador, 64 miles from Childress. The atmosphere was too unsettled, and I was unwilling to risk getting caught again by a violent storm in the 31 empty miles between Matador and Floydada. Actually, from the look of the sky, I had no confidence that I'd even make Matador without another drubbing from above.

But I did. In my anxious state, it seemed as if Matador would never appear. My arms and shoulders, which normally ached a little at the end of a long day clutching the handlebars, were especially painful now — tension, I suppose. Finally, about six miles out, I spotted Matador's water tower, the object I usually saw first approaching prairie towns. I began watching for the Church of Christ sign.

I'll explain. I'd noticed a similar pattern of visual signals as one neared these little communities. First, from a long way off, the water tower was visible. Then, a mile or more before the town limits, there'd be a sign advertising a church, and most of the time, it was the Church of Christ. Following that, not far from the edge of the hamlet, a sign announcing "Reduced Speed Ahead" appeared. Shortly thereafter there would be the town limits sign and then a sign stating the in-town speed limit. A moment after that, I'd be in the center of the community.

In Matador's case, the main street was a block long, and ran at a right angle to 62. I spotted a motel, and with the weather still threatening, I headed for it. The office was in an adjacent restaurant that was closed for the evening, but there were people inside, and a young man waved me in. Inside, I found three generations of the motel owner's family, and the grandmother seemed to be the person in charge. As she got out the paperwork to rent me a room, I asked the other people what they'd heard about the prospects for improving weather conditions. The reports were not encouraging, they said, and there was a likelihood storms would rumble through the area for yet another day.

Since I couldn't afford the day to wait the storm out, I asked if they knew of anyone who might be going into Lubbock the next morning — someone with whom I could catch a ride. Lubbock was about 70 miles down 62, and I hoped it would get me out of the storm area.

"Would you be willing to go at 6 o'clock?" a young woman asked.

When I said yes, she said that she and a friend were heading for Lubbock in the morning and would give me a ride. She introduced herself as "Seven" and told me to be at the convenience store across the street at 6. Meet Seven at six. Got it.

The older woman then handed me the key for room #1, and a little girl spoke up to say, "Oh, that's a good room." I headed for it, grateful for the sanctuary from the weather.

Once inside, I inspected my stuff. Despite the pounding rain, it had not fared too badly. I had most of my clothing in plastic bags inside the panniers, and it had stayed reasonably dry. But the outer clothing I'd removed earlier in the day was wet. When I'd taken it off, I'd merely shoved it in outside pockets of my saddlebags, and they were not waterproof. Also, my bike shoes were sopping. I hung up the wet garments around the room and shoved motel washcloths in the shoes to soak up the moisture. After a hot shower, I ate a microwaved meal at the convenience store and then, as the rain was still in abeyance, made a quick prowl of the town — all shuttered up for Sunday evening. Finally, I settled down in the room for a quiet evening and soon fell into a deep sleep.

While I waited for Seven in the convenience store the next morning, four men arrived in a pickup and came inside to buy coffee. Dressed in work shirts and jeans, mud-caked chaps, worn boots complete with spurs and sweat-stained Stetsons, these men were working cowboys. When one eyed me in my tight-fitting jersey and riding tights, I braced for a wisecrack. But all he said was "Did you catch any of that storm yesterday?" I told him I had and where I'd been at the time. "Lucky you were where you were," he said. "There was a tornado in that storm, but it touched down about 15 miles south of the highway. It didn't stay on the ground too long, but it was there."

Seven pulled up in an SUV, and I went outside to load my steed into the vehicle's cargo area. Then I climbed into the back seat, which I shared with a child safety seat. Seven was behind the wheel and another young woman occupied the passenger seat. Seven introduced her as Sheila. Seven steered the vehicle into the predawn darkness, heading west on 62.

Both women were EMTs, emergency medical technicians, and helped staff the local ambulance squad. They traveled to Lubbock once a week to receive paramedic training, an advance over their EMT skills. Their squad, headquartered in Matador, was the only ambulance service in the entire county. The nearest major hospital was in Lubbock, 70 miles away.

I asked about the problems the distance creates. "We call the life-flight helicopter for anything serious," Sheila said. "That happens about six times a year. But since that takes 20 minutes to get here, even our police and firefighters are trained about when to call the chopper in."

As the sun began to rise, we came into Floydada and Sheila mentioned that that town had 3,800 people. "That's more than in our entire county," she said. Indeed it was. I later looked up the population of Motley County where Seven and Sheila lived. It was only 1,300 people, and that was a drop of more than 200 from eight years before.

I told them about the empty stores I'd seen in Paducah, and Seven had an explanation different from the man in Paducah. "They built a new Wal-Mart in Childress, and people started going up there. That just killed the Paducah stores."

I asked Seven the origin of her unusual name. She said, "Most people guess that I must be the seventh child in my family, but that's not it. My dad was one of seven children, and when I was born, he named me Seven in honor of all of them. I like my name."

We were nearing Lubbock, and Seven asked where I wanted to be dropped off. We settled on a truckstop on the eastern edge of the city, where the women's route diverged from 62. When we pulled into the lot, I proffered some cash to Seven for gas. "No, we don't want it," she said. "We were coming here anyway."

"Then use it to have lunch on me," I said.

"No way," Seven said, and Sheila joined in the refusal. "We enjoyed your company. Have a good ride."

As they pulled away and I put the money back in my wallet, I thought about how many times people had helped me in tight spots on my two long trips across America. Not once had anyone accepted money for doing so. I wouldn't have thought less of the women if they had accepted it, but it made me feel good to witness their spontaneous generosity.

Following 62 into Lubbock, I passed a park called the American Wind Power Center. From the road, I could see a few windmills, and I thought at first it was some sort of experiment in electric power generation, but as I poked around a bit, I found that the place was actually a museum of old-time windmills. These devices had played an important role in the settlement of the Great Plains, so it was appropriate that Lubbock, in the heart of the plains, would host such a facility. It is said that more than any other invention, the windmill made settlement of the West possible, giving railroads access to underground water, permitting ranchers to fence and breed cattle and farmers to live on land with no lakes, rivers or streams nearby.

Pushing further into town, I rode under a bridge carrying I-27, an Interstate that runs into Lubbock from the north. Interstates, though a problem for the bike, are a significant part of the American highway story. In fact, as the largest public works project in history, the Interstate system is a sizable chunk of the tale. These 41,000 miles of divided, limited-access roads were given life by the Federal-Aid Highway Act of 1956 and the system was 40 years in the building. It consumed as much acreage in right of ways as is in the entire state of Delaware and moved enough earth as to cover the state of Connecticut knee-deep. Its paved surface is equivalent to the state of West Virginia and the concrete used would build six sidewalks to the moon. The drainpipes on the system would handle the water and sewer needs of six Chicagos.

The need for an interstate system of multilane highways had become apparent to highway planners some years earlier. By the 1940s the existing highway system was caught up in a losing spiral with the automobile. Each time a road was improved to better accommodate its existing traffic level, more drivers were drawn to use it, rendering it inadequate again almost at once. Further, improved roads encouraged manufacturers to produce faster cars and heavier trucks, which in turn overtaxed the roads. World War II brought road construction to a halt, but attempts to curtail travel to save gasoline and rubber for the war effort revealed how much citizens had come to depend on mobility for all facets of their lives.

Unlike during the first World War, America's railroads performed well in this one, though at least part of that was because trucks were now carrying some of the load. But wartime reminded military leaders of how vulnerable a country is without a good system of roads. In many places, the railroads where simply a single track; cut that and the trains stop. Road vehicles, however, could get through even when roads are damaged. Also, with the threat of nuclear warfare, many believed it was vital that urban areas be served by highways that would provide evacuation routes in case of nuclear attack. Though later traffic jams would prove the evacuation route implausible, the defense argument helped sell the Interstate system to Congress.

That the act authorizing the Interstate program was passed during President Eisenhower's administration was no accident. In fact, some say the real beginning of the Interstate program was in 1919 when Eisenhower, then a young military officer, accompanied a motorized column of 79 military vehicles from Washington DC to San Francisco. The trip took 56 days, proving the inadequacy of U.S roads for military purposes. Just west of North Platte, Nebraska, 25 trucks skidded off the road and the convoy lost two days getting them back on the road. At another place, it took seven hours to go 200 feet. Eisenhower later referred to the trip as "60 days and 6,000 breakdowns." Twenty-five years later, as the supreme commander of the Allied forces in Europe, Eisenhower saw firsthand the German autobahns and their usefulness in military actions.

A key provision of the 1956 legislation was the new way of funding the roads for the Interstate system. The act established the

Highway Trust Fund, setting federal taxes on gasoline and diesel fuel, tires and tubes, new buses, trucks and trailers and a use tax on heavy trucks. Thus, the more people drove, the more money was available for the road building. The Trust Fund paid 90 percent of the cost of building the Interstates with the states underwriting the rest, as well as subsequent maintenance. The highway would be built to federal standards but along routes approved by the states.

In Lubbock, 62 conveyed me past a building dedicated to one of the city's famous sons, rock-and-roll artist, Buddy Holly. The center was not yet open for the day, but it contains a collection of memorabilia related to the late singer and has displays highlighting other performing musicians from Texas. The building housing the Buddy Holly Center is a former railroad depot, and the whole area surrounding it appeared to be restored historic structures.

I first became aware of Lubbock several years earlier thanks to another musician who was born there, Mac Davis. His song, "Texas in My Rear View Mirror," contained the memorable line, "Happiness is Lubbock, Texas, in my rear view mirror." Later in the song, however, the singer has a change of heart and is happy to return home.

It took me about 45 minutes to work my way through this city of 200,000, passing Texas Tech University on the way. At the far edge of Lubbock, 62 bends steeply southwest, and I rolled out into open country, paralleling tracks of the West Texas and Lubbock Railroad, though I saw no trains moving on them.

My destination for the day was Seminole. My uncle Hal lived in Midland, just 70 miles from Route 62, and we'd agreed to rendezvous in Seminole. Because of my car ride with Seven and Sheila, I would arrive there a day earlier than planned, but I had phoned Hal from Lubbock, and he had no problem switching days.

The journey from Lubbock to Seminole was 87 miles, most of it on four-lane highway. But unlike the frantic-paced expressways I encountered elsewhere, this one carried only moderate traffic. It was an enjoyable ride, with a light wind at my back. The land was flat and had a uniform prairie character for the whole way, but there were periodic agri-businesses — peanut processing plants, cotton gins, feed mills, irrigation equipment sales firms — and small towns to break the monotony. And after the stress of yesterday's storm, I was quite content to have an uneventful ride this day.

This section of the Great Plains, with Lubbock at its heart, is known as the Llano Estacado, which means "staked plain." In the 16th century, Spanish explorer Francisco Vasquez de Coronado found this grassland region so flat and lacking in landmarks that he marked his route through it with piles of bones and dung as guideposts for his return trip. Later explorers labeled the area part of the Great American Desert and predicted that it would remain forever uninhabited.

But once the area was opened to settlement, people did move in. Irrigation was introduced and the endless miles of grasslands that once supported huge herds of buffalo became agricultural lands. Eventually, discovery of oil and gas fields brought further development.

In Brownfield, the halfway point between Lubbock and Seminole, several highways intersect, including four routes of the Numbered Highway System and a major state route, so the town is rife with restaurants and motels. I ate lunch there, at last finding the spaghetti dinner I had been hungering for. Long-distance cycling burns so many calories that carbo-craving is a natural state. When I'm home, I like spaghetti now and then, but when cycling, pasta moves high on my list of favorites because of its carbohydrate concentration.

In midafternoon, I entered Gaines County at the small town of Seagraves. A sign at the county line declared Gaines County the number one producer of cotton, peanuts and oil in the state.

Later, out on the highway a little way above Seminole, a motorist heading the opposite direction tooted his horn at me. This was not particularly unusual; something similar happened every other day or so. I've never been sure what the motorists are trying to communicate. Many people have told me that they'd love to be doing what I was doing, so the tooting may simply be an expression of camaraderie. Or perhaps some drivers are fellow cyclists and the toot implies solidarity. In any case, I perceive the honks as friendly gestures.

But this time, the driver made a U-turn and pulled to the roadside ahead of me. It was my uncle Hal, my father's older brother.

He's 84, but only his white hair gives that away. Most mornings, he begins his day by running several miles. He's sharp and savvy, and retains the outgoing personality and people skills that made him a top-ranking professional fundraiser during his working years. Living several states apart, I didn't get to see him often, but I always found it enjoyable when I did.

He exited the car and after a quick hug, he asked if I'd be willing to cover the remaining few miles to Seminole in his car. After the exceptions I'd already made, this was a no-brainer. Besides, I was looking forward to spending time with Hal.

True to his smart business practices, Hal had arrived in Seminole, a town of 6,300 people, a few hours ahead of time and scouted things out. He'd determined which was the best motel and arranged for a room. Next, from the motel clerk, he solicited dining recommendations and received two. He checked the first of these out by eating lunch there, and decided it wasn't to his liking. So, after I'd showered and changed, he took me for dinner to the other establishment, where I had the most deluxe meal of my trip. Hal has a gift for drawing people out, and by the time we'd finished eating, he had captivated the young waitress, asking her about her life and work. He also flooded her with lavish praise of my bike endeavor. He told her so much about my previous cross-country trip that she ended up writing down the name of my book about it. Hal left her a generous tip.

We spent an enjoyable evening in conversation about family, my trip, Hal's life in Midland and life in general — the kind of small talk that is really the stuff of life. And after a comfortable night at the motel, Hal took me to breakfast. As to where to eat this first meal of the new day, he had gotten two additional recommendations. We selected one and walked in. It was a little diner, with most tables full. Every customer looked up startled when Hal boomed a hearty "Good morning," to the entire assemblage. Hal started his usual friendly banter with this waitress as well, and we received excellent service and her well wishes when we were finished. The time with Hal was great.

In Seminole, 62 turns directly west again, and aims for Hobbs, New Mexico. Pedaling beyond the Seminole city limits, I saw evidence to support the county's claim to be number one in oil production. There was field after field of oil wells, their pumps bobbing up and down like giant birds dipping for worms.

Next followed thousands of acres under irrigation. All of these used the "center pivot" setup, where a long arm of pipes with many nozzles is hung from a series of wheeled movable towers that slowly rotate around a well head in the center. A single rotation takes several hours, allowing time for the water to soak in uniformly over a large acreage.

Although these fields were being farmed, I couldn't see where the farmers lived. The few occupied areas along the way included an oil refinery and several agri-businesses, but hardly any houses.

Texas provides a "picnic area" at roadside halfway between Seminole and Hobbs, but like the previous ones I'd seen in the Lone Star state, it wasn't much more use than a place to get off the road. Most of these areas include a couple of picnic tables, each under a roof, but none offer what most travelers really need, restrooms. And with these areas being on the wide prairie, they don't even have a tree one can stand behind. For its anti-litter campaign, the state uses the motto, "Don't mess with Texas." For its picnic areas, it could be, "Don't mess IN Texas"!

The New Mexico border was marked with a bright yellow welcome sign, and as I rolled past it, I entered the Mountain Time zone. Minutes later, I was in Hobbs.

Chapter 16

From Hobbs, 62 plows across New Mexico's southeast corner and then re-enters Texas in that state's western extremity. Frontiersmen referred to this area as "The Shears," the region where whites found themselves between the blades of the Comanches and the Apaches. Before those tribes were subdued, whites who ventured into the area were considered either extremely brave or extremely careless.

Hobbs also marks a change in geography. The Llano Estacado ends in the vicinity of the community. Beyond it, I would enter the desert, where I would find out if I were extremely brave or extremely careless. The map showed nothing between Hobbs and Carlsbad. I'd asked a trucker if that were indeed the case. "There might be some jackrabbits," he had said. Maybe I would just be extremely lucky.

In town, 62 skirts the business district, but runs through the edge of the community. I stopped long enough to eat a quick lunch and purchase an extra bottle of water for the 70-mile stretch ahead.

Leaving Hobbs, I passed the county airport, and saw a building identified as the Confederate Air Force Flying Museum. It's an organization devoted to restoring and preserving World War II combat aircraft. The name dates back to 1957, when the group founders had acquired a few old planes. Upon arriving at the Texas airfield they were then using, the men discovered that as a joke, someone had painted a sign on the fuselage of one of the vintage planes, reading "Confederate Air Force." All the members were pleased with the name, saluted each other and decided it should stay.

Another sign near the airport, showing a glider plane, labeled Hobbs as the "Soaring Capital of the World."

The road to Carlsbad is a four-laner in excellent condition. A wide shoulder provided me a private lane for the entire run to Carlsbad. It ambled out across a hardscrabble and sagebrush terrain, real desert. No longer did I see irrigated fields, or crops of any sort. This was waste land in the usual meaning of the term, but to me, a resident of a green eastern state, it had a certain dry-land beauty. But it was clearly heartbreak land for anyone who might have tried to settle there.

A short way out of Hobbs I saw the first sign related to my final destination. It read, "El Paso, 223 miles." I also got another clue that the land I was entering held its own challenges. Two highway workers were making some repairs at the edge of the road. As I pedaled by their truck, one waved and shouted, "Good luck!"

Although the ride was long and offered remarkably similar scenery mile after mile, it was also uneventful. And it turned out that about halfway between the two towns, there was a small eatery, appropriately named the Halfway Café. I didn't need food, but did stop for a cold drink. A sign on the door announced that its bathrooms were for customers only. Since they were the only bathrooms for 70 miles, I imagined that usage requirement generated considerable business for the establishment.

From that point on, I began seeing signs of another sort of land use that was neither agriculture nor oil. Several chemical plants had set up shop on it. Periodically I'd see buildings or tanks off in the distance and occasional signs gave company names for chemical compacting plants.

But the most graphic evidence of how the land was being used were the several "lakes" along the road filled with a white, briny-looking substance. The surrounding area contains potash mines. Potash is an ingredient in fertilizer, and the pools were evaporation ponds, an element of the mining process. There are five potash-mining companies in the area, and that industry employs much of Carlsbad's work force. The community is known as the potash capital of the world.

The "waste" nature of the land also led to the region being selected for the construction of a Waste Isolation Pilot Project, a facility of the Department of Energy built to permanently store radioactive waste from the defense industry in salt beds 2,150 feet underground. More than two billion dollars were poured into the project over 20 years, but legal struggles kept the facility from opening for several years after its completion. But in 1999, the first shipment of waste arrived and operations began.

Those who say that there is "nothing out there" in the desert aren't correct, though little of what is there is designed to charm or comfort a traveler.

About 25 miles out from Carlsbad, I began seeing the purpled outline of mountains ahead of me. These were the Guadalupe Mountains, and 62 would eventually take me to them, but they were still more than 60 miles away.

This first day of riding across desert had gone well. The temperature had warmed a lot by midafternoon, but never became oppressive, and I arrived in Carlsbad feeling fine, though a little sunbaked.

Carlsbad, a city of 27,000, is a thriving community. And because of its low-tax structure, many people select it as a place to retire. In fact, a national magazine had recently designated it as among the top 20 best places to live in America from a retirement standpoint.

Wheeling into town, I crossed the Pecos River and proceeded through town to an RV campground, which, while adequate even for a tenter, charged a fee that made my stay the most expensive non-motel night of my entire trip. Mileage-wise, this was also my longest day; I'd ridden 102 miles.

At breakfast in a Carlsbad restaurant the next morning, I listened in to the small talk of the guys who shared the counter with me. One man was clearly a local and another the driver of the semi sitting outside. I figured they'd know about the road ahead.

"Excuse me." I said. "Are either of you familiar with Route 62 between Guadalupe Park and El Paso?" The two points were separated by 115 miles of desert.

"Sure," said the trucker. "What would you like to know?"

"I was wondering if there'll be anyplace to get water. I'm on a bicycle and I want to figure out how much I'll need to carry."

"There's a café at Cornudas," he said, referring to a spot roughly halfway between. "You can get water there."

The local man joined in. "Yeah, and you can get good food there too. They serve a hamburger this big." He held his hands far enough apart to suggest a Frisbee-sized meat patty. "When we go there, my wife and I order one hamburger between us, and sometimes we can't finish it."

I was glad to hear about the café. I already knew there'd be no services for a long way after I left Whites City, the next community down the line, but water would be available at Guadalupe Park. Someone back in Lubbock had told me there was absolutely nothing between there and El Paso, and that had me concerned. I wasn't worried about food; I could carry enough of that. But enough water for an extended desert crossing would amount to a lot of weight. Now, with both men certain about the café, my concern was alleviated.

My mention of the bicycle had gotten both men's attention, and they asked about my trip. They seemed especially impressed that I had pedaled the length of 62, even when I told them I'd done the first half the year before. I hit the road to the tune of their good wishes.

This day at morning was already as warm as the previous one had been at midday, but I pumped the bike easily over the 22 miles to Whites City. On the way, I noticed a change in the desert. Now, in addition to the sagebrush and hardscrabble, there began to be a lot of cactus, in several varieties.

I soon came to Whites City. When applied to that location, "city" is a euphemism for a small commercial settlement plopped down where a side road leaves 62 for the seven-mile trip to the entrance of Carlsbad Caverns. Whites City includes a couple of motels, some gift shops, a post office, a gas station and a small grocery. There must have been some housing for the service staff somewhere nearby, but I didn't see it.

I had given some thought to visiting the caverns. I was planning to ride only to the primitive campground at Guadalupe National Park this day, just 48 miles from Carlsbad, so I probably had time. But I wasn't crazy about adding a 14-mile round trip to the day, especially after I learned that the route into the caverns involved a long and steep upgrade. I knew I was already facing a stiff climb to the Park, and the day was even now plenty warm. With some reluctance, I decided to forego the visit. And the way the day played out, that proved to be the right decision.

From Whites City to the Guadalupe campground is 26 miles, and about halfway, I would re-enter Texas, dropping into the state's far western arm. As I headed for the border, the air temperature soared. With the sun directly overhead and nothing to throw shade, there was no escaping its intense rays. My arms, already a weathered brown, began to sting from the sun and turn red. Riding into the oven that the desert had become, I rolled on, but slowly. It was too hot to push fast or hard.

Eventually the Welcome to Texas sign hove into view. Just beyond the sign stood an old van with a worn travel trailer hitched behind. Above the trailer's rear window was a sign reading "Walk-N-Roll 99." When I stopped to take a photo of my bike by the state sign, a 40-something woman stepped out of the trailer, saw me and said hello. I wandered over. "You're getting really red out here in the sun," she said. "Why don't you come inside for a few minutes." A man sat immediately inside, and when he too invited me in, I accepted, grateful for the shade.

Inside, the woman introduced herself as Susan Hobbs. Her companion was David Large. "Walk-N-Roll" was an endeavor the pair had begun the year before as an informational and fundraising journey for Raynaud's — a circulatory disease — and glaucoma. With David following with the van and trailer, Susan was in-line skating from New York to California, and then from Vancouver to the Peace Bridge at Niagara Falls. They had not been successful soliciting sponsors, so they funded the project themselves. One potential sponsor told them they weren't "big enough" to receive funding, David said.

The pair was managing to raise consciousness about the two ailments as newspapers in the communities Susan skated through carried their story. David showed me a front-page photo and account about them that had appeared in the Carlsbad paper the previous day. With the heat, Susan was doing her skating in the morning and evening, and laying low in the middle of the day. She looked at my red arms, legs, ears and nose, and warned me to take the sun seriously. From previous experience I knew I'd be brown again by morning, but Susan looked skeptical. She was in the process of preparing lunch, and suggested I eat with them. "That will keep you out of the sun a while longer." she said.

Over sandwiches and cold drinks, I asked David how many sets of wheels Susan had worn out so far. "Nine," he said, "and 12 sets of bearings." She'd also fallen and skinned herself up a few times, but they were determined to complete the trip. Since they'd gotten this far from New York, I suspected they'd make it. I respected what they were doing and I told them so.

As I got ready to go, Susan insisted I take some aloe ointment with me to rub on my skin later. She found a small medicine container and filled it with aloe from a larger bottle. Susan was a gentle but determined woman, so I didn't argue. Both David and Susan suggested I stay longer until things cooled off, but I thought the few miles remaining would be doable. My normal preference is to get my work done first, and then rest. Holing up with miles yet to go went against my nature.

But as it turned out, I probably should have taken them up on the offer. As I chugged on, the day got hotter and the sun, if anything, became more intense. It became difficult to gauge my progress. In the distance, I could see El Capitan, a prominent landmark outcrop of the Guadalupes, but no matter how long I rode, it never seemed to get any closer. I knew, of course, that this was an illusion, common in the clear desert air, but the illusion worked. I seemed to be getting nowhere.

I desperately needed some shade, and for all the bad mouthing of Texas picnic areas I had done, I'd have given quite a lot at that moment to have one appear at the roadside. The roofed shelter over the picnic table would have cast a most welcome shadow.

And then, all at once, there *was* a picnic shelter, this one complete with restroom and a water fountain. I blinked to make sure it wasn't a mirage. I pulled in immediately, parked under a shelter, and stretched out on the table. It must have been at least 10 degrees cooler in the shade.

I stayed there for about an hour, drank lots of water and snacked on food from my saddlebags, until finally, I began to feel better. Though the day was still hot, the sun was no longer directly over-head. I calculated that I still had about 10 miles to the campground, and decided to head for it.

After the heat I'd endured before the rest stop, the temperature now, though still uncomfortably high, seemed more bearable. But I was now climbing. With the exception of a few dips, the entire 10 miles was up, and the added labor that required brought me back to the edge of heat exhaustion again and again. I combated that by stopping whenever I felt my body temperature get too high. Also, the highway now passed periodically through cuts in the rock, and now that the sun had passed its zenith, the rock walls were tall enough to cast shadows. In addition, as I gained altitude, there was an occasional roadside tree to throw a little shade. With all of this, the shady spots were still spaced widely apart, but whenever I came to one, I rested in the shadow. I made progress, but more slowly than I would have liked.

The campground was at the summit of the pass, which, a sign informed me, was 5,695 feet above sea level. That explained why I was having a harder time getting my breath — the air was thinner. Granted, 5,700 feet isn't that high, not if you normally live in, say, Denver, but my hometown is at 1,000 feet. The Llano Estacado had been a little over 3,000 feet, but I'd climbed to that gradually. Now I was puffing upward all at once. Without acclimatization, climbing to more than a mile high takes a toll.

My map showed a spot called Pine Springs nearby, which was not a town but merely a small cluster of housing for the park em-ployees. The camping area was across the road in a beautiful can-yon, a pocket formed by El Capitan, Guadalupe Peak (which at 8,749 feet, is the highest point in Texas) and the nearly as tall Hunter's Peak. All three were powerfully dominant, but it was easy to under-stand why El Capitan was given its name. Though not quite as high as the other two, and more a shear cliff than a peak, it thrust for-ward into the sky, a promontory seemly leading the adjacent pin-nacles into the magnificent desolation of the region. It was indeed "The Captain."

The national park campground offered a good choice of sites, all with breathtaking views of the surrounding mountains. I selected one, set up my tent, and then cooked supper on my camp stove. In the fading light, several small deer wandered the grounds, never getting too close to the campers, but not appearing afraid either.

I had worked hard to get to this location, but I felt a deep satisfaction about it. This was the most gorgeous spot I'd encountered along the entire length of 62, and it was worth every pedal stroke.

When the daylight was almost gone, two cyclists, with loads similar to mine, rolled into the campground. I gave them some time to get set up and then moseyed over. Before I could introduce myself, one of the young men asked, "Are you Stan?"

I was dumbfounded. "Yes. How did you know?"

"The skater-lady told us about you." Susan and David had entertained these two as well.

We talked for a few minutes while the two, Justus and Tyler, waited for their supper to cook (pasta with spaghetti sauce!). They were college students from Seattle, but had arranged enough time off for an extended bike tour. With the vigor of youth, they frequently covered 120 or more miles a day. They were planning to be in El Paso the following evening. I expected to arrive there the day after that.

We exchanged a few tales from our respective journeys. They had had one bad experience. While both were in a store in Louisiana, Tyler's bike was stolen. The pair notified the police, who responded quickly, apprehended the thief and rescued the bike unharmed. But in the thief's attempt to elude the police, he had thrown Tyler's saddlebags into a bog. The young men retrieved them, but had to do a lot of cleaning of the bags and their contents.

They hadn't let that incident sour them on the trip, though. These young men were having the time of their lives.

I was up early the next morning, but Justus and Tyler were already gone. I cooked my breakfast and packed up. The air was warm even then. Before leaving the park, I browsed for a few minutes in the Visitor Center, looking at the displays that told the geological history of the mountains. A park ranger who asked about my journey told me that in addition to the Cornudas Café, I'd also find a place to eat at Salt Flat, about halfway between the park and Cornudas.

A footpath near the Visitor Center led me to an old stone wall, the remains of a Butterfield stage station — the highest station on the Butterfield route. As I mentioned previously, 62 had touched the Butterfield route back in Arkansas. It did so again here, but in between, they had pursued different paths.

The first 10 miles of the day's ride was downhill, and I hit speeds as high as 37 mph. This side of the pass was even more barren than the north side, but also provided grandly majestic views of the mountains. The road here was also considerably steeper than the approach from the north had been, so I was glad I was not riding this journey in the opposite direction.

Throughout the trip downhill and for at least another 10 miles after that, El Capitan remained fully visible from one and then another and then another perspective. In fact, the headland dominated the landscape like a sentinel in every direction. El Capitan was one powerful piece of geography. A sign beside the highway declared that 62 now possessed an additional name, the Texas Mountain Trail. The reason was evident all around me. In addition to the Guadalupes behind me, there were also mountain ranges in the distance on both my left and right.

From a vantage point partway down the mountain, I had been able to see the desert stretched out ahead, between these ranges. Also visible in the far distance as a white band across the land were the salt flats. Once I was down on the level ground, I lost sight of them for a while, but eventually I spied them again, spread across the terrain ahead, a stark irregularity on an already stark land. They appeared to be close at hand, but that was another desert illusion. I did finally come to them, and followed 62 across them, but only after several more miles of pedaling.

For centuries, native peoples of the surrounding area had taken salt from the flats as needed, but in 1877, one Charles Howard filed claim to the flats and imposed a fee for the salt. This invoked bitter resentment from villagers who said the salt had always been theirs, and they threatened to take the salt without payment. The resulting conflict, known as the El Paso Salt War, cost several lives. It ended when Howard and two companions were shot to death by an armed mob.

By noon, I had crossed the salty band and come to the spot that bore the name Salt Flat. The entire place consisted of a café with a couple of houses behind it, and a little farther on, an RV park, which was little more than a parking lot in the desert. A sign on the café door reminded all who entered that restrooms were for customers only. No problem; I fully intended to be a customer.

A young woman operated the place, assisted by an older woman who spoke mostly in Spanish. This was a good arrangement, for while I was there, a customer came in who spoke only Spanish. Both women were pleasant, and the meal was excellent. A girl of about 11, apparently the younger woman's daughter, was also behind the counter. I asked her if she lived in one of the houses behind the café. She did. How did she like living way out there so far from everything? She liked it just fine, she said.

The little café was air conditioned, though it wasn't cooling the place very well, but when I stepped outside after eating, the heat hit me like a fist. After my experience with the afternoon heat the previous day, I was tempted to go back inside and wait out the midday sun. But today, I wasn't facing a climb, and I had a slight tailwind. Besides, I didn't relish spending six hours in the café, no matter how congenial the staff. Still, I was surprised how much the day had heated up while I'd been eating.

It was 28 miles to the Cornudas Café, and for the first 10 or so, things went smoothly despite the heat. I even found another café no one had mentioned. It was tiny and shabby, but the cold drink I purchased there from a man who reminded me of Popeye in both appearance and speech tasted good. Before I left, he warned me not to die in the heat. He even followed me outside to say, "If you kill yourself, I'll never forgive you," and sauntered back inside yuk, yuk, yukking at his own strange humor.

Cycling through this inhospitable land, I was surprised to come upon mile after mile of signs announcing 10-acre lots available for sale. Additional signage advised that the property could be had for $95 down, $105 a month. Electric and telephone service was also available, the signs said. I noticed, however, that none said anything about water. Who would settle out here? I wondered. Not many, apparently, for none of the parcels were homesteaded.

Soon after my cold drink stop, the wind reversed and strengthened, and I found myself battling a headwind. Having to work against that in the heat soon had me feeling unwell, and when, despite the temperature, I started shivering, I knew I was headed for heat exhaustion. I needed to get out of the sun. The only problem was, there was nowhere to do that, and nothing tall enough to cast shade. I still had water, but it was so warm that it offered no refreshment.

Having no other choice, I pushed on through what became the longest couple of hours in my cycling experience. As I became weaker, my progress slowed to a crawl, and I began to think I could not go on. Just as I felt near the end of my resources, I crested a small upgrade. There, a downhill mile ahead, was the Cornudas Café. I pushed on the pedals to start the bike in motion, and coasted down to it as eagerly as if I were a crusader and it were the Holy Grail.

Arriving at last, I limped in, headed straight for the cold case, and grabbed an icy drink. Then I wobbled toward a table, gulping the beverage as I dropped into the chair. Finally, my initial thirst slaked, I looked around.

The place was a unique sanctuary. Several hundred hats, each bearing the name of a different farm implement dealer, trucking firm or other industry hung from the ceiling — gifts from customers, I later learned. The walls were covered with correspondence the café staff had received from people who had written after visiting the restaurant. The legs of the tables had been covered with the pantlegs from blue jeans, each ending in a pair of boots. The table tops were covered with clear plastic tablecloths, and under these, satisfied customers had shoved napkins on which they'd written complimentary notes about the food and service of the café, or other thoughts of the moment. An adjoining room was a gift shop, stocked with high-quality crafts and mementos. The building also included some motel rooms, and there was an RV park out back. The compound comprised all there was of Cornudas, so the woman who owned the place was known as "Mayor May." She was also the cook.

When I entered the cafe, I noticed a Wal-Mart semi on the highway shoulder outside. The driver, easily recognizable in his official Wal-Mart shirt, was seated at a table eating a sandwich. I had seen Wal-Mart tractor-trailers on 62 frequently across Oklahoma, but all across Texas, it seemed as if every third 18-wheeler in either direction bore the Wal-Mart name. I struck up a conversation with the driver, who invited me to join him at his table. He told me that the discount store giant had 6,000 trucks in its fleet. Most of the big rigs were busy shuttling goods from Wal-Mart warehouses to regional distribution centers. From there, local trucks disbursed the products to the area Wal-Mart stores.

I gathered he ate at Cornudas often. "The food is great and the atmosphere is friendly," he said. "Also, it's one of the few places where there's room to park the truck. There are a lot of places I can't get into."

In addition to May, who appeared to be in her 60s, there was another woman of similar age working there. When I mentioned to the driver the 10-acre desert lots I'd seen for sale, he pointed to this second woman and said, "There's the person you should ask. She runs cattle on some of that land."

The woman overheard the comment and came over. She was Mary Foster. She and her husband had been ranchers, and when he died, she continued to run the ranch, working in the café in the afternoons. Her daughter and grandson helped with the ranch. I repeated my comment about the land for sale. "It's a scam," Mary said vehemently. "A lot of Mexican immigrants get caught in it. They hear they can have a homestead out there with easy financing. When they finally figure out what a bad deal it is, they give it up, and the same land gets sold again."

"I noticed the signs said there was electric and telephone, but none mentioned water," I said.

"Yes, but a lot of people don't notice that until too late. And even the business about electric is deceptive. Unless your land happens to be right under where the power line crosses, it costs thousands of dollars to run it to where you are."

"I didn't notice any houses at all. Does anyone stay?"

"Oh, a few do. They'll put up a shack. And then they have to have water hauled in. Most who try don't stick it out too long. The only reason we've been able to live at the ranch is because we drilled an 800-foot well. And the well here," she said, indicating the café, "is 1000 feet deep. Few people starting out can afford that type of investment. These people end up paying $175 an acre for land we wouldn't pay more than $5 an acre for. There's so little grass on the land that you need lots of acres for each cow out here, so you can't pay more than that."

"How many acres do you need per cow?"

"It takes 640 acres to feed 10 cows. Between owning and leasing, I have 70,000 acres, and I'm running 400 cows."

"Longhorns?" I asked.

"No, we have to raise what beef buyers are looking for, and that changes from time to time. Nobody wants longhorns now. I'm currently raising Angus, Limousines and Charolais."

"With that much land, how do you roundup your cattle?"

"We do it in sections. My grandson brings some of his high school friends. They've all been raised on ranches and know what to do."

I spent three hours at the café, sitting at a table, catching up on my notes, and finally, eating an excellent dinner — or at least part of an excellent dinner. The servings were Texas sized, and though I made a heroic attempt, there was no way I could finish them. Neither May nor Mary seemed bothered in the least that I hung around so long.

At one point a 60-ish couple came in, apparently to use the bathroom, but evidently they weren't clear on the meaning of "customer." They quizzed Mary about it, who explained that they could purchase anything. The pair then had a huddled discussion and asked to see a menu. They inquired about several items of food and finally each ordered pie and ice cream. Only after they had been served and had eaten did they head for the restrooms. I wondered if they were holding it all that time thinking they had to complete being customers before they were allowed to use the facilities!

A little after 6, I decided to resume riding. According to the café's thermometer, the air had only dropped to 91 degrees, but the sun was no longer directly overhead and the air would cool more as the sun set. Mary told me of a picnic shelter about 20 miles farther on, and I decided to make for it.

It was a good plan. The day cooled quickly, making twilight riding very comfortable. My progress was still slow, thanks to the constant headwind, but I felt good. My only concern came when the sun had fully set. There was no visible moon, and the night became very dark, so black that I envisioned riding right past the picnic area without knowing it. The traffic was light, so only occasionally was I helped by the headlights of a passing vehicle. Once I could no longer see more than a few feet ahead, I got out my flashlight, and at every highway sign I passed, I flicked it on to read what the sign said. The first several signs merely confirmed that I was indeed traveling 62 and that the speed limit was 65, but just as I was beginning to think I was going to have to camp on the hardscrabble at roadside, I came to a sign announcing the picnic area one mile ahead. Even with this advance notice, I could easily have missed the rest area had it not been for the glowing amber lights of a semi idling in the parking lot. I aimed for the truck, and as I drew near, my flashlight beam illuminated a picnic shelter. In minutes I had my air mattress and sleeping bag unrolled next to the table, and I settled down to sleep.

Almost right away, I had to make an adjustment. The wind that had impeded my riding continued to blow, and without thinking about it, I had positioned my sleeping bag with the open end toward the wind. The now cool breeze kept invading the bag, chilling me. So I turned the bag 180 degrees aiming the closed foot end into the wind, and with that, climbed back into the bag and snuggled into the arms of Morpheus.

Occasionally throughout the night, I awoke momentarily as trucks pulled in or out of the area, but the sounds were not bothersome, and I had a restful sleep.

At dawn, the wind still blew from the west, but I felt like a new man. Only one truck — a Wal-Mart unit — remained in the rest area, but I saw no one moving in the cab.

I fired up my stove to make breakfast, and while it cooked, I packed up my gear. Just as I was ready to leave, the driver emerged from the truck, a large man carrying a Colman stove. He proceeded to the other table and began heating coffee. I stopped to say good morning as I walked my bike toward the highway, and the driver offered me a cup. Since I'd already eaten, I declined, but I lingered for a few minutes to answer his questions about my trip. He also told me a little more about why I saw so many Wal-Mart trucks. "We double team a lot of them. One guy will drive it for a few days, and when he gets his time off, another driver uses the same truck. So they don't stay off the road for long."

The morning was warm but not hot, and I worked into the wind without problem. After I'd been on the road about 20 minutes, a truck passed and gave me a light toot of the horn. It was my buddy from the rest area, and I waved. Later, just before noon, he passed me again near El Paso, this time heading back the other way. He tapped his horn again and waved.

The land now had some undulations — no serious climbing, but enough variation to make the ride interesting and add contour to the landscape.

About 30 miles out from El Paso, I began seeing shacks and beat-up mobile homes spread over the hills with dirt roads leading to them. These dusty tracks were identified as "streets" with signs as grand as any you'd see in an upscale suburban neighborhood. They bore names like Sunset Boulevard, Sunshine Place and Moonbeam Street, and the whole business reeked of some shyster realtor trying to convince low-income people that they were really getting something valuable when they purchased a lot. More realistic designations might include Mule Dung Alley, Ripped T-Shirt Trail and Underbelly Strip. The grandiose naming continued on the other side of the highway where a swarm of tarpaper dwellings was identified as "Mountain Estates."

Near those was a Border Patrol station and checkpoint. Orange pylons placed in the eastbound lane caused traffic heading that way to slow. Then a Border Patrol officer either waved the occupants on or instructed them to stop for questioning. There wasn't much traffic to occupy him, so I asked the officer why they were checking here, 30 miles from the border. He explained that some people who slip into the country illegally manage to hitch a ride, thinking they have evaded the Patrol. This interior checkpoint catches some of them.

When I told him I was heading for El Paso, he pointed to the top of the next rise on the highway. "When you get over that," he said, "it will be downhill all the way there."

He was right. After I crested the hump, I found myself sailing down a pass between mountains. The Texas Mountain Trail had mountains at this end as well. The downgrade continued sharply for several miles and then became less steep, eventually appearing almost level. But judging from how easily the bike rolled, I could tell I was still descending.

Within the hour, I would arrive in El Paso. Route 62 had conveyed me all the way there from Niagara Falls. But even as I completed this journey on a route of the U.S. Numbered Highway System, I wondered how much longer the system would function. For years, its routes had been considered the most important in the country, but this gradually changed as segments of the Interstate System were completed. And in some places, the construction of major state routes siphoned traffic off the U.S. Numbered Highways as well. Now these changes were reflected in federal rules regulating commercial motor vehicles. A 1982 transportation act required the states to identify routes for use by larger-dimensioned vehicles without regard to any numbering system.

Then, in 1995, prompted by a mandate in the Intermodal Surface Transportation Efficiency Act of 1991, the Department of Transportation proposed a new nationwide plan: a 161,108-mile National Highway System (NHS). Unlike the Interstate Highway program, the NHS does not call for the building of new roads, but the designation of a new set of routes to better serve today's traffic needs.

The NHS, under development as I write, consists of the most important rural and urban roads and streets in the nation, including the Interstate System and other principal arterials. Although the NHS includes a mere four percent of total rural and urban highways, it serves about 42 percent of total highway vehicle travel, and significantly, nearly 70 percent of commercial vehicle travel. In addition to the Interstate System, the NHS includes some, but not all of the U.S. Numbered Routes. It also uses important State routes and even some unnumbered roads and streets, especially in urban areas. Thus the new system sprawls across the spectrum of existing route numbering systems.

Although I was still several miles from the city limits, I felt as if I had already arrived, for tentacles of the city had snaked well beyond the official boundary. El Paso itself, the 22nd largest city in America, has 600,000 people, but the whole metropolitan area, including Juarez on the Mexican side of the river, has 1.7 million. As I rode on toward the city, 62 became a business strip serving the population of this growing metroplex. The most outlying of these businesses aimed at a Spanish-speaking clientele, often with hand-painted signs. The closer I got to the city, the more mainstream-looking the establishments became.

The outreaching city was growing right over the foothills of the mountain range, and "over" is the right word. I saw a couple of the mini mountains that were in the process of being torn down, presumably for gravel and rock, but it also made more space.

When I finally hit the actual city limits of El Paso, I still had eight city miles left on 62, which runs right to the U.S-Mexican border at the Rio Grand.

Somewhere in El Paso, 62 crosses what was once the path of El Camino Real de Tierra Adentro — the Royal Highway of the Interior Land. This old road, running some 1,800 miles from Mexico City to Santa Fe, claims fame as the first highway in North America built by Europeans, though for much of its distance, it took advantage of trails already in use by indigenous peoples. Spaniards began to use the route that would become El Camino Real soon after Hernán Cortés conquered Mexico in the 1520s. The first well-documented trip over its length was in 1598.

In 1610, Santa Fe was established as the capital of the Spanish province of New Mexico, and for the next three centuries, the Camino Real was the main corridor between Old and New Mexico. Commerce, colonization, missionary supply, military campaigns and travel took place over its route.

In 1821, two events boosted the importance of the Camino Real even more. First, Mexico gained its independence from Spain, making trade with the fledging United States more important. Second, the Santa Fe Trail was set up between Santa Fe and Independence, Missouri, meaning there was now a continuous trade route all the way from Mexico City to the interior of the United States.

With the building of the railroads along the route in 1882, the use of El Camino Real began to decline. Later still, it was replaced by modern roads. Today, although perhaps a third of the old El Camino Real still exists as ruts and traces, its route is paralleled by the Panamerican Highway of Mexico, Interstate 10 from El Paso to Las Cruces and Interstate 25 from Las Cruces to Santa Fe.

I entered El Paso proper about 11:30, and the day was starting to cook. After miles of empty country, the sprawling city seemed distasteful to me — too crowded, too busy, too noisy, too jarring. But this was yet another of 62's identities, and I meant to know them all, so I pursued the highway, mile after urban mile, aiming toward the river.

The closer I got, the more Spanish the districts became, until finally, a couple blocks before the border, I encountered a steady flow of people walking from the bridge from Ciudad Juarez, El Paso's Mexican sister.

And then, after riding Route 62 for nearly 2,300 miles, I lost it a half mile from its terminus. For the last couple of miles, 62 had been paralleling the river. Then, according to my map, 62 makes a left turn and runs on a one-way street a few blocks to the river crossing. At the turn, the city street 62 was following becomes U.S 85. I had been watching for a sign announcing the turn, but if the sign existed, I missed it. All I know is that when I next spotted a highway sign, I was on 85. I turned around and retraced my path all the way back to the last 62 sign, but still saw no marked turn. I turned around again but even on this third pass, I saw no indication of where 62 branched off. Finally, I stopped at a street with an arrow sign pointing down it reading "Footbridge to Mexico." This street, however, was one-way *away* from the river. It was probably the return lane of 62, though no sign confirmed that. The traffic on this street, both vehicle and pedestrian, was so thick that riding down it the wrong way was out of the question.

I moved over to the next street paralleling the one-way thoroughfare. If my map was right, this should have been the one-way street *toward* the river, but it was not. Exasperated, and growing extremely uncomfortable under the broiling sun, I maneuvered down this avenue toward the river. It did not take me to the bridge. Instead, it dumped me out on a road passing under the bridge. I followed this, made a right at the next turn and then cut through a parking lot and at last found myself at the bridge at the end of the first one-way street. I was still without proof that this was the long sought after endpoint of 62, but I reasoned that it had to be. There were no other bridges.

In the end, I declared it to be.

And so, for me, it was, and is, and always will be, now and forevermore.

A Guide to Route 62

For the most part, all you need for following Route 62 are ordinary highway maps of the 10 states through which 62 passes. However, if you are on a bicycle, there are a few places where you have to leave 62 because it joins Interstate highways where bikes are not permitted. There are also a few places where scenic alternatives are warranted. These directions, made from my notes while on the trip, were accurate at the time, but because streets and roads are rerouted from time to time and highway signs get knocked down, it's always a good idea to check with local residents before heading off on a bypass. Besides, that gives you a great excuse to talk to people and learn about the area.

All routes described are from north to south. All mileages are approximate.

Sharon, Pennsylvania

East of Sharon, 62-Business splits off from the main route, which bypasses downtown Sharon. The business route goes through a long commercial strip of stores and restaurants and then right down the main street of town. It next doubles back on a parallel street and rejoins the main route. The business route is four miles long. The regular route is three but sees a lot of truck traffic. Cyclists can use either one, but I recommend the business route.

Youngstown, Ohio

In Youngstown, 62 briefly joins I-680, an Interstate route. Use the following alternative:

Route 62 enters Youngstown on Hubbard Road, which becomes Albert Street in town. Continue on Albert for about a mile. Watch for McGuffy Road, which crosses Albert. Turn right on McGuffy, ride to the top of the hill and turn left on Wick Avenue. After passing through the center city, continue straight on across the bridge over the Mahoning

River. On the south side of the bridge, the street name changes to Market Street and the bridge itself is referred to as "Market Street Bridge." Route 62 joins Market Street shortly after the bridge, although you may not see any 62 signs until the next turn. Continue straight on Market for approximately a mile and half. Turn right on Indianola. This turn is marked with a Route 62 sign. Continue to follow the 62 signs out of town.

A scenic alternative in Youngstown

This route is in Mill Creek Park, through which I could have ridden as a scenic alternative to Youngstown's south side. I chose not to use it because I had formerly lived in the area and had ridden in the park many times, but the park is a slice of wilderness beauty that offers a complete change of environment to the city ride.

The park follows a rugged six-mile-long wilderness gorge — an exceptionally beautiful wilderness park that is a pleasant surprise in the midst of the city. Riding through the park allows you to skip the entire south side of Youngstown.

To use this alternative, follow the directions given above until the Market Street Bridge. Then, instead of crossing the bridge, turn right on Front Street immediately before the bridge. After three blocks, turn left onto a steel bridge and then proceed through the underpass beyond it. You will be on Marshall Avenue. Continue one more block and turn right on Hogue. Go one block and then turn left on Mahoning Avenue. Proceed on Mahoning several blocks to Glenwood Avenue. Turn left on Glenwood, cross the Interstate on an overpass and turn right into Mill Creek Park. You will be on East Glacier Drive, although you may not see any road signs. Once in the park, there is a paved road on each side of the creek (which widens into small lakes at a couple of places), and it doesn't matter which one you use, as both will bring you out on 62 (a couple of bridges within park let you cross back and forth across the creek. Simply stay on the roads that meander through the gorge, avoiding the occasional cross roads that lead out of the park. Eventually you will intersect with Canfield Road, which crosses the gorge on a high bridge. Canfield is also 62. If you are on the east side of the gorge, you'll see a sign for Lanterman's Mill parking area right before Canfield Road. (By the way, the mill, built in 1845 and now fully restored, is well worth seeing. It's actually on the far side of Canfield Road, but a path from the parking lot will take you under the road.) The park roads do continue beyond Canfield Road, but you need to turn right on Canfield, and you'll be back on 62.

Salem, Ohio

Route 62 used to go through Salem but now bypasses it on a four-lane road that is less interesting than riding through the community. To ride "old 62" instead of turning right onto the four-lane, simply proceed straight ahead into Salem — the road becomes Lincoln Avenue. When you hit State Street, turn right and keep riding. You will eventually rejoin current 62.

Alliance through Canton, Ohio

Restrictions for cyclists begin on the west edge of Alliance where 62 turns onto a high-speed four-lane highway. In Canton, 62 joins I-77 and then Route 30, both of which do not permit cyclists. Instead, use the following route, which was the path of 62 before the four-lane superslabs were built:

At the west edge of Alliance, continue straight on State Street (also marked Route 173). After 2.75 miles, 173 proceeds straight ahead but the main highway curves left, becoming Columbus Road. Follow Columbus Road 10.5 miles until it merges with 62, which is unrestricted at this point, but very heavily traveled. Exercise extra caution. Follow 62 for 1.25 miles. (You will cross a bridge over a railroad track and a small stream). Watch for the exit marked "Market Ave. Route 43" which will be straight ahead. Take this exit. (Bicycles are restricted on 62 beyond this exit.) This becomes 30st Street N.E. Follow it one block to a major intersection and traffic light. Turn left there onto Market Avenue.* Follow this for 2.75 miles to Navarre Road S.W. (also marked 11th Street S.E.). Turn right onto Navarre Road and follow it for approximately two miles to where it empties onto 17th Street S.W. Turn right onto 17th and continue straight across Raff Avenue. 17th becomes Southway Avenue as you cross Raff. Continue one-half mile to the next

---

*The exit ramp is one way only. Northbound riders should use these directions after turning right from Market Avenue onto 30th: Stay on 30th Street as it makes a left turn onto Martindale. Go one block north and turn right on 31st Street. At the first stop sign, turn right onto Rowland N.E. Go to the traffic light and there turn left onto 62.

light. Turn left on Whipple. Go under U.S. 62, which is still restricted. Turn right at the next light. This is the resumption of Navarre Road. Stay on Navarre Road for about five miles to Erie Avenue. Turn left on Erie. You are now back on 62.

An attraction-laden side trip in Canton

Use the following directions to visit the Football Hall of Fame and the McKinley Memorial and Museum. This route will also take you through two attractive city parks.

To use this alternative, follow the directions given above to Market Avenue. Proceed south on Market to 25th Street. Turn right onto 25th and follow it until it ends on Fulton Drive, a four-lane street. Turn right onto Fulton and go one block. Turn left onto Stadium Park Drive. Take the first right turn, which will take you immediately under I-77 and directly to the Football Hall of Fame, a distance of about one block.

From the Hall of Fame, retrace your route one block to Stadium Park Drive and turn right. Follow Stadium Park Drive straight across 12th Street into Monument Park. Continue through Monument Park to the McKinley Memorial, which will be on your right. The Museum is directly to the left of the Memorial.

Leaving the Memorial, return to Monument Park Drive and continue on it to 7th Street. Turn right on 7th. Go two blocks and turn left on Hazlett. Go two blocks and turn right on 4th Street. Follow 4th across I-77 on a bridge. Immediately after the bridge, turn left onto Harrison Avenue. Proceed several blocks on Harrison to Navarre Road. Turn right onto Navarre. You are now back on the bypass route described above.

Killbuck, Ohio

Route 62 has been relocated to bypass Killbuck. You can easily stay on the main road, but I found the old route more interesting. When you leave Millersburg, Route 62 and Ohio Route 83 run together. A few miles south of Millersburg, 62 turns right and 83 continues straight. From that split, ride 62 about four miles, and watch for County Road 622 splitting off on your right (there should also be a "Killbuck, 1 mile" sign at that juncture). Follow 622 into Killbuck, where 622 becomes Main Street. At the central four-way stop, turn right onto Front Street. Follow this just over a block to the bridge and continue straight across the bridge. Front Street becomes County Road 621 at the bridge. Follow 621 until it ends on Ohio Route 520, a distance of about one-fourth mile. Turn left onto 520 and follow it about a mile until it rejoins current 62.

Columbus, Ohio

In Columbus, Route 62 joins I-670 for about four miles. Instead, use the following passage:

At the community of Gahanna, just northeast of Columbus, Route 62 makes a right turn and crosses a bridge over Big Walnut Creek. Get into the left turn lane and turn left at the traffic light onto Old Ridenour Road. After one block, turn right onto Johnstown Road, which is old 62. Follow this to Steltzer Road. Turn left onto Steltzer and take it about 2.5 miles to Broad Street (also marked Ohio Route 16 and U.S. Route 40). Turn right onto Broad, which is the main east-west street through Columbus. Follow Broad about six miles, straight through the heart of the city. Route 62 joins Broad for part of this stretch but leaves it again before the bridge over the Scioto River. I suggest you remain on Broad Street however. About 1.5 miles after crossing the bridge, turn left onto Central, which, after a few blocks, becomes 62.

Fayetteville, Arkansas

Routes 62 and 102 run concurrently through Rogers. When 62 turns onto 71 (on which bicycles are prohibited), continue straight on 102 to 112. Turn left onto 112 to South Walton Boulevard (which is 71B and 12). Turn right onto this road. When 71B veers to the right, stay on 12 to the lower portion of 112. Turn left onto 112. Take 112 all the way to Fayetteville where it intersects 62 (which is W. Sixth Street in Fayetteville). Turn right on 62.

Okmulgee-Henryetta-Okemah, Oklahoma

Route 62 is a bicycle-forbidding freeway from Okmulgee to Henryetta. From Henryetta to Okemah, 62 runs on Interstate-40, also closed to bicycles. By asking directions in Henryetta, I found a pleasant but wandering back route from Okmulgee to Henryetta, which, unfortunately, I did not record, but the road from Henryetta to Okemah, (which is old 62) was so broken up that it was very difficult and jarring riding, and I do not recommend it. (If you want to take it anyway, it leaves Henryetta as Hornbeam Road, and seems to change names a few times, but is a straight, continuous road to Okemah.)

The best bicycle alternative is probably to head west out of Okmulgee on State Route 56, passing though Park Wheeler Corner, Okfuskee and Haydenville. Eventually 56 turns south and brings you to Okemah, where you can rejoin Route 62. The mileage should be approximately the same as if you had stayed on 62.

Oklahoma City, Oklahoma

As I explain in the text, even a longtime resident of Oklahoma City could not think of a way for me on a bicycle to get out of that community that would put me anywhere near Route 62. I needed to cross the Canadian River but the two bridges over it are both Interstates. In the end, he arranged for me to be driven across the river. Short of a huge detour way to the north or way to the south of Oklahoma City, there seems no other alternative.

One suggestion: Use the Internet to locate an area bike club or bike shop and contact them, explaining when you are coming through. More than likely, someone in the club or the shop will help a fellow cyclist and drive you across the river.

Lawton, Oklahoma

About five miles north of Lawton, Route 62 drops onto I-44, a route closed to bicycles, but here there is a wonderful alternative that takes you through the Wichita Mountains Wildlife Refuge. As you are nearing Lawton on 62, watch for Meers Porter Hill Road, a right turn (west) off of 62. Stay on Meers Porter Hill Road until it meets Stony Point Road. Jog south on Stony Point to E 1540 Road, which continues west. After you cross State Route 58, E 1540 becomes Meers Road. Follow it to the tiny community of Meers. Turn south on Route 115 to Route 62. Because I was driven through this bypass, I was unable to record mileages, but the total miles on the bypass should be about the same as if you had been able to stay on 62.

For Further Reading

In addition to the sources listed here, some of the historical and place information in this book came from community websites, pamphlets obtained at the locations and newspaper archives, as well as from conversations with people who live or work along U.S. Route 62.

America's Highways 1776-1976: A History of the Federal-Aid Program (Washington, D.C.: U.S. Department of Transportation, Federal Highway Administration, n.d., Stock No. 050-001-00123-3).

Butler, John L., *First Highways of America* (Iola, Wis.: Krause Publications, 1994).

Butterfield, Jim, *Driving the Amish* (Scottdale, Penn.: Herald Press, 1997).

Cantor, George, *Old Roads of the Midwest* (Ann Arbor: The University of Michigan Press, 1997).

Davis, William C., *A Way Through the Wilderness: The Natchez Trace and the Civilization of the Southern Frontier* (New York: HarperCollins, 1995).

Dunlop, Richard, *Great Trails of the West* (Nashville: Abingdon Press, 1971).

Eyewitness to the American West (New York: Viking, 1998), David Colbert, ed.

Federal Writers' Project of the Works Project Administration, *Arkansas: A Guide to the State* (New York: Hastings House, 1941). Sponsored by the Arkansas State Planning Board.

Federal Writers' Project of the Works Project Administration, *Kentucky: A Guide to the Bluegrass State* (New York: Hastings House, 1939). Sponsored by the University of Kentucky.

Federal Writers' Project of the Works Project Administration, *New Mexico: A Guide to the Colorful State* New, Completely Revised Edition (New York: Hastings House, 1940, 1962). Sponsored by the University of New Mexico.

Federal Writers' Project of the Works Project Administration, *Oklahoma: A Guide to the Sooner State* Second Edition (Norman, Okla.: University of Oklahoma Press, 1941, 1955). Sponsored by the University of Oklahoma.

Federal Writers' Project of the Works Project Administration, *Pennsylvania: A Guide to the Keystone State* (New York: Oxford University Press, 1940). Co-sponsored by the Pennsylvania Historical Commission and the University of Pennsylvania.

Federal Writers' Project of the Works Project Administration, *Texas: A Guide to the Lone Star State* (New York: Hastings House, 1940). Sponsored by the Texas State Highway Commission.

Fleishman, Glen, *The Cherokee Removal, 1838: An Entire Indian Nation Is Forced Out of Its Homeland* (New York: Franklin Watts, Inc., 1971).

Forester, John, *Effective Cycling*, (Cambridge, Mass.: The MIT Press, 1993) 6th Edition.

Good, Merle, *Who Are the Amish?* (Intercourse, Penn.: Good Books, 1985)

Guthrie, Woody, *Pastures of Plenty: A Self-Portrait* (New York: HarperCollins, 1990), Dave Marsh and Harold Leventhal, eds.

Hickerson, Thomas F., *Route Location and Design*, Fifth Edition, (New York: McGraw-Hill Book Company, 1964).

Hokanson, Drake, *The Lincoln Highway: Main Street Across America* (Iowa City: University of Iowa Press, 1988).

Hurt, R. Douglas, *The Ohio Frontier: Crucible of the Old Northwest 1720-1830* (Bloomington, In.: Indiana University Press, 1996).

Jensen, Jamie, *Road Trip USA: Cross-Country Adventures on America's Two-Lane Highways* (Chico, Calif.: Moon Publications, Inc., 1999) Second Edition.

Kincaid, Robert L., *The Wilderness Road* (Indianapolis: The Bobbs-Merrill Company, 1947).

Klein. Joe, *Woody Guthrie: A Life* (New York: Alfred A. Knopf, 1980).

Labatut, Jean, and Lane, Wheaton J., eds., *Highways in Our National Life: A Symposium* (Princeton, N.J.: Princeton University Press, 1950).

Lewis, Tom, *Divided Highways: Building the Interstate Highways; Transforming American Life* (New York: Viking, 1997).

Loomis, Noel M., *Wells Fargo: An Illustrated History* (New York: Clarkson N. Potter, Inc., 1968).

McClain, Meredith, "The Alluring Myth of the Desert: European Fascination with the Llano Estacado," *Desert Development: The Endless Frontier. Proceedings of the Fifth International Conference on Desert Development* Vol. II (Lubbock, Tex.: Texas Tech Press, 1999) Traylor, Dregne, and Mathis, eds, 930-937.

Morgan, James, *The Distance to the Moon: A Road Trip Into the American Dream* (New York: Riverhead Books, 1999).

Observing the 175th Anniversary of the Evangelical Friends Church — Eastern Region (Canton, Ohio: Evangelical Friends Church — Eastern Region, 1987).

Patton, Phil, *Open Road: A Celebration of the American Highway* (New York: Simon and Schuster, 1986).

Pelta, Kathy, *The Royal Roads: Spanish Trails in North America* (Austin, Tex.: Raintree Steck-Vaughn Publishers, 1997).

Quaker Sesqui-Centennial 1812-1962 (Damascus, Ohio: The Friends Church, Ohio Yearly Meeting, 1962).

Rae, John Bell, *The Road and the Car in American Life* (Cambridge, Mass.: MIT Press, 1971).

Richardson, Rupert Norvel, *Texas: The Lone Star State*, 2nd Edition (Englewood Cliffs, N.J.: Prentice-Hall, 1958).

Schneider, Norris F., *The National Road: Main Street of America* (Columbus, Ohio: The Ohio Historical Society, 1975).

Schneider, Norris F. and Stebbins, Clair C., *Zane's Trace: The First Road in Ohio* (Zanesville, Ohio: Mathes Printing Company, 1973).

Scott, Quinta and Kelly, Susan Croce, *Route 66: The Highway and Its People* (Norman, Okla.: University of Oklahoma Press, 1988).

Sherwood Anderson's Winesburg, Ohio: With Variant Readings and Annotations, Ray Lewis White, ed. (Athens, Ohio: Ohio University Press, 1997).

Snyder, Tom, *The Route 66 Traveler's Guide and Roadside Companion* (New York: St. Martin's Press, 1990).

The Statutes at Large of the United States of America From December 1915 to March 1917, Vol. XXXIX (Washington, D.C.: Government Printing Office, 1917). This contains the Highway Act of 1916.

The Statutes at Large of the United States of America From April 1921 to March 1923, Vol. XLII (Washington, D.C.: Government Printing Office, 1923). This contains the Highway Act of 1921.

Steele, William O., *The Old Wilderness Road: An American Journey* (New York: Harcourt, Brace & World, Inc., 1968).

"The Story of the U.S. Numbered Highway System," *American Highways*, April 1956, 11-15, 31.

"Survey Says ..." *Bicycling*. (May 1999) 70.

United States Numbered Highways, (Washington, D.C.: AASHTO, 1989).

Utter, William T., *The Frontier State 1803-1825*, Volume II of The History of the State of Ohio, Carl Wittke, ed. (Columbus, Ohio: Ohio State Archaeological and Historical Society, 1942). See especially Utter's chapter, "The Building of Roads."

Wood, Frederic J., *The Turnpikes of New England* (originally published by Marshall Jones Company, Boston, 1919) reissued with abridgement and introduction by Ronald Dale Karr (Pepperell, Mass.: Branch Line Press, 1997).

Yates, Brock, *Outlaw Machine: Harley-Davidson and the Search for the American Soul* (Boston: Little, Brown and Company, 1999).

Acknowledgements

I owe a great debt to many people who, one way or another, made my journey, or the telling of it afterward, possible.

A special thank you to those who pedaled portions of the route with me: Dave Barnas, Mark Phillips, Scott Purdum and Ron Breedlove.

I am grateful to those who gave their time to drive me to jumping off or ending points: John Burns, Jane Wagner, Joel Becher, Jeanine Purdum, Nick Karman, Rebecca Purdum and Scott Purdum.

Warm hospitality and genuine help came my way several times while on the road. My sincere appreciation to Mallie Shirley, Joe Greenslade, Hal Purdum, Ray and Dixie Fallis and their family, Tony, Randy and Ryan Fallis, Coy and Gail Bush, Rev. Scott and Polly Shafer, Mary Foster, Seven Alexander and Sheila Womack, Susan Hobbs and David Large, Cloetta Johnson. Their contributions to my journey are detailed in the text. Dennis Egler came to my rescue by locating a bike shop through the World Wide Web and relaying the information to me on the road.

No single source contains the full story of America's highways, but I had a lot of help in piecing it together. My thanks to Congressman Ralph Regula's office, especially the congressman's District Staff Director, Daryl Revoldt, for procuring for me the text of the Highway Acts of 1916 and 1921, as well as for putting me in touch with state highway officials. The staff at North Canton (Ohio) Library and the staff of the Stark County (Ohio) Library helped me obtain many out-of-print but pertinent books on the history of roads, trails and journeys. Myra Hardy of the Mason County (Kentucky) Museum, located a trove of information on the Maysville Turnpike Company.

My thanks also to people who shared their knowledge with me: The Reverends Edwin Mosher and Kenneth Albright explained

Quaker faith and history to me, as did Jan Anderson, reference librarian at Malone College, Canton, Ohio. Glenda Arnold, staffer at the Killbuck Valley (Ohio) Museum, Ann Page, librarian at Central City, Kentucky, and Ann Raheem, Chamber of Commerce, Hardy, Missouri, all told me about their hometowns. Ken Theil, former bass player in the Route 62 band, provided information about the band and sent me their CD. Rick Boyle, an engineer at the Ohio Department of Transportation assisted me in understanding highway grade standards, and Sharon Todd, State Bicycle Coordinator for Ohio, explained standards for traffic lanes. Paul Svercl at the Federal Highway Administration answered my questions about National Highway System.

Several friends and family members were kind enough to read the manuscript and offer helpful comments: Randy Coy, Alan Purdum, David McCoy, Rebecca Purdum, Sherry Lowry and John McDonald.

Thanks to Jane France, Peggy Ferrell and Nancy Miller who proofread the manuscript and corrected my not infrequent typos.

Years ago, I made a good choice when I married Jeanine, and I am always in her debt for her love and moral support, as well as her financial monitoring and patient endurance of my wanderings.

Stan Purdum is a writer, editor and pastor. His published works include material as varied as a study of the Gospel of John, a how-to book for newsletter editors, numerous direct-mail campaigns, articles on preaching, sermons, short stories, family humor columns and bicycle-travel narratives. He lives in North Canton, Ohio.